D1236207

PENOLOGY FOR PROFIT

NUMBER SEVEN
Texas A&M Southwestern Studies
Robert A. Calvert and Larry D. Hill
GENERAL EDITORS

A History of the Texas Prison System 1867–1912

By Donald R. Walker

TEXAS A&M UNIVERSITY PRESS
College Station

First Edition

The paper used in this book meets the minimum requirements
of the American National Standard for Permanence
of Paper for Printed Library Materials, Z39.48-1984.
Binding materials have been chosen for durability.

LIBRARY OF CONGRESS CATALOGING-IN-PUBLICATION DATA

Walker, Donald R. (Donald Roy), 1941–
Penology for profit.

(Texas A&M southwestern studies ; no. 7)
Bibliography: p.
Includes index.
1. Convict labor—Texas—History. I. Title.
II. Series.
HV8929.T42W34 1988 365′.65′09764 87-18048
ISBN 0-89096-315-0 (alk. paper)

For

NEAT AND DOBIE

who, I think, would have been pleased.

CONTENTS

List of Illustrations		*page* ix
List of Tables		xi
Acknowledgments		xiii
Introduction		3
Chapter I.	Background to Leasing: The Early Years of the Texas Penitentiary	13
II.	Early Failures, 1867–1878	18
III.	The Successful Lease, 1878–1883	46
IV.	The State as Lessor, 1883–1912	78
V.	The Prisoner's Lot	112
VI.	The Powers That Were: Leadership of the Prison System	143
VII.	The End of Leasing	163
VIII.	The Texas Experience in Perspective	191
Afterword		198
Selected Bibliography		201
Index		211

ILLUSTRATIONS

Guard Force, with Dogs, 1887 *following page* 101
Prisoners Quarrying Granite, 1887
Blast Furnace at Rusk Penitentiary, 1908
Rusk Prison, Interior, 1908
Inmates Working Sugarcane, 1910
Prisoner with Mules for Hauling Cane, 1910
Superintendent Thomas J. Goree
Huntsville Prison, Interior, ca. 1877
Meal at Huntsville Prison, 1911
Edward M. House
Governor Thomas M. Campbell
Governor Oscar B. Colquitt

TABLES

1. Prison Population, 1870–1912 *page* 113
2. Prison Population by Race or Ethnic/Nationality Group, 1880–1912 114
3. Prison Population by Age, 1880–1912 117
4. Classification of Prison Population by Sex, 1880–1912 118
5. Educational Level of Prison Population, 1880–1912 118
6. Percentage of Prison Population Born in Texas, 1880–1912 119
7. Percentage of Prison Population Listed as Having No Trade or Occupation, 1880–1912 120
8. Principal Crimes, 1880–1912 121
9. Terms of Sentence, 1880–1912 122
10. Commitments and Recommitments, 1880–1912 123
11. Number of Escapes and Deaths per Biennium, 1880–1912 125

ACKNOWLEDGMENTS

In the course of preparing this manuscript, a number of debts have been incurred that I want to acknowledge. To James V. Reese goes my appreciation for suggesting the topic and guiding the initial research. Alwyn Barr also made helpful recommendations for the research, and supervised the writing. Both of these men, profoundly committed to the rigorous demands of history, gave considerable amounts of their time to assist me and I shall be in their debt always.

To Otto Nelson, George Flynn, Key Ray Chong, and Marietta Morrissey I wish to express my thanks for reading the manuscript thoroughly and offering suggestions to improve the style of the writing and to clarify points of potential misunderstanding. Joan Weldon and Susan Underwood labored diligently and cheerfully to decipher an extensively amended draft and produce a professional typed copy. For their timely efforts, I thank them sincerely.

Mention must also be made of the many librarians and archivists who provided valuable assistance in locating obscure sources and photographs. The staff of the State Archives, especially John Anderson, and the personnel at the Barker Texas History Center were especially helpful in this regard, as were Mary Rainey and Charles Dwyer of the Thomason Room at Sam Houston State University. Mrs. Rainey combines an understanding of sources with an eagerness to help that can ease significantly the amount of work facing any researcher. Mr. Dwyer, with the vast knowledge and broad intellectual perspective that comes only from a lifelong love affair with good books, provided keen insights into the development of the prison system and shared with me his enormous store of information on the history of Texas. It was truly delightful to work with both of these persons, and I hope to be able to rely on their expertise in future projects.

And finally, to my wife, Jonette, and my daughters, Jolie and Jennie, who persevered through this with me, I apologize for all the weekends and vacations they had to give up, and I promise to make amends.

PENOLOGY FOR PROFIT

INTRODUCTION

A criminal justice system generally is considered to be composed of three separate, yet closely related, entities: the police, the courts, and the correctional facilities. Although each of the three acts within its own jurisdiction and from its own unique internal requirements, they labor in unison to enforce and maintain those standards of behavior society has deemed necessary to guarantee stability.[1] If a society is to endure and flourish, it must be willing to exercise its inherent right to protect itself from those of its members who violate the established laws. The criminal justice system serves as the medium through which such protection is accomplished.

Most Americans have occasion, at some time during their lives, to become somewhat familiar with the workings of the police and the courts. Relatively few, however, ever know much about the prison system. Most prisons are located in remote, rural areas and remain out of the public consciousness until a riot or some other type of notoriety focuses attention on them. The general population, as a rule, understands little of how prisons are administered or the daily activities that make up prison life. In the words of the President's Commission on Law Enforcement and Administration of Justice, prisons are places that serve as "a rug under which disturbing problems and people can be swept." They incarcerate the "misfits and the failures, the unrespectable and the irresponsible." For this reason, the public "has been well content to keep them out of sight."[2]

This book will examine one part of the criminal justice system in Texas—the prisons. Specifically, it will look at the state penitentiaries as they functioned in the period between the end of the Civil War and the outbreak of World War I, a time when the state routinely hired out prison inmates to private individuals and corporations. In return for the labor of the prisoners, the private contractors agreed to pay the state

[1]The President's Commission on Law Enforcement and Administration of Justice, *The Challenge of Crime in a Free Society* (Washington, D.C.: United States Government Printing Office, 1967), p. 7.

[2]Ibid., pp. 11–12, 159.

either a specified amount of money or, in the case of share farms, a certain percentage of monies received from the sale of crops grown by inmates.

Previous studies of the state prison system during the same period generally have not presented a complete picture. Some have focused attention only on the political and institutional history of the system, providing little information on the prisoners themselves, the prison contractors, or the economics of leasing. Others have attempted to argue that state leaders in the post–Civil War period conspired to use the prison system as a means of exerting social control over minority groups in the Texas population. This study proposes to enlarge upon the earlier works and prove that the management of the state penal system during the late nineteenth and early twentieth centuries did not evolve as a result of any clearly conceived and well-executed master plan. Instead it developed from the plodding and often haphazard efforts of state officials to provide for a growing inmate population at a time when there was little money for state spending and limited public support for innovation in prison policy.[3]

For the purposes of this study, convict labor will be defined as any arrangement in which private individuals or business entities profited from the labor of prisoners in a state penitentiary. No attempt will be made to examine conditions and practices in the county jails even though state laws permitted county officials to set up workhouses and road gangs to employ jail inmates.[4] The inclusion of material at the county level would result in a work of unmanageable size and scope; hence the decision to exclude it.

All major dimensions of the Texas convict labor system will be explored. In particular, the study will seek to determine why the state decided to hire out the prisoners, the nature of the political, legal, and economic framework under which the system flourished, how the system endured and was able to deflect criticism from its opponents, and the reasons it came to an end in the early twentieth century. Attention also will be directed toward identifying the individuals who hired the

[3]See theses and dissertations: William E. Blatner, "Some Aspects of the Convict Lease System in the Southern States"; Herman Lee Crow, "A Political History of the Texas Penal System, 1829–1951"; James Robertson Nowlin, "A Political History of the Texas Prison System, 1849–1957"; Thomas Michael Parrish, "This Species of Slave Labor: The Convict Lease System in Texas, 1871–1914"; James Robert Reynolds, "The Administration of the Texas Prison System"; Thomas E. Sullenberger, "An Interpretive History of the Texas Convict Lease System, 1871–1914" (M.A. thesis, the Institute of Contemporary Corrections and the Behavioral Sciences, Sam Houston State University, 1974).

[4]United States Commissioner of Labor, *Second Annual Report of the Commissioner of Labor, 1886: Convict Labor* (Washington: United States Government Printing Office, 1887), pp. 592–94.

convicts, drawing a profile of the prisoners themselves, and describing conditions in the contract camps. The concluding chapter will place the major findings within the historiography of Progressivism and will compare the system as it existed in Texas with examples from other Southern states and with national developments in penology through the same period.

The agitation for prison reform in the United States originated in the general reform impulse associated with the early decades of the nineteenth century. The emerging nationalism and religious awakening of the period, coupled with the Enlightenment legacy of the American Revolution, produced an intellectual climate in which much of traditional society came under close scrutiny. Long-established institutions, customs, and beliefs received careful evaluation in light of the new nation's feelings regarding itself and its future. Practices found to be antiquated, inefficient, and ineffective became the targets of reformers bent on bringing a measure of rationality into the conduct of everyday life.[5]

Those who thought about crime and the problems it presented for early American society believed criminal conduct to be an antisocial aberration that could be corrected. Unlike their colonial predecessors, they did not see humans as naturally depraved beings, easily corrupted by evil influences, whose good conduct could be guaranteed only by the fear of harsh, swift corporal punishment. Criminal behavior, in their view, arose out of the combined pressures of poverty and ignorance, coupled with the absence of any sense of civility or moral restraint. It naturally followed, therefore, that society, in order to correct criminal behavior, had only to remove the offender from the surroundings and circumstances that had given birth to crime, and provide the training and moral discipline that would make for good citizenship. The penitentiary became the institution, the instrument, that society established to bring about reform of the criminal offender.[6]

Early American penitentiaries were designed to be places where convicted felons not only could be removed from the rest of society, but kept separate from the rest of the prison population as well. Prison officials hoped such forced solitude would give inmates ample time to repent of the wrongs they had committed against society and change their behavior for the better. Prisoners would be forced into the discipline of hard work and self-control and would be surrounded only by wholesome, uplifting influences that would inculcate in them the moral lessons and restraint they had not learned earlier in their lives. Upon

[5]David J. Rothman, *The Discovery of the Asylum: Social Order and Disorder in the New Republic* (Boston: Little, Brown, 1971), pp. 57–62.

[6]Ibid., pp. 53–56, 62–72.

completion of their terms of confinement, they could return to society prepared in every way to be productive, law-abiding citizens.[7]

The debate over how best to achieve the goals of penitentiary incarceration gave rise to two schools of thought, one centered in Pennsylvania, the other in New York. Both laid great stress on the moral component of reformation and, to a greater or lesser degree, sought to keep inmates isolated from each other. Most importantly, both theories emphasized that inmates were to be kept busy at productive labor, the performance of which would instill in them habits of punctuality, sacrifice, and discipline. The major difference between the two systems involved the degree to which prisoners were to be kept apart from each other, a question that ultimately determined the design of the prison and the kind of work done by inmates.[8]

The Pennsylvania system of penitentiary management had its origins with the Philadelphia Society for Alleviating the Miseries of Public Prisons. This Quaker group, founded in 1787, studied with considerable interest the works of leading European penal reformers, especially John Howard in England and Cesare Beccaria in Italy. The successful culmination of its study and effort came in 1829 with the completion of the Cherry Hill penitentiary in Philadelphia.[9]

Under the Pennsylvania system, prison inmates were kept completely isolated from each other at all times. They could not make contact with other prisoners who might exert a negative influence on the process of reformation. All inmates had their own private cell, with adjoining private exercise yard, and remained within these confines for the entire period of incarceration. Prisoners could speak only with prison officials or with ministers who provided Bibles and other religious literature upon request.[10]

The total isolation of each prisoner, the sine qua non of the Pennsylvania system, proved to be extraordinarily costly. Rooms had to be relatively large because inmates lived and worked entirely within their cells. Efforts had to be made to conceal all pipes, and walls had to be a certain thickness to prevent any communication, spoken or in code, between prisoners. The adoption of such stringent design requirements caused construction expenses for the Cherry Hill penitentiary to reach $750,000 – a sum that, in the words of one author, "staggered" the minds

[7] Ibid., pp. 82–85.

[8] Ibid.

[9] Blake McKelvey, *American Prisons: A Study in American Social History Prior to 1915,* pp. 5–11.

[10] Ibid.; Rothman, *Discovery,* pp. 84–85; Samuel Walker, *Popular Justice: A History of American Criminal Justice,* pp. 66–67.

of contemporaneous penal experts. And as the prison began to operate and implement its reform program, it became apparent that inordinately high costs would continue.[11]

Because prisoners could not leave their cells, except to exercise, they could do only limited kinds of work. Generally, small handcrafted items were all that could be produced. Production levels depended wholly on the varying speeds at which individual prisoners could work.[12] Under such conditions, officials found it almost impossible to control either the uniform quality of finished goods or the amount produced in any given period of time. Prison administrators, thus, could not count on prisoner-made goods as a dependable source of operating revenue.

Although the Pennsylvania system had its fervent admirers, its expense factors kept it from becoming popular with the rest of the nation. Most states found that they needed a system that would permit comparatively low initial construction outlays and provide for a more dependable source of income once the prison began operation. The model for just such a facility was offered by the state of New York at its Auburn penitentiary.[13]

The New York system, which began operation in 1823, also gave all inmates their own cell. Unlike Pennsylvania, however, New York prisoners were not kept in their cell at all times. During the day they labored in large workshops where, using steam-powered manufacturing equipment, they produced a variety of goods. The use of machinery afforded greater levels of production, more uniform quality of the finished product, and higher earnings for the prison—results guaranteed to please even the most cost-conscious legislators and prison administrators.[14]

While the prisoners were out of their cells and working together, they were forced to abide by strict rules of silence. No conversation among prisoners was permitted at any time, nor could any prisoner look another squarely in the face. Those guilty of violating any of the rules usually received whippings for their transgressions.[15]

Advocates of the Auburn system could argue that theirs was a realistic compromise solution to the problems of penal administration. Because inmates used their cells only for sleeping, individual units could

[11]McKelvey, *Prisons,* p. 11; Rothman, *Discovery,* pp. 87–88.

[12]Rothman, *Discovery,* pp. 83–88; Henry C. Mohler, "Convict Labor Policies," *Journal of the American Institute of Criminal Law and Criminology,* 15 (May, 1924–Feb., 1925): 557.

[13]Walker, *Popular Justice,* pp. 67–68; Rothman, *Discovery,* pp. 87–88.

[14]McKelvey, *Prisons,* pp. 12–13; Walker, *Popular Justice,* pp. 66–67; Harry E. Allen and Clifford E. Simonsen, *Corrections in America: An Introduction,* 2nd ed. (Encino, Calif.: Glencoe Publishing, 1978), pp. 39–40.

[15]Walker, *Popular Justice,* p. 67.

be smaller in size. This translated into lower construction costs and permitted more persons to be housed in a given amount of space. Prison labor brought in more money, and vigorous enforcement of the rules of silence enabled Auburn officials to argue that they too were preventing their charges from being further corrupted by fellow prisoners.[16]

Despite the intensity of the debate over prison management, both schools of thought were in fundamental agreement as to the causes of criminal behavior and the steps necessary to bring about reform. The fruits of idleness and wanton conduct that had brought inmates to the prison were to be eradicated through strict regimentation and hard work. Old habits were to be broken and new ones learned. Harsh discipline became an essential tool to force prisoners to adapt to the rigors of prison life.[17]

The universal conviction among leading prison reformers that hard work and discipline brought about the reform of criminal behavior led almost inevitably to the working of prison inmates for a profit. Administrators and legislators could hire out the labor of prisoners, secure in the realization that they were helping to reform the individual. At the same time, the proceeds from the inmate labor eased the financial burdens of taxpayers dissatisfied at the thought of having to support prisoners in idleness.[18] The desirability of working prisoners at some form of profitable employment so fixed itself in the minds of public officials that it became a hallmark of nineteenth-century prison management in the United States.

There were four basic forms of convict labor: the contract, piece-price, public account, and lease systems. Each had the same basic goal—to keep prisoners working—but differed somewhat in structure. Some yielded greater profits; some required greater skill on the part of convicts; and some gave greater authority to private contractors. All, however, shared the common objective of securing the highest level of production at the lowest possible labor cost.[19]

The contract system, the type used at the Auburn penitentiary, became the most popular of the four types of prison labor. Under this arrangement, prison officials, at the instruction of their state legislatures, advertised for bids from private contractors who wished to work the prison inmates within the walls of the prison. Contracts usually were awarded to the highest responsible bidder. As a general rule, contractors provided all necessary raw materials and furnished such skilled

[16]McKelvey, *Prisons,* p. 13; Rothman, *Discovery,* p. 88.
[17]Rothman, *Discovery,* p. 82.
[18]McKelvey, *Prisons,* p. 12; Rothman, *Discovery,* pp. 103–04.
[19]U.S. Commissioner of Labor, *Second Annual Report, 1886,* pp. 371–82.

craftsmen and foremen as were needed to train and supervise the prisoners. The state, for its part, received a fixed price per prisoner per day for the labor. Depending upon the terms of the contract, the contractor might also provide tools, machinery, and the power required to operate the equipment. Finished products manufactured by inmates were taken by the contractor, who would market them.[20]

The popularity of the contract system derived chiefly from its profitability. Next to the lease system, contract labor brought in the largest return on state money. Once a contract was made, the state was guaranteed a regular source of income. Contractors had to bear the burden of keeping prisoners employed even if economic downturns or other reverses intervened. To default on a contract usually meant the automatic forfeiture of a rather substantial bond made at the time the contract was signed.[21]

The state's responsibilities usually were considerably less onerous. The principal areas of state concern included maintenance of the prison plus the provision of food and medical care for prisoners.[22] To guarantee that these costs were covered, the state could set a minimum contract bid at whatever level it decided.

Although the contract system offered much to the states that adopted it, it also brought criticisms and problems. Nonprison workers as well as prison reformers, as early as 1834, began to oppose the system and urge its immediate discontinuance. Workers resented the unfair competition of prison labor and argued that it depressed wages and demeaned the status of all workers. Prison reformers agreed with worker complaints and further contended that basic steps leading toward the moral reformation of prisoners were impossible as long as the state viewed its prison population as simply a source of revenue. Both groups, often working in concert, prevailed upon state legislatures to stop the exploitation of prisoners by private interests.[23]

In an effort to appease and pacify the critics, some states modified the contract system. Under the piece-price arrangement, which developed in Northern prisons during the Civil War, prisoners worked within the prison for private contractors and corporations. They supplied raw materials and paid a fixed price for each item manufactured. The work

[20] Ibid., p. 372; Walker, *Popular Justice,* p. 71.

[21] U.S. Commissioner of Labor, *Second Annual Report,* p. 372.

[22] Ibid.; E. T. Hiller, "Labor Unionism and Convict Labor," *Journal of Criminal Law, Criminology, and Police Science,* 5 (1914–15): 862–63; Glen Albert Gildemeister, "Prison Labor and Convict Competition with Free Workers in Industrializing America, 1840–1890," pp. 33–34.

[23] U.S. Commissioner of Labor, *Second Annual Report,* pp. 373–79; McKelvey, *Prisons,* p. 13.

itself, however, was supervised exclusively by state employees. Inasmuch as they were public officials and not in the hire of contractors, they were less likely to be concerned with profits and more likely to be solicitous about the well-being and morale of prisoners. Neither the contractors themselves nor any of their employees were permitted to enter the prison compounds where the work was taking place.[24]

Goods manufactured under the piece-price system were taken by contractors and sold on the free market. The arrangement, thus, did nothing to alleviate the problem of competition with nonprison labor. Prison officials, nonetheless, saw it as an improvement over the contract arrangement. By bringing inmates under the exclusive control of the state, reform efforts—such as opportunities for religious instruction and basic education—could proceed free of any disruptive influences from representatives of private contractors.[25]

Under both the contract and piece-price systems, the states attempted to retain at least a modicum of control over inmates. Although their labor was given over to contractors, the states continued to provide housing, food, clothing, and medical care. This permitted state officials to discharge the responsibilities of stewardship assigned them by the state penal code. At the same time, money received from outside employers helped defray at least part of the prison operating expenses, thereby reducing the amount that would have to come from legislative appropriation.

States interested solely in the money they could make from prison labor generally chose the lease system, the most profitable form of penitentiary management. Although leasing reached the peak of its popularity in the post–Civil War South, the system had come into existence many years earlier in other parts of the nation. As early as 1798, the Massachusetts legislature authorized prison officials to hire out state prisoners to private lessees. California adopted leasing for a short time in the late 1840s and several Northern prisons did the same during the early 1860s when wartime manufacturers ran short of labor. Not until the Reconstruction South embraced the system, however, did it become entrenched.[26]

The terms of the lease contract usually called for the state to yield control of its prisons, along with all equipment, buildings, other property, and inmates, to the highest competitive bidder. Lessees could then

[24] Ibid., p. 379; Harry Elmer Barnes, *The Story of Punishment. A Record of Man's Inhumanity to Man,* 2nd ed. (Montclair, N.J.: Patterson Smith, 1972), p. 219.

[25] U.S. Commissioner of Labor, *Second Annual Report,* p. 379.

[26] Hilda Jane Zimmerman, "Penal Systems and Penal Reforms in the South Since the Civil War," pp. 22–24; Barnes, *Story of Punishment,* p. 219.

employ prisoners in any way they chose, even subcontract them to other individuals, subject only to very minimal state regulation and control. In return for the lease of the prison, the lessee paid the state a specified amount of money at regular intervals, as a rule annually.[27]

In adopting the lease system, a state abdicated virtually all responsibility for the welfare of its prisoners. As a result, the typical leased institution lodged prisoners who were poorly fed, poorly clothed, poorly housed, without proper medical care, and worked beyond reasonable limits. Unless state officials were particularly diligent in seeing to it that their prisoners were cared for properly, lessees, most of whom had personal profit uppermost in mind, did as they chose. Most states did not exercise such diligence, and the lease system came to be characterized by unconscionable levels of brutality, cruelty, and neglect.[28]

The ideal form of prison labor—the one endorsed to a greater or lesser degree by both reformers and nonprison workers—was the public account, or public use, system, which came into effect in the 1870s as a result of pressure from organized workers. Under this arrangement, prisoners worked within the prison walls completely under state control manufacturing goods for use by state institutions. Any articles produced in excess of state needs were sold on the free market; profits, if any, went into public coffers. Under the public account system, private individuals did not gain from the labor of prisoners.[29]

Although the public account system forestalled the exploitation of prison inmates by private interests, it was not without other problems. The functioning it envisioned required leadership by prison officials who were competent both as correctional officers and as practical businessmen—individuals who could see to the proper care and discipline of inmates as well as plan and implement business policies that would be successful in a competitive and unpredictable market. Judging by the relatively small number of states that adopted the public account system, one may conclude that individuals possessing both qualities were not easy to find.[30]

Organized labor responded to the public account system in a somewhat mixed manner. American workers preferred the system over the other forms of prison labor. But they resented the selling of surplus goods on the free market, particularly at the low prices for which those

[27] U.S. Commissioner of Labor, *Second Annual Report,* pp. 381–82; Robert T. Devlin, "Prison Labor," *Overland Monthly,* 7 (May, 1886): 505.

[28] McKelvey, *Prisons,* pp. 180–85; George W. Cable, *The Silent South Together with the Freedman's Case in Equity and the Convict Lease System,* p. 122.

[29] U.S. Commissioner of Labor, *Second Annual Report,* pp. 379–81.

[30] Ibid.

goods could be sold. The states had paid nothing for the labor to manufacture the products, and so they only had to recoup the cost of the raw materials to avoid a financial loss. The goods produced by free workers simply could not compete successfully with prison-made products.[31]

Labor argued for reforms that would make the system less destructive of the free market system. For one thing, it wanted prison industries to become as diversified as possible so as to diminish the amount of injurious competition that would fall on any one sector of the free work force. Prisoners would produce small amounts of many products rather than large amounts of a single item. The resulting competition thus would be minimal for many industries rather than destructive to any one. Free workers also wanted prisoners to be paid for their labor. The money, they contended, could be used to help support prisoners' families, left without a source of income.[32] Labor also must have known, although there is no record of it, that by paying the prisoners a wage, the states would have had to raise the prices of prisoner-made products, a situation that could only have benefited free workers.

The debate over prison labor, including assessments of the relative advantages and disadvantages of each system, consumed a great deal of the time and effort of early penitentiary administrators. As individual states began taking steps to establish their own prisons, they studied closely the experiences of others and selected the type of management and labor system best suited to their needs. When Texas legislators turned their attention toward providing for a state prison system in the mid-1800s, they did so at a time when prison matters were a major topic of national discussion. The state was thus at an advantage in that it was able to start from the experience of others and modify proven policies to fit the Texas setting.

[31] Ibid.; "Sanity in Solving Prison Labor Problem," *American Federationist,* 2 (Sept., 1904): 774–77.

[32] E. Stagg Whitin, "Trade Unions and Prison Labor," *Case and Comments,* 19 (Sept., 1912): 243–44.

CHAPTER I

BACKGROUND TO LEASING: THE EARLY YEARS OF THE TEXAS PENITENTIARY

The idea that prisoners should work to redeem themselves and defray at least part of the costs of their incarceration has been characteristic of penology in Texas since the advent of organized government in the state. Beginning when Texas was part of Mexico and continuing through statehood, legislators and other public officials sought to keep prisoners busy performing some type of useful and remunerative labor. Although the various plans and programs of prison labor did not always attain the desired results, state officials nonetheless maintained their belief that supervised work formed a vital part of prison rehabilitation efforts.

As early as 1829, public officials governing the Mexican state of Coahuila and Texas directed their attention toward establishing an organized state penal system to ease the burden on local jails. In that year the congress of the state empowered the governor to enter into contract with private individuals to build two prisons, one in the department of Béxar, the other in the district of Parras. Under the contract terms, the contractors were permitted to use inmate labor to construct the prisons. Upon completion, the contractors would be entitled to receive all profits from the inmates' labor for two years. They would then share the profits equally with the state for an additional three years. At the end of the five years, the prisons would become the exclusive property of the state.[1]

The 1829 law also contained provisions designed to guarantee that individuals sentenced to the new prisons would emerge from their confinement better equipped to become productive members of society. Contractors were required to teach the inmates a useful trade and to provide them, upon their release, with $30 and the tools to continue the trade in free society.[2]

Although the two prisons were never built, the provisions of the 1829

[1] H. P. N. Gammel, comp., *The Laws of Texas, 1822–1897,* I, 130–31.
[2] Ibid.

law reflected the latest in penological theory. Like their counterparts in the United States, especially those in New York, the Mexican officials believed prisons could be profitable for the state. At the same time, inmates forced to work during their time of incarceration would be prepared for useful citizenship upon their release.[3]

With the demise of the 1829 law, punishment of convicted lawbreakers again became a function of local officials. This situation continued throughout the Republic period, though there were several unsuccessful attempts to get the Congress of the Republic to establish a national prison.[4] It was not until the early years of statehood, following the end of the war with Mexico, that the Texas legislature passed formal legislation providing for the construction of a state prison.[5]

The bill that made the Texas penitentiary a reality received legislative approval on March 13, 1848.[6] To a large degree, its passage reflected the growing realization that in an organized society, the state must assume responsibility for and take the lead in penal matters.[7] The various provisions in the law seemed to anticipate any eventualities that might arise, and are worth examining as a basis for comparisons with modifications and amendments that had to be made later as new and unforeseen problems arose.

The language of the penitentiary act indicated quite clearly the intentions of the legislature with regard to both the construction of the facility as well as the later management of inmates. The governor was required to appoint immediately three persons to locate a site for the new prison. The spot chosen should be no larger than one hundred acres and should not cost more than $5 per acre. It should be in a healthy climate and near a navigable body of water so as to permit "the importation of machinery, tools, [and] materials to be . . . manufactured, and for the transportation of articles made . . . by the convicts to a market."[8]

Once the state located and purchased a suitable site, the governor, acting with the consent of the senate, was to appoint an individual to serve as superintendent and be responsible for the daily operation of the facility. This position would carry with it an annual salary of $1,000.[9]

[3] Ibid.

[4] Herman Lee Crow, "A Political History of the Texas Penal System, 1829–1951," pp. 21–31; James Robertson Nowlin, "A Political History of the Texas Prison System, 1849–1957," pp. 3–7.

[5] Crow, "Texas Penal System," pp. 21–27; Gammel, *Laws,* III, 79–84; Nowlin, "Texas Prison System," pp. 2–7.

[6] Gammel, *Laws,* III, 79–84.

[7] Nowlin, "Texas Prison System," pp. 7–10.

[8] Gammel, *Laws,* III, 79.

[9] Ibid., p. 84.

The law made no statement as to any qualifications or prior experience required of the individual appointed, an omission that would allow the position to become a plum of patronage.

The first duty of the superintendent was to procure a plan for the new prison and submit it to the governor for approval. Once this was done, he then could hire such workers as were necessary to begin construction. As soon as "part of the main buildings" was completed, the superintendent could discharge the paid workers and complete the work with prison inmates.[10]

The legislators spoke also about the type of facility they desired and how it was to be administered. The language of the law reveals quite clearly that the state lawmakers wished to emulate, as nearly as possible, the Auburn system of prison management. The buildings of the new facility should be constructed of "substantial materials" and surrounded by a "secure wall . . . placed at such a distance from the main building as to enclose a yard of sufficient dimensions as to allow room for the erection of workshops." Inmates were to be kept busy at whatever labor state officials "deemed most profitable and useful to the State." When prisoners were not working, they were to be confined in their "solitary" cells. The prison superintendent had the responsibility of guaranteeing that the institution operate in accordance with legislative dictates.[11]

In addition to the superintendent, the governor also was required to appoint three persons, subject to senate confirmation, to serve as directors of the prison. These men would be responsible for establishing prison policy by rules, regulations, and bylaws. They were to see to it that inmates were fed a "sufficient quantity" of "common but wholesome" food; were clothed in uniforms that were "comfortable but of coarse material"; and were punished when necessary, "provided that no cruel or unusual punishment shall be inflicted."[12]

The directors were required to visit and inspect the prison at least once a month and were to be paid $3 per day for their services up to a limit of $100 per year. As in the case of the superintendent, the state demanded no particular qualifications of the persons who might be appointed to serve as directors.[13] This fact, coupled with the low salaries, dictated that the individuals chosen by the governor would have to be persons with independent sources of income who would, therefore, likely take care of prison affairs only in their spare time.

[10]Ibid., p. 80.
[11]Ibid.
[12]Ibid., pp. 80–81.
[13]Ibid., pp. 80–84.

Following the passage of the penitentiary act, events moved fairly quickly. The three commissioners selected the town of Huntsville as the site of the new prison and construction began on August 5, 1848.[14] Although it would take several years to complete all the buildings specified in the original plan, the first prisoner arrived to begin serving his sentence on October 1, 1849.[15]

For the first several years of its existence, the population of the prison grew at a relatively slow pace. As of January 1, 1850, for example, there were only three inmates. By the same date in 1855, the number had increased to 75, and by 1860 it totaled 182.[16] During these early years there appears to have been no particular problem accommodating all the inmates.[17] Problems did arise, however, in other areas of prison management.

Very early in the life of the prison, the chief executives, along with the prison officials, recognized the reluctance of the legislature to appropriate large sums of money for penitentiary affairs. Accordingly, Gov. P. H. Bell, in 1853, asked the state lawmakers for $35,000 to install a cotton and woolen mill in the prison. Bell hoped that this would make the prison self-sustaining financially and provide labor for all inmates and thus contribute significantly to their moral reformation.[18]

The mill became operational over the objections of Bell's successor, Gov. E. M. Pease, who wanted to complete the several workshops in the prison plan and then lease the entire facility to private contractors. The legislature refused to accede to Pease's wishes, choosing instead to implement Bell's plan and make available all necessary monies. By June, 1856, the prison operation consisted of 40 looms with 896 spindles for cotton and 200 for wool. When functioning, the mill could process into cloth 500 bales of cotton and 6,000 pounds of wool annually.[19]

The investment in the prison mill proved to be a wise one. The cloth products were eagerly purchased by the planters and merchants of Texas, thereby enabling the prison to reduce accordingly the appropriation needed from the state. Under Gov. Hardin Runnels's guidance, the legislature agreed to purchase additional equipment for the mill, hoping

[14]Nowlin, "Texas Prison System," p. 8.

[15]Bowen C. Tatum, "The Penitentiary Movement in Texas, 1847–1849," p. 72; James Robert Reynolds, "The Administration of the Texas Prison System," p. 4.

[16]*Reports of the Superintendent and Financial Agent for the Texas State Penitentiaries, Embodying the Proceedings of the Penitentiary Board, and Statistical and Financial Exhibits: Also Reports of Subordinate Officers of the Texas State Penitentiaries* (Austin: Ben C. Jones, State Printer, 1892), p. 34 (hereafter referred to as *Biennial Report,* followed by the year of issue and the page number).

[17]Crow, "Texas Penal System," pp. 39–40.

[18]Ibid., pp. 47–48.

[19]Ibid., pp. 49–50.

to increase prison profits even more.[20] Unfortunately at this point events outside the state became the focus of general attention and ushered in a new period in the history of the prison.

During the Civil War, the Texas penitentiary became an institution of critical importance to the state. The inmate population from January 1, 1860, to January 1, 1865, decreased from 182 to 165.[21] The reduction in the number of inmates, however, did not have an adverse effect on production from the prison textile mills.

Prisoner-made cotton and woolen cloth constituted a major source of revenue for Texas during the war. For the period from December 1, 1861, to August 31, 1863, for example, Texas prison inmates produced 2,258,660 yards of cotton and 293,298 yards of wool. Selling both to the civilian population and to the Confederacy, the state earned a total of $1,174,439.07. After paying expenses and buying additional supplies, $800,000 of the total amount was deposited as earnings in the state treasury.[22] The wartime prosperity, however, which benefited both the state and the prison, did not extend beyond the cessation of hostilities.

The end of the Civil War and the defeat of the Confederacy in 1865 also brought a downturn in the fortunes of the prison. The coarse fabric that once had found a ready market as clothing for slaves no longer appealed to Texas consumers. There were, in addition, chronic problems in procuring sufficient quantities of the raw fiber to keep the machinery in operation. These difficulties, coupled with the rapid increase in the prison population following the war, soon led Texas officials to consider leasing the prison, the most drastic method of penitentiary management ever adopted in the state.[23]

[20] Ibid., pp. 52–54.
[21] *Biennial Report,* 1892, p. 34.
[22] Crow, "Texas Penal System," pp. 62–63.
[23] *Biennial Report,* 1892, p. 34; Crow, "Texas Penal System," pp. 85–86.

CHAPTER II

EARLY FAILURES, 1867–1878

The defeat of the Confederate forces in the spring of 1865 and the ensuing years of Reconstruction brought many changes to Texas society. Through the remainder of the nineteenth century Texans witnessed former slaves make the often painful transition to freedom while the state received a flood of immigrants from other parts of the South. The economy diversified and grew stronger, adding new wealth to the state. In the immediate aftermath of the fighting, however, the only changes appeared to be for the worse as political unrest and civil turmoil engulfed the state.

Out of the turbulence came fundamental changes in the prison system. The postwar political officials quickly found themselves with an abundance of prisoners and very little money. To solve their dilemma, they decided to lease the prison to outside parties. Although leasing ultimately proved to be very profitable, the early attempts failed in virtually every measure.

The first decade or so following the end of the war brought lawlessness, a near collapse of the state's finances, and a weakening of state government to the point that, at times, it seemed almost incapable of maintaining any control at all. Property taxes formed the major source of income for the state, but poor collection procedures, coupled with citizen reluctance to pay what were perceived as unduly high taxes, resulted in relatively little money flowing into state coffers. One author has described the financial situation of Texas during the immediate postwar period as being characterized by a "large growth of expenditures, great increase in taxation, and the rapid accumulation of comparatively heavy debt."[1]

A picture of the general prostration of the state can be seen by examining certain elements of the postwar economy in Texas. At the end of the war, the state treasury showed a balance of $3,368,510.07. Of this amount, however, only some $145,000 represented currency of any value. The remainder consisted of worthless Confederate and state wartime

[1]Edmund T. Miller, *A Financial History of Texas,* pp. 165–66, 195.

paper issues. The major industry in the state—agriculture—showed similar reverses. From 1865 to 1870, the value of all farms declined by 45.4 percent. Cotton production, which had reached 431,463 bales in 1859, dropped to 350,628 bales ten years later. Along with the reduced production came a drop in cotton prices from forty-three cents per pound to seventeen cents per pound.[2]

The financial plight of the state government, as severe as it was, was not the only difficulty with which state officials had to contend. Increasing levels of lawlessness also plagued Texas. All sorts of petty offenses increased, as well as the more serious depredations and terror perpetrated by bands of brigands that roamed about the state preying on the populace. The statistics on crime for this period are suspect at best, particularly those that attempt to attribute certain crimes to certain groups in society. There seems to be little doubt, however, that the state did in fact suffer an alarming breakdown of law and order in the postwar period.[3]

As early as the fall of 1866, the increased lawlessness became apparent in the larger number of committals to the state penitentiary. Gov. James Throckmorton, in an address to the eleventh legislature, pointed out that in the few months since the end of the war, the prison population had increased from 146 to 264 persons. This had resulted in a serious overcrowding problem. He suggested that the lawmakers consider enlarging the prison facility to handle the growing population. Barring that, he urged a revision of the penal code so as to change the definitions of grand and petty larceny. According to the governor, the prison population could be reduced significantly if persons convicted of stealing goods worth less than $20 were kept in county jails rather than sent to the penitentiary.[4]

The legislature chose not to act in accordance with the governor's recommendations. It sought instead to relieve the overcrowding by adopting new procedures for working the inmates. In "An Act to Provide for the Employment of Convict Labor on Works of Public Utility," passed on November 12, 1866, the legislature created a body known as the Board of Public Labor to superintend prison inmates. The board was to be composed of the governor, the secretary of state, the comptroller, the attorney-general, and the treasurer. A majority of three members would constitute a quorum for conducting business.[5]

[2] Ibid., pp. 157–58.

[3] Alwyn Barr, *Reconstruction to Reform: Texas Politics, 1876–1906,* pp. 7–8; Charles W. Ramsdell, *Reconstruction in Texas,* pp. 65–70; Ernest Wallace, *Texas in Turmoil,* pp. 139–46.

[4] *Journal of the House of Representatives, Eleventh Legislature, State of Texas* (Austin: Office of the State Gazette, 1866), pp. 86–87.

[5] H. P. N. Gammel, comp., *Laws of Texas, 1822–1897,* V, 1110–13; "Minutes of the

The law required the board to divide the prison inmates into two categories, first and second class. First-class prisoners would be those convicted of "murder, arson, rape, horse stealing, burglary, perjury, or robbery." Owing to the more serious nature of these offenses, first-class convicts were to be kept at their labors within prison walls. They were not to be worked outside the confines of the prison itself.[6]

The second class of convicts would be made up of persons sentenced to the penitentiary for crimes other than those listed in the first-class designation. Second-class prisoners could be put to work at the board's discretion on "works of public utility." The law contemplated that such works would be outside the walls of the prison.[7]

The law defined "works of public utility" as "The building of railroads, including . . . the making of the grade, the cutting and laying of ties, and the laying of track; all works for improvement of navigation of rivers, bays, channels, and harbors; for irrigating lands; [and] all workings of mines of iron, lead, copper, or of gold."[8]

Second-class prisoners also could be employed in iron foundries if railroad iron was being made. The board was authorized to hire out the inmates on any project that satisfied the definition of public utility regardless of whether the project belonged to the state or to private individuals.[9]

The law made no mention as to the type of housing required for prison inmates who worked outside the prison. In every other regard, however, it sought to keep prisoners firmly under state control. The state would yield the labor of the prisoners but not their supervision and care. State agents working directly for the Board of Public Labor would hire and supervise all guards, make certain prisoners were adequately fed and, by hiring a private physician, would see to the necessary medical care.[10] This concern and active intervention by state officials to try to guarantee proper care for prisoners would be one of the more difficult goals to attain.

The rules and bylaws adopted by the Board of Public Labor early in 1867 maintained the spirit of the 1866 act. In clarifying and elaborating on the specific duties and responsibilities of the supervisory personnel, the board manifested considerable concern for the welfare of

---

Board of Public Labor" (unpublished manuscript, Archives, Texas State Library, Austin), p. 3.

[6]Gammel, *Laws,* V, 1110–11.

[7]Ibid.

[8]Ibid.

[9]Ibid.

[10]Ibid.

prisoners. The duties of guards and physicians were carefully spelled out, food requirements were listed, and the hirers of labor were told the precise amount of time that prisoners should be worked, reserving a designated hour or hour and one-half for lunch, depending on the season of the year. The board further specified that it preferred to hire out the prisoners in groups of one hundred or more, and stipulated that private contractors would pay all expenses incurred in transporting prisoners from Huntsville to the work site.[11]

At its first meeting, the Board of Public Labor authorized advertisements for bids to hire prison inmates. The ads were run in newspapers in Marshall, Houston, San Antonio, and Galveston. Bids would be received until February 1, 1867, and notices specified that potential bidders should be interested in hiring labor for a period of twelve months. Upon receipt of the bids, the board contracted 100 prisoners to the Airline Railroad and 150 to the Brazos Branch Railroad. Both companies agreed to pay $12.50 per month per man.[12]

Despite the planning and attention given to detail, the Board of Public Labor encountered a number of problems in implementing the terms of the contracts. State agents did not fully understand their duties, so were often dilatory in fulfilling their responsibilities. Serious and protracted disagreements arose between the state and contractors over their respective obligations. State officials, moreover, expressed alarm at the large number of escapes from the railroad camps and the number of men killed or seriously wounded attempting to escape—an indication that guards were not performing their duty in a satisfactory manner. These problems, coupled with a failure on the part of contractors to make regular payments, induced the board late in 1867 to begin canceling contracts upon their expiration.[13]

Even though the contracts made by the Board of Public Labor lasted only a few months, the difficulties that surfaced in that short time portended the kind of problems that would plague the state for many years to come. Inherent in the process of hiring out state prisoners was a fundamental clash between the interests of the state and the interests of contractors. The state discovered it could not easily guarantee that its provisions for the welfare and safekeeping of its prisoners would be

[11] *Rules and By-Laws Adopted by the Board of Public Labor, Relative to Employment of Convicts on Works of Public Utility* (Austin: Jo. Walker, State Printer, at the Gazette Office, 1867), pp. 1–8; "Minutes of the Board of Public Labor," pp. 9–18.

[12] "Minutes of the Board of Public Labor," pp. 3–6.

[13] John T. Allen, Secretary, Board of Public Labor to President of the Airline Railroad, Dec. 4, 1867, "Minutes of the Board of Public Labor"; *Journal of the Reconstruction Convention, Which Met at Austin, Texas, June 1, A. D. 1868* (Austin: Tracy, Siemering and Company, Printers, 1870), p. 772.

faithfully adhered to by private parties who employed prisoners for private gain. State supervision proved especially difficult when prison inmates were scattered in work camps far from the scrutiny of the officials responsible for them.

Upon termination of the contracts with the railroads, the state returned the prison inmates to Huntsville. There the twin problems of overcrowding and expense again became critical and demanded the attention of state leaders. During the time that prisoners had been working for the railroads, the commander of the Fifth Military District, which included Texas, had removed Governor Throckmorton from office and named former governor Elisha M. Pease to replace him.[14] Pease, who had advocated leasing the prison during his earlier term of office, served only until September, 1869, when he resigned.[15] During this second period of his service to the state, however, the idea of leasing the prison moved further along the path of realization.

In early summer, 1868, delegates convened in Austin to draft a new state constitution. The convention met in two sessions between June 1, 1868, and February 8, 1869. The state prison was one of the areas to which the members of the convention turned their attention shortly after the beginning of the first session.[16]

The president of the convention, Edmund J. Davis, appointed a committee of five members to go to Huntsville, examine conditions in the prison, and report back to the convention. He urged the committee to look into the finances of the prison, the care that inmates were receiving, the number of inmates, and the types of crimes for which they had been convicted. The report submitted by the committee following its investigation painted a most dismal picture.[17]

The committee found that there were more than four hundred inmates in the prison and that overcrowding was a serious problem. Prisoners appeared to be adequately fed and clothed, but the crowded conditions made it impossible for inmates to be provided for in the manner contemplated by the law and the penal code. The report suggested that a good many inmates were either sufficiently reformed or had been incarcerated under such questionable circumstances that the governor could extend executive pardons and greatly ease the overcrowding.[18]

[14] Barr, *Reconstruction to Reform,* pp. 7–8; Wallace, *Texas in Turmoil,* p. 196.

[15] Barr, *Reconstruction to Reform,* p. 8; Seymour V. Connor, *Texas: A History,* p. 221; Wallace, *Texas in Turmoil,* p. 210.

[16] *Journal of the Reconstruction Convention,* I, 63, 74.

[17] Ibid., pp. 18, 74, 534–35.

[18] Ibid., pp. 534–35.

On the subject of prison finances, the committee had nothing favorable to report. In the past there had been no organized system whatsoever for keeping the penitentiary books and accounts. There was no specified food or clothing ration for inmates. Supplies were routinely purchased and turned over to prison officials with no requisitions, receipts, or other forms of general accountability required. Indeed, there was no way to determine how much of the supplies even reached the inmates. The committee concluded that in the absence of accepted bookkeeping procedures, mismanagement would be an inevitable problem and that in all likelihood the prison would be "a source of great corruption" and a drain on the state treasury.[19]

The committee speculated that under proper management the prison ought to make about $25,000 per year. To this end, it recommended that the state lease the facility to private individuals who would make regular payments for the labor of the prisoners. The state should retain full authority in the areas of inmate care and supervision; lessees would be entitled only to the labor of the prisoners.[20]

Governor Pease fully shared the committee's sentiments regarding a lease of the prison. On August 18, 1868, he sent a message to the convention in which he outlined his feelings respecting the prison and its future management. His remarks were very much in keeping with earlier statements he had made on the subject.

Pease pointed out that the indebtedness of the prison system stood at approximately $50,000; that since January 1, 1868, the state had had to spend $14,000 to meet prison operating costs, and that another $20,000 likely would be needed to operate the facility until October 1, 1868. The machinery in the prison could employ only about half the inmates, he argued, and the profits from the goods produced were so low as to be hardly worth the effort. He believed that private individuals could manage the prison more efficiently than state officials had been able to do.[21]

Pease further contended that mismanagement had been the most important factor creating the unsatisfactory state of prison affairs. According to the governor, on September 4, 1866, the date the prison had been turned over to the financial agent appointed by Governor Throckmorton, there had been on hand a stock of goods, material, and money amounting to approximately $80,000 over and above all outstanding debts. The Throckmorton administration had so botched things that when the new financial agent appointed by Pease took over in January, 1868, there remained only about "$1,900 worth of goods, very few

[19]Ibid., pp. 803–04.
[20]Ibid., p. 805.
[21]Ibid., pp. 771–73.

materials, and no money, with debts outstanding . . . not far from $40,000."[22] Pease's comments regarding the management of the prison under his predecessor were virtually identical to those made by each incoming administration throughout the period of this study. All existing problems were blamed on previous administrators, while boasts were made that the new management was correcting many of the inherited difficulties. It has proven next to impossible to determine from the reports the financial condition of the prison at any given time.

In keeping with his earlier sentiments regarding the prison, Governor Pease urged the convention to consider leasing the facility to the highest competitive bidder. To provide additional guidance to the convention, and perhaps to convey the urgency of the situation, the governor also submitted a proposed lease arrangement for the convention members to consider. Although the draft did not make provision for every aspect of a lease agreement, it did, to a large degree, foreshadow the type of contractual agreement ultimately entered into by the state.[23]

The Pease proposal would have required the governor of the state to lease the penitentiary for at least five but not more than ten years. The lessees would have had full use of all prison lands, buildings, machinery, and other property and could have directed the labor of the prisoners as they saw fit subject to one stipulation: the prisoners could be worked only within the prison itself. The lessees would have been obligated to take care of state property and to construct such additional buildings as the state might direct at some future time. The proposal made no mention of any amount the lessees should pay the state but did suggest that a $50,000 bond be executed as a guarantee of financial capability.[24]

Upon receiving the lease proposal, E. J. Davis appointed a special committee of five men to consider the whole matter and make a recommendation to the entire convention. Two of the five committee members deserve special mention. Nathan Patton, a Republican manufacturer from McLennan County, would later develop a personal interest in the lease system and be a partner in the company with which the state would make the first lease. George T. Ruby, president of the Union League in Texas, had become, without question, one of the more respected black leaders in the state, and when the final vote was taken, he too supported leasing the prison.[25]

[22] Ibid., pp. 771–72.
[23] Ibid., pp. 773–75.
[24] Ibid.
[25] Ibid., p. 775; Wallace, *Texas in Turmoil,* p. 202; Carl H. Moneyhon, "George T. Ruby and the Politics of Expediency in Texas," in Howard N. Rabinowitz, ed., *Southern Black*

The committee as a whole, after some deliberation, unanimously recommended the adoption of the Pease lease agreement with certain amendments. The members wanted the lease to be undertaken "without unnecessary delay" and they wanted the lessees to be persons who could hold office under the terms of the Fourteenth Amendment to the United States Constitution—that is, lessees should be persons who had never "engaged in insurrection or rebellion" against the United States. This last recommendation occasioned some controversy within the committee itself. One of the members, James Burnett, a Republican and former United States Army captain, objected to the requirement, stating that the lease of the prison was a purely business proposition and that the Fourteenth Amendment was irrelevant. He ventured that a good many persons would make excellent lessees even though they were not qualified to hold office under the terms of the amendment. In the final vote, the members of the convention disregarded the proposed amendments and approved the original lease proposal.[26]

All the convention efforts on behalf of the prison yielded no immediate results. Governor Pease began to devote increasing amounts of his time to problems he believed to have emanated from attempts by the federal military authorities to meddle in state politics. By September, 1869, his frustrations had reached such a point that he resigned from office. There ensued a period of some four months when the United States Army general commanding Texas, J. J. Reynolds, assumed the duties of governor. Reynolds finally relinquished control in early January, 1870, to Edmund J. Davis, who had been elected to fill the governor's chair in November, 1869.[27]

Shortly after assuming office, Governor Davis received a report on the prison from Col. N. A. M. Dudley, who had been appointed superintendent of the facility in November, 1869. The report offered little encouraging news. In a very few months, the prison seemingly had gone from bad to worse. Dudley described the prison as being in a "miserably filthy condition," without money and with very little credit. Nearly nine-tenths of the inmates were kept locked in their cells because there was no work for them to do. Moreover, prison hygiene and sanitation facili-

---

Leaders of the Reconstruction Era, pp. 372–73. Accounts of the 1868 convention list the delegate from McLennan County as Nathan Patten, a forty-five-year-old manufacturer. In all the published works on the prison lease, however, the name is given as Nathan Patton, a prominent citizen of Galveston. Chances are very good that the two names refer to the same man though I could not find definite proof of it. See Carl H. Moneyhon, *Republicanism in Reconstruction Texas,* p. 244.

[26] *Journal of the Reconstruction Convention,* I, 783–84, 832–33.

[27] Wallace, *Texas in Turmoil,* pp. 208–10.

ties remained in such a poor state that "a great many" of the inmates became ill and would have been unable to work had there been something for them to do.[28]

At the time Dudley took control, he found 489 prisoners under his care. During the year 1869, a total of 201 persons had arrived in Huntsville to begin serving their sentences. The counties sending the largest number of persons to the prison included Harris County, 24 prisoners, 12 white and 12 black; Galveston County, 41 prisoners, 27 white and 14 black; Bexar County, 15 prisoners, 9 white and 6 black; and Marion County, 10 prisoners, 5 white and 5 black.[29]

Dudley had managed to convince one local citizen, Dr. W. A. Rawlings, to advance the prison some $10,000 worth of cotton on credit so the prison factories could be put into limited operation.[30] Such assistance, he stressed to the governor, represented only a temporary expedient. Much more money would be needed to get the prison industries running on a solid financial basis. Dudley suggested that something just short of $125,000 would be required.[31] He further recommended that a chapel be built in the prison and that a hospital for the treatment of infirm prisoners was desperately needed. Dr. H. C. Oliphant, the prison physician, supported the request for a hospital, noting that under conditions then prevailing sick prisoners were either treated in their poorly ventilated cells or in the "alleys" through which all the inmates had to pass as they moved about the prison.[32]

Dudley's requests for assistance drew virtually no response. Approximately five weeks after his report had been submitted, military rule ended in Texas, and shortly thereafter, Governor Davis appointed a civilian, A. J. Bennett, to serve as prison superintendent. The new superintendent, in his first report a few months later, demonstrated quite forcefully the continued decline of the prison.[33]

At the time Bennett became superindentent, prison finances had reached their lowest point. The institution had no credit, and inmates had to be kept locked in their cells for want of anything to do. The legislature had failed to act on earlier financial requests by prison officials for appropriations to maintain prisoners and prison employees. The situation was so depressed that Bennett assumed the state contem-

[28]*Biennial Report,* 1870, pp. 5–6.

[29]Ibid., pp. 14–17.

[30]Ibid., pp. 5–6.

[31]Ibid., p. 8.

[32]Ibid., pp. 7, 32.

[33]Wallace, *Texas in Turmoil,* p. 210; Herman Lee Crow, "A Political History of the Texas Penal System, 1829–1951, pp. 78–79.

plated ending any support for the prison, that the facility would be "no longer an institution of the state."[34]

Like his predecessor, Bennett requested that an infirmary be built inside the prison. He also explained that the shortage of cells had made it necessary to house male and female prisoners in the same building. The improprieties that resulted from such an arrangement, he explained, could not be avoided under the circumstances.[35]

As for finances, the superintendent stated he had been able to borrow some money locally to feed prisoners but much more would be needed to get the prison going again. The looms in the prison factory could make only low-grade cotton jeans and wool garments, commonly called "nigger cloth." The former slaves, now that they were free, would not buy the cheaper grade clothing. Bennett recommended the precise sum of $247,611.98 to get the prison factory back into shape to begin earning a profit. Anything less than this would mean that the institution would remain a burden on the state treasury.[36]

The financial agent of the penitentiary, Louis W. Stevenson, confirmed Bennett's estimate of the amount of money needed to revitalize the prison factories, but went on to recommend leasing the prison as the only practical solution. By adopting the lease system, the state would be spared the immense expense "absolutely necessary" to resume factory operations. At the same time, leasing the prisoners and placing them under someone else's care would enable the state to "do away with the large corps of officers and employees . . . now required to keep the Penitentiary running."[37]

Evidently, the remarks by Bennett and Stevenson impressed the governor. Shortly after receiving their report, Davis delivered his message to the twelfth legislature and spoke, among other things, of the penitentiary. He told the legislators that the prison was not self-supporting and could not be made so without major changes of equipment. Large amounts of money would be required to replace existing machinery with a type that could produce a commercially competitive fabric. Davis went on to note that prison officials desperately needed an appropriation of about $50,000 and that additional appropriations would be required to cover the mounting indebtedness of the institution.[38]

Acting on Governor Davis's remarks, the Speaker of the House, Ira H.

[34] *Biennial Report,* 1871, pp. 3–6.

[35] Ibid., pp. 5, 17.

[36] Ibid., pp. 6–10.

[37] Ibid., p. 27.

[38] *Message of Governor Edmund J. Davis of the State of Texas* (Austin: J. G. Tracy, State Printer, 1871), p. 16; *Galveston Daily News,* Jan. 20, 1871, p. 2.

Evans, appointed Representatives J. W. Lane, R. L. Moore, and Robert Zapp as a special committee to examine conditions in the prison and report their findings back to the legislature with appropriate recommendations. The investigation revealed problems similar to the ones discovered by the committee of the Reconstruction Convention some two years earlier. The more serious matters that needed attention included the continued indebtedness of the system, proper care of inmates, and the need for large amounts of money to restore prison industries. The committee recommended that an appropriation large enough to retire the indebtedness be voted by the legislature at once. Because the problem of prisoner care was intimately related to overcrowding, the committee suggested that a law be passed to provide for commuting, or shortening, sentences for good behavior. Such legislation would not only be an inducement to proper conduct on the part of prisoners, but also would result in a reduction in the number of persons in the prison.[39]

As its final recommendation, the House committee urged that the prison be leased to outside bidders. The members believed this was the only way the system could be made self-sustaining. In advocating lease, the committee strongly urged that the state not abdicate its responsibilities to guarantee proper care for inmates. The duties of the superintendent should be defined in such a way that they would focus almost exclusively on seeing to it that prisoners were not abused or neglected by the private parties who hired them.[40]

The Texas Senate, meanwhile, had conducted its own investigation of the prison. The Senate committee found virtually the same problems as had its counterpart in the House—that is, no money, sizable debt, and outmoded manufacturing equipment. When Senate members confronted the enormity of the problem and considered the amount of money that would be required to make the institution a going concern, they too opted in favor of leasing the entire facility.[41]

With the members of both chambers of the legislature convinced of the necessity of leasing the prison, events moved rather rapidly. Bills introduced in both chambers passed quickly. After brief deliberations to reconcile minor differences between the House and Senate versions, the legislature approved the lease bill and Governor Davis signed it into

[39] *Journal of the House of Representatives of the Twelfth Legislature, Part First* (Austin: J. G. Tracy, State Printer, 1871), pp. 252, 593–602; *Report of Special Committee on Penitentiary, State of Texas* (Austin: J. G. Tracy, State Printer, 1871), pp. 7–9.

[40] *Report of Special Committee on Penitentiary,* pp. 9–10.

[41] *Senate Journal of the Twelfth Legislature of the State of Texas* (Austin: J. G. Tracy, State Printer, 1871), pp. 48–52.

law on March 22, 1871.[42] Texas was thus committed to the convict lease system.

The prison facility the state offered to private bidders in 1871 had changed rather dramatically from its days of prosperity during the Civil War. In addition to the increasingly acute problems concerning lack of money, growing indebtedness, and outmoded equipment, the prison was overcrowded and unsanitary. Furthermore, the state seemed unable to take the kind of action needed to reverse the decline. The decision to lease the entire facility to outside parties clearly represented an admission, albeit tacitly, that the state was either unable or unwilling to shoulder its responsibilities toward its convicted felons.

Texas awarded its first prison lease to Ward, Dewey, and Company of Galveston. The principal individuals involved in the company included A. J. Ward, E. C. Dewey, and Nathan Patton. All three had reputations as relatively successful businessmen and at least one was very active in state Republican party politics.[43]

Patton had been a member of the committee in the Reconstruction Convention that had supported Governor Pease's lease proposal. He also served during Governor Pease's term as the customs collector for the port of Galveston.[44] According to one source, Patton, whose considerable political talents had earned him the nickname "The Fox," played the preeminent role in Ward, Dewey, and Company. He also was reputed to exert a powerful influence among the directors of the Port of Galveston and the Bolivar Point Wharf and Cotton Press Company.[45]

A. J. Ward served as the director of both the Port of Galveston and the Bolivar Point Wharf and Cotton Press Company. In addition, he and Dewey sat on the board of directors of the Texas Mutual Life Insurance Company, which had been chartered by the Texas legislature in September, 1870.[46] Ward was present in Austin during most of the time the legislature debated the lease bill. Rumors made him a very strong contender for the lease because of his "large experience with the same duties in other states."[47]

[42] *House Journal, Twelfth Legislature,* pp. 534, 605; *Senate Journal, Twelfth Legislature,* pp. 139, 453; *Report of the Commission Appointed by the Governor of Texas, April 10, 1875, to Investigate the Alleged Mismanagement and Cruel Treatment of the Convicts* (Houston: A. C. Gray, State Printer, 1875), p. 9.

[43] Moneyhon, *Republicanism,* p. 158; *Galveston Daily News,* Mar. 14, 1871, p. 2; *Austin Daily Statesman,* Aug. 20, 1874, p. 3.

[44] Gov. E. J. Davis to Nathan Patton, Jan. 30, 1871, Davis Letterpress Books, Archives, Texas State Library, Austin.

[45] *Galveston Daily News,* Mar. 14, 1871, p. 2.

[46] Ibid., Dallas *Herald,* Sept. 14, 1870, p. 4; Mar. 11, 1871, p. 2.

[47] *Galveston Daily News,* Mar. 14, 1871, p. 2; Mar. 18, 1871, p. 2; Apr. 27, 1871, p.

The lease law drawn up by the state contained fairly specific provisions. The duties and responsibilities of each party were spelled out and a mechanism was established to protect the financial interests of each side. Another provision called for the appointment of a state official to be present in the prison to safeguard the state's interests.[48]

The act "authorized and required" the governor to lease the prison for a period of not less than ten or more than fifteen years. The lessees would have the right to direct the labor of the prisoners and could construct such additional buildings and alter existing structures in any manner they saw fit to keep the prisoners at profitable labor. They were given full use of all lands, buildings, machinery, tools, and other property belonging to the prison, with the stipulation that all property was to be kept in good repair.[49]

The lessees were required to pay all costs "necessary for the support and maintenance of the penitentiary." This would include all food, clothing, and medical care for the prisoners as well as the salaries of all guards and prison officials. They were further obligated to pay county sheriffs for costs incurred in transporting prisoners from the county of conviction to Huntsville. These payments were not to exceed $10,000 a year.[50]

Prior to the commencement of the lease contract, there would be an inventory and appraisal of all prison property. The governor and the company would each appoint an appraiser. In the event these two could not reconcile differences of opinion, they could choose someone to serve as mediator. A similar evaluation would take place upon termination of the lease contract to determine the nature of any final financial settlement between the two parties. To protect the interests of the state, the law required the leasing party to execute a bond payable to the state of at least $50,000 but not more than $100,000.[51]

The state's interest in the prison would be supervised by a board of three directors who would appoint a chaplain and a physician. To make certain that the care of prisoners always conformed to state law, an in-

---

2. The "experience" attributed to Ward was never specifically defined by the newspaper reporter. Other research, however, has revealed that during the early 1860s, an A. J. Ward was the lessee of the Arkansas State Prison. Ward fled Arkansas in 1863, shortly before the arrival of Federal troops. The temptation is great to assume that the two men were one and the same even though no evidence to substantiate such a belief has been found. See Harry Williams Gilmore, "The Convict Lease System in Arkansas" (M.A. thesis, George Peabody College for Teachers, 1930), p. 1.

[48] *Report of the Commission Appointed by the Governor, 1875,* pp. 10–11.

[49] Ibid.

[50] Ibid., pp. 10–14.

[51] Ibid.

dividual would be appointed to serve as state inspector of prisons. The act required the inspector as part of his duties to submit a monthly written report to the governor discussing the management of the prison and the treatment of inmates.[52]

On April 29, 1871, the state entered officially into a lease agreement with Ward, Dewey, and Company. The lessees submitted their required bond on June 9 and took possession of the prison on July 5, 1871.[53] The lease agreement gave the use of the prison to the lessees for a period of fifteen years. In return for the labor of the prisoners, the lessees agreed to pay the state $5,000 per year for the first five years of the lease. For the ensuing five years, they were to pay $10,000 per year. The amount increased to $20,000 per year for the remaining five years. These amounts, added to the $10,000 per year the lessees agreed to pay sheriffs, meant that the lease would have a value of $325,000 to the state.[54]

Ward, Dewey and Company acquired a prison valued by the appraisers at $236,099.32, although it was in a deplorable condition.[55] Directors Strother Green, Peter Royal, and Sandford Gibbs, all long-time residents of the town of Huntsville, described the prison at that time as "being without means, credit, or resources of any kind, and the inmates greatly demoralized by idleness and want of discipline."[56]

The lessees, in a similar view, spoke of the financial problems and described the prisoners as being confined to their vermin-infested cells, fed only beef and cornbread, and suffering from scurvy. There were no eating utensils of any kind in the prison, "nor had there ever been any." The prison contained 238 cells for 607 inmates with "neither hospital, dining-room, nor chapel."[57]

During the first few months of their lease, Ward-Dewey made several improvements. They built a dining room that could be used for church services on Sunday, made room for an infirmary, built forty additional cells, constructed new work shops, and bought new machinery and equipment for use by the prisoners. By December, 1872, the lessees had the prisoners busy making high-quality wool and cotton garments, "furniture, doors, sash, blinds, wagons, boots, and shoes," all of which found

[52]Ibid.

[53]Ibid., pp. 13–14.

[54]Ibid., pp. 13–16.

[55]Ibid., p. 36.

[56]*Biennial Report,* 1871–72, p. 3. The director, Strother Green, was a prominent black educator in Huntsville. See Mae Wynne McFarland, "A History of Huntsville," in *Huntsville and Walker County, Texas. A Bicentennial History,* compiled and edited by D'Anne McAdams Crews (Huntsville: Sam Houston State University Press, 1976), p. 42.

[57]McFarland, "History of Huntsville," p. 5; *Report of the Commission Appointed by the Governor, 1875,* p. 40.

a good market in Texas.[58] The total prison population had increased to 944 inmates. Of this number 638 were employed in and about the prison at Huntsville. The remaining 306 worked on construction crews for the Houston and Texas Central Railroad and the Houston and Great Northern Railroad.[59]

The initial burst of activity to improve the prison physical plant met with everyone's approval. The lessees received considerable praise for the manner in which they were managing and providing for the prisoners. Although the prison population had increased substantially during the first year and a half of the lease, the lessees had encountered few difficulties in housing, feeding, or clothing the prisoners. The Inspector, Ed T. Randle, reported that the lessees were complying with all parts of the lease agreement. The prison was clean, strict sanitation regulations were in force, and illness and disease were at a minimum. Randle mentioned only the perennial problem of overcrowding and urged the governor to take this up with the legislature at the earliest opportunity.[60]

The prison physician, Dr. H. C. Oliphant, echoed Randle's kind words for the lessees. According to the doctor, the low incidence of disease was directly attributable to the new sanitation regimen and the ready availability of medical care in the infirmary. Of the sixteen inmate deaths since the lessees took charge, nine had resulted from diseases and infirmities contracted by the prisoners when they were in various county jails prior to their arrival in Huntsville. Of the others, three died of dropsy, one from consumption, one from tetanus, and one "from the effects of wounds," the nature of which the doctor failed to specify.[61]

The three individuals who served as chaplains all acknowledged the good work they had been able to do since a chapel had been provided for them. Attendance at Sunday services was excellent and "quite a number" of the inmates "entertain hopes of everlasting life." The chaplains did ask the governor to assist them in obtaining an annual appropriation from the legislature to buy books for a prison library so that prisoners would have a means of filling their leisure hours, "the most gloomy of their prison lives."[62]

The general mood of euphoria soon spread beyond the small circle of state officials responsible for the management of the penitentiary. A leading newspaper of the state, the *Galveston News,* commended the lessees for having brought about badly needed changes in the prison.

[58] *Biennial Report,* 1871–72, pp. 3–4.
[59] Ibid., p. 66.
[60] Ibid., pp. 7–9.
[61] Ibid., pp. 10–11.
[62] Ibid., pp. 11–12.

The life of the average inmate had been improved substantially and at no cost to Texas taxpayers. The paper lamented the fact that few Texans knew or cared very much about prison matters, but asserted that those who did would agree that Texas "has just cause to be satisfied with the experiments instituted by Messrs. Ward, Dewey and Company, and should, both from policy and humanity, enlarge and perfect the system introduced."[63]

Despite the general improvement in conditions, two problems of a serious nature had developed. One of these involved the payment of money to the county sheriffs for transporting prisoners to Huntsville, and the other concerned the treatment of prisoners by one of the lessees.

As early as August, 1871, Ward-Dewey balked at having to pay the charges incurred by the sheriffs who brought prisoners to Huntsville. Governor Davis wrote to the lessees, quoting the part of the lease contract that required such charges to be borne by them up to a maximum of $10,000 per year. The governor said the charges should be paid as the sheriffs presented them and that failure to do so could result in a revocation of the lease.[64]

Despite the governor's threats, the problem persisted. Davis heard that Ward-Dewey was discounting sheriffs' bills for payment. He instructed Inspector Randle to investigate the matter and inform the lessees that such procedures were illegal and should cease.[65]

Davis further instructed the inspector to institute new policies respecting the payment of sheriffs. In a letter to Randle, copies of which were dispatched to all county sheriffs, the governor announced that henceforth limits would be placed on the number of guards that could be used to transport convicted felons to the state prison. The number of guards would depend on the number of prisoners to be supervised. In addition, the governor instructed sheriffs to practice economy in their trips to Huntsville. They were to wait until their local courts had adjourned and then bring all persons convicted at that session at one time to the state prison. Davis authorized the prison inspector to examine carefully all requests for payment and to approve only those he deemed to be legitimate.[66]

This persistent problem of reimbursing county sheriffs did not attract the serious attention of lawmakers until April, 1879. At that time, the sixteenth legislature approved a bill that allowed the state to enter

[63] *Galveston Daily News,* May 4, 1873, p. 1.

[64] Governor Davis to Ward-Dewey, Aug. 10, 1871, Davis Letterpress Books.

[65] Governor Davis to Ed T. Randle, Apr. 10, 1872, Davis Letterpress Books.

[66] Governor Davis to Ed T. Randle, Apr. 10, 12, 1872; Davis to Ward-Dewey, Aug. 28, 1872, Davis Letterpress Books.

into contracts with private individuals to transport prisoners from the counties of conviction to Huntsville.[67] As a result of the contract legislation, the average cost of transporting prisoners dropped from slightly over $77 per prisoner to approximately $39 per prisoner.[68] Subsequent contracts would reduce the price even more.[69]

Guaranteeing humane treatment for persons incarcerated in the penitentiary proved to be much more difficult. Despite all the provisions concerning prisoner care in both the state penal code as well as the lease contract, evidence of abuse and neglect appeared soon after the lease system was instituted. In April, 1872, Governor Davis wrote to the inspector that there had been reports that Dewey had been mistreating the prisoners. Davis suggested that Dewey stay away from the inmates and leave all direct relationships between prisoners and lessees to Ward, who the governor believed to be much more qualified and experienced.[70]

In other communications with the inspector, Davis ordered a complete investigation into charges that prisoners working in a railroad camp near Bremond had been brutally beaten by guards.[71] In response to a letter from the county judge in Crockett, Texas, Davis ordered Randle to look into the treatment of prisoners working on the Great Northern Railroad near that East Texas town. According to the judge, L. W. Cooper, prisoners were not even "half-fed," were made to work on Sunday, required to do more work "than men can do," were "cursed and abused," and were crowded at night into pens "where they suffer a want of ventilation." Prisoners were punished by being placed naked in stocks, raised off the ground, and whipped cruelly. The governor wanted all guilty individuals in these matters punished severely.[72]

Inspector Randle quickly discovered that complying with the governor's requests was no easy task. Prisoners were reluctant to tell the inspector the truth about their treatment, knowing they might later suffer the wrath of the guards. Moreover, the state penal code specifically prohibited the testimony of convicted felons in legal proceedings. Thus charges could not be filed and prosecutions instituted unless guards testified against their colleagues, a most unlikely prospect, or some local citizen who had witnessed the mistreatment of prisoners came forward to testify.[73]

[67]H. P. N. Gammel, comp., *The Laws of Texas, 1822–1897,* VIII, 1439–40.
[68]*Biennial Report,* 1880, p. 11.
[69]*Biennial Report,* 1882, p. 7.
[70]Governor Davis to Ed T. Randle, Apr. 10, 1872, Davis Letterpress Books.
[71]Ibid., Feb. 29, 1872.
[72]Ibid., June 11, 1872.
[73]George W. Paschal, *A Digest of the Laws of Texas: Containing Laws in Force, and the Repealed Laws on Which Rights Rest,* p. 531.

Reports of the abuse of prisoners by lessees and guards continued throughout the duration of the Ward-Dewey lease. In fact, the evidence of brutality became worse the longer the Galveston company held the contract. By the spring of 1873, however, matters concerning prisoner care were overshadowed by other problems that both state officials and the lessees considered to be of much greater importance.

In their zeal to reestablish prison industries, a process that had involved considerable renovation and construction of new buildings as well as equipment purchases, the lessees found that their expenses quickly outstripped the income from the labor of the prisoners. As a result, in May, 1873, they appealed to the legislature for a delay in making payments that would be due to the state under the terms of the lease contract. The state lawmakers, the majority of whom were Democrats, consented to the delay, believing it to be much more important that the prison industries be firmly established and the permanent facilities well built. Governor Davis vetoed the bill granting the delay, arguing that such action constituted a loan of state money to the lessees and, as such, was constitutionally prohibited. The legislature, however, overrode the governor's veto and permitted Ward-Dewey to postpone payment of both the annual lease sum of $5,000 as well as the $10,000 annual payment for sheriff's transportation charges. The lessees were authorized to make no payments to the state for the years 1873, 1874, and 1875, but would pay upon expiration of the lease the total sum of $45,000 plus 7 percent interest.[74]

Having been given something of a financial reprieve, the lessees devoted more of their attention to managing the prison. In 1874, the first Democratic appointees of Gov. Richard Coke gave unqualified praise to Ward-Dewey. The inspector, J. K. P. Campbell, considered the lease to be a most "fortunate circumstance" for the state. All provisions of the lease contract were fully complied with by the lessees: prisoners were well fed, well clothed, and adequately disciplined. Campbell even asserted that the prison was "more than self-sustaining" financially. Inasmuch as no payments were made to the state, he must have meant that enough money was available to provide adequately for prisoners as well as for permanent improvements to the prison facility.[75]

The prison directors—J. W. Bush, B. W. Walker, and Thomas J. Goree—fully supported Campbell's assessment of the prison and its operation. The three men expressed complete agreement with the in-

[74] *Report of the Commission Appointed by the Governor, 1875,* pp. 16–18.
[75] *Biennial Report,* 1873–74, pp. 6–14.

spector's findings. Further concurrence came from Dr. W. A. Rawlings, the prison physician, who said that he had first been associated with the prison during the gubernatorial term of Sam Houston and that at no time since then had the institution seen "better discipline and management."[76]

Governor Coke, in a message to state lawmakers in January, 1875, said of the prison: "The management of the penitentiary in all its departments is excellent, the discipline is admirable, because while strict it is humane. The convicts are well-fed and clothed, and are not overworked, and all the apartments and cells in the prison are in good condition."[77] The governor also commented favorably on the "system, skill, and enterprise" with which the prison industries were managed.[78]

Regarding the overcrowding and the resultant necessity of placing prisoners in outside work camps, Coke stated that under the existing conditions little else could be done. The prison at Huntsville simply was not large enough to house the growing prison population. To remedy the situation, he requested that the legislature authorize the construction of additional prisons. He further recommended a house of corrections for juveniles serving their sentences in the Texas prison system.[79]

The legislature responded to the governor's message by approving a bill "to provide for the building and completing of two State Penitentiaries." One of the new prisons was to be built "northeastward of the Trinity river," to exploit the iron ores in that part of the state. The other was to be located west of the Colorado River where state prisoners would engage in the "manufacture of cotton, wool, leather, and other goods."[80]

The western prison would never be built. The commission empowered to locate a site for a prison in northeast Texas ultimately selected a location near the town of Rusk in Cherokee County.[81] The legislature appropriated $5,000 for the initial work to establish the East Texas penitentiary.[82]

The general mood of satisfaction with prison affairs, as manifested by the governor and other state officials, failed to reflect accurately the

[76]Ibid., pp. 14–15.

[77]*Governors' Messages, Coke to Ross, 1874–1891,* edited by and for the Archive and History Department of the Texas State Library, p. 84.

[78]Ibid.

[79]Ibid., pp. 84–87.

[80]Gammel, *Laws,* VIII, 400–401.

[81]*Governors' Messages, Coke to Ross,* p. 733; James Robertson Nowlin, "A Political History of the Texas Prison System, 1849–1957," p. 31.

[82]Gammel, *Laws,* V, 403.

deplorable conditions inside the prison. Indeed, the official statements contrasted so sharply with the true situation as to exceed the bounds of acceptable political hyperbole. Perhaps state leaders spoke from ignorance and simply repeated information passed on to them by prison officials. Or, possibly, knowing something of the abuses, they preferred, nonetheless, to ignore them, fearing that to do otherwise would risk a public outcry that would force the state to abrogate the lease. Whatever the case, as charges against the management of the prison began to be heard, state officials were forced to take action.

The earliest criticism of the Texas prison system came from officials in the state of Kansas. According to the superintendent of the Kansas penitentiary, during the months of July and November, 1874, a group of sixty-seven United States Army prisoners had been transferred from Huntsville to the state prison in Kansas. Upon their arrival, the prisoners appeared to be in a "horrible condition": "Most of them were emaciated and sick, reminding the prison authorities more of returned Andersonville war prisoners than of military prisoners, some of whom had committed only trivial offenses."[83]

The prisoners themselves described their treatment in Texas as brutal. The food they had received was of poor quality, often spoiled, and in short supply. They never had adequate clothing to protect against extremes of weather, and were forced to work all day long despite rain, cold, or their physical condition. The cruelties perpetrated against them did not differ substantially from the abuse meted out to all Texas inmates. The principal culprits included not only guards and sergeants, but the lessees themselves, especially Ward. One inmate told of Ward's ordering a hospital attendant not to feed a sick prisoner. Another said that Ward instructed a prison guard to kill a particular inmate who recently had attempted to escape.[84]

Most Texans first became aware of the charges made by the Kansas officials in an article that appeared in a New Orleans newspaper (the *Times*) in March, 1875. The Texas press subsequently picked up the story and generated a good deal of controversy and debate.[85]

Governor Coke, responding to all the publicity, appointed a three-man committee led by the assistant attorney-general to undertake a full investigation of state prison affairs. Committee members spent two weeks talking with inmates, guards, lessees, directors, and other prison officials. They visited the outside camps where prisoners worked, as well

[83] *Report of the Commission Appointed by the Governor, 1875,* p. 68.
[84] Ibid., pp. 68–81.
[85] Ibid., pp. 67–68.

as the main prison at Huntsville. Although the committee did not have subpoena powers, it did take all testimony under oath.[86]

The committee concluded that there was indeed room for legitimate criticism. Prisoners received insufficient clothing during the winter; they were overcrowded, especially in their sleeping arrangements, and were forced to sleep on bedding that was "disgustingly filthy." Moreover, they were not fed a sufficiently varied diet. Inmates received generally good medical care but the committee was at a loss for words "sufficiently strong to condemn as inhuman and unfit for the purpose, the place in the Penitentiary miscalled a 'hospital.'" The medical facility was located on the second floor of a building directly over the kitchen with its large oven and cauldrons. During the summer the heat from the kitchen made the infirmary insufferable.[87]

The committee reserved its strongest condemnation for the manner in and degree to which prisoners were punished. Even trivial offenses against prison regulations could result in a punitive ordeal so severe that gags had to be placed in the suffering prisoner's mouth to stifle the screams. Guards often inflicted punishment at night so there would be no witnesses. Citizens living near some of the prison work camps stated that "the groans and entreaties of the convicts *at night* were often so absolutely heart rending as to prevent . . . sleeping."[88]

Having defined what it perceived as the major failures of the prison administration, the committee next turned its attention to suggesting remedies. To ease the overcrowding, committee members recommended a house of correction for inmates under the age of twenty-one. The committee further argued that too many persons were being sent to the prison for theft of items of comparatively little value. It suggested a change be made in the penal code to decrease the number of penitentiary offenses but stopped short of making a specific recommendation to that effect.[89]

In its concluding remarks, the committee spoke of those fundamental weaknesses in the administrative structure of the prison system that rendered it difficult to prevent mistreatment of prisoners. Committee members pointed out, for example, that it was to the "conduct of guards, more than anything else, that the abuses of convicts may be traced." Many of the persons who worked as guards had no qualifications for the job. They were paid only $20 per month so that many who sought the position did so only as a last resort. Because of the large number

[86]Ibid., pp. 3–7.
[87]Ibid., pp. 92–99.
[88]Ibid., pp. 100–105.
[89]Ibid., pp. 127–29.

of guards required, the lessees found it impossible to conduct thorough investigations into the character of persons hired.[90]

The committee also criticized the provision in the lease contract that left the salaries of prison officials to the lessees. Those who served as guards, directors, physician, and chaplain were supposed to be employees of the state who looked after the interests of the state. By permitting the lessees to control their salaries, however, the lease contract place state prison officials in the awkward position of serving two masters. To correct this predicament, the committee recommended that all prison officials be paid directly by the state.[91]

On the subject of punishment, the committee recommended that definite procedures be instituted to prevent arbitrary and capricious conduct of guards. Corporal punishment, for example, should be permitted only with the approval of the inspector or one of the directors. In addition, complete written reports of all punishment should be prepared and given to the inspector, who would have the responsibility of keeping them in a permanent file. Any irregularities, such as unauthorized punishment, or the escape or death of a prisoner, should be investigated thoroughly by the inspector and reports made for submission to the proper authorities.[92]

Acting on the recommendations of the investigating committee, Governor Coke and the directors drew up new regulations and bylaws for the prison. Specific duties were assigned each officer, with the inspector being given much greater authority in matters concerning the proper care and discipline of prisoners. Regulations required all punishment to be carefully supervised, with no corporal punishment to be administered at night under any circumstances. New reporting requirements were instituted so that elected public officials could be kept better informed on matters taking place in the prison. The new regulations took effect in late July, 1875.[93]

In addition to alerting state officials to the necessity of reforms, the committee report represented a watershed in the relationships between the state and the lessees of the prison. Following its publication, the two parties to the lease contract seemed bent on a collision course that would result in the demise of the Ward-Dewey lease. The harmonious, mutually satisfactory state of affairs that had existed prior to the late

[90] Ibid., pp. 133–34.

[91] Ibid., pp. 133–35.

[92] Ibid., pp. 136–37.

[93] *Rules and By-Laws for the Government of the Texas State Prison. Adopted by the Board of Directors July 16, 1875, and Approved by the Governor, July 22, 1875* (Houston: A. C. Gray, Printer, 1875), pp. 4–6, 11–12.

spring of 1875 gave way to suspicion, mistrust, and recrimination. Texans were treated to what must have seemed a bizarre and rather inexplicable about-face on the part of their elected officials, as the generous expressions of satisfaction with prison affairs abruptly changed to accusations, heated rebuttals, and reciprocal hostility.

Governor Coke grew increasingly critical of the lessees following the submission of the report of the prison investigating committee. The governor expressed anger at the number of prisoners who either had been killed or had escaped. He wanted a full report from Inspector Campbell on each death. Coke believed that the large number of escapes from the prison reflected "inexcusable mismanagement."[94]

The governor also wanted the inspector to make certain that all inmate deaths were followed by a proper legal inquest and wanted the name of the presiding judicial officer in each case. Campbell was instructed particularly to see that the lessees fully honored those parts of the lease agreement and the penal code that sought to guarantee humane care of prisoners, including adequate medical treatment.[95] To assist Inspector Campbell in his duties, Governor Coke appointed Henry K. White of Ennis to serve as assistant inspector of the prison.[96]

Dissatisfaction with the prison management under Ward-Dewey also began to appear in other arenas of state affairs. In early September, 1875, delegates met to write a new state constitution to replace the one drafted in 1868.[97] In calling for the constitutional convention, Governor Coke referred to the 1869 document as an "extremely defective instrument." Many of its provisions were "repugnant . . . oppressive . . . [and] at war with the view of proper policy of the people of Texas." It had been written at a time of political turbulence, when the threat of federal intrusion into state politics loomed large. In 1875, however, Texas citizens no longer feared "Federal interference" and could draft a governing document more to their liking.[98]

Shortly after the convention assembled, it launched its own investigation of the prison. The investigation findings asserted that reform of inmates was virtually impossible under the management of Ward-Dewey and that no matter how stringent the rules and regulations providing for inmate care, they would be essentially unenforceable as long

[94]Governor Coke to J. K. P. Campbell, May 5, 1875, Coke Letterpress, Archives, Texas State Library, Austin.

[95]Governor Coke to J. K. P. Campbell, May 5, 1875; June 3, 1875; July 3, 25, 1875; Dec. 11, 1875, Coke Letterpress.

[96]Governor Coke to H. K. White, November 27, 1875, Coke Letterpress.

[97]*Journal of the Constitutional Convention of the State of Texas, 1875* (n.p., n.d.), pp. 35–38.

[98]*Governors' Messages, Coke to Ross,* p. 73.

as prisoners were scattered about the state in isolated camps. State leaders should take positive steps, such as establishing a house of corrections, commuting sentences, and decreasing the number of penitentiary offenses. The results of such policies would likely reduce the prison population to such an extent that additional prisons would be unnecessary. Convention members warned state officials to take immediate action with regard to the prison, for there was a strong possibility that at any moment it would "suddenly be thrown back upon the State."[99]

The arrival of the new year, 1876, brought a continuing decline in the fortunes of Ward-Dewey. In separate actions the inspector and the directors scored the lessees for their poor management of the prison and for their failure to carry out all the provisions of the lease contract. Reports pictured Ward and Dewey as unfit for the responsible positions they held and described them as being indifferent, if not completely callous, to the numerous cruelties perpetrated against the prisoners in their care.

In his report, Inspector Campbell did little more than reiterate the charges and complaints made against the lessees in the 1875 investigative report—namely, Ward-Dewey was not complying with the provisions of the lease contract. The inspector explained the large number of escapes as resulting, in part at least, from the practice of placing prisoners serving long sentences, those with little left to lose, at work in outside camps. Campbell urged the governor to resume possession of the prison. The lessees had demonstrated their inability or unwillingness to manage the prison properly as the law provided so that humane considerations and "the good name of our state" left only one recourse—resumption of administration.[100]

The director's report carried much the same message as had that of the inspector. All admitted that the prison was being run poorly, but the directors attributed much of the lessees' failure to a critical shortage of money needed to put the institution on a sound footing and not to any deliberate intention to ignore responsibilities. They pointed out that the penitentiary was, under any circumstance, a costly and unwieldy institution, and would likely remain so no matter who administered it. The implication in their message was that resumption of administration might not be the answer to all the problems.[101]

The directors additionally noted that a serious conflict of authority existed between the lessees and the inspector, and that possibly this had

[99] *Journal of the Constitutional Convention, 1875,* pp. 170–74, 541–42.

[100] *Biennial Report,* 1874–76, pp. 4–21.

[101] *Report of the Board of Directors of the Texas State Penitentiary to the Governor, March, 1876* (Houston: A. C. Gray, State Printer, 1876), pp. 6–10.

been the cause for much of the problem in prison management. The rules and bylaws adopted in July, 1875, had given the inspector considerable power to act against guards who were either brutal in their handling of prisoners or incompetent. Yet the lessees paid the guards' salaries. The directors reasoned that the only way to solve this dilemma was either to leave discipline exclusively to the lessees or have the state pay the guards.[102]

Within a few weeks of the directors' report, Ward-Dewey submitted a report of its own in response to all the criticism it had received. In a tone that revealed a curious sort of contentious bewilderment, the lessees seemed to be at a loss to explain the attacks made against them. They pointed out that all the reports on the prison prior to the early months of 1875 had been very good. In late spring of that year, however, following the Kansas report, the mood of state officials had changed abruptly. The same inspector and directors who had worked so closely with the prison and who had found so much to compliment just a few months earlier began to find much to criticize. Using the inspector's reports of 1874 and 1876, the lessees pointed out the complete reversal of opinion concerning the same topics and material.[103]

Ward-Dewey concluded its appeal to the governor by admitting that it had encountered many difficulties with the lease of the prison. The severe economic crisis that had begun in late summer, 1873, had forced cancellation of many work projects, leaving them with over a thousand prisoners who were without work but who, nevertheless, had to be fed and cared for. This had placed a severe financial drain on their resources. The lessees argued that their losses had been such that it likely would be at least a year, or perhaps two, before they could recover financially, but at that future time they would be willing to return the prison to the state.[104]

The lessees' appeal had little effect in reversing or even slowing down the growing antipathy toward the lease. The die having been cast, events proceeded along an inexorable path to resumption of administration. The next step came when the fifteenth legislature, convened in mid-April, 1876, sent yet another investigating committee to examine prison affairs under the lessees.[105]

[102]Ibid., p. 6.

[103]*Report of the Lessees of the Texas State Penitentiary, April, 1876* (Houston: Telegraph Steam Book and Job Print, 1876), pp. 3–8; *Biennial Report, 1873–74,* p. 13; *Biennial Report,* 1874, 1875, 1876, pp. 4–6, 12–13, 16–17.

[104]*Report of the Lessees, 1876,* pp. 23–28.

[105]*Journal of the House of Representatives of the State of Texas, Being the First Session of the 15th Legislature, Begun and Held at the City of Austin, April 18, 1876* (Galveston: Shaw and Blaylock, State Printers, 1876), pp. 395–402.

The report submitted by this committee simply restated the findings of earlier investigations. Ward-Dewey's management of the prison in all its aspects was roundly condemned and the state was urged to assume its responsibility. The final blow came on August 19, 1876, when the legislature approved a bill requiring the governor to abrogate the lease and resume possession of the penitentiary, "at such time and in such manner as he may deem necessary or expedient."[106]

The state did not immediately resume possession of the penitentiary. Following passage of the resumption bill, there ensued lengthy deliberations between the state and the lessees seeking to determine the nature and size of a final financial settlement. An appraisal of all prison property, including all permanent improvements made during the lease period, was initiated. The lessees, fearing that their interests might be jeopardized, or at least not considered equal to the interests of the state, hired legal counsel to protect themselves.[107]

Further delays came when, in the midst of the resumption negotiations, the state changed governors. On December 1, 1876, Governor Coke resigned to accept a seat in the United States Senate. Upon Coke's resignation, the mantle of state leadership passed to the lieutenant-governor, Richard B. Hubbard. Governor Hubbard on April 2, 1977, officially took possession of the state penitentiary and ended the Ward-Dewey lease.[108]

In assessing this first lease of the state prison, a somewhat clouded picture emerges. It is extremely difficult to measure how well, or how poorly, Ward-Dewey administered the prison. There can be no doubt that problems existed. Everyone, even the lessees, admitted this. Given the general agreement that there were difficulties, however, raises the more important question: Were the problems so severe as to warrant terminating the lease? The available evidence suggests that they were not.

The charges that prisoners had been abused and neglected no doubt were true. Similar charges had been made during the late 1860s, before the Ward-Dewey lease, when prisoners were put to work on the rail-

[106] Ibid., Gammel, *Laws,* VIII, 1029–32. The *Galveston Daily News* charged that during debate on the bill to cancel the Ward-Dewey lease, Rep. William Lang of Falls County led the pro-lease forces. The paper hinted that Lang, Worthy Master of the state Grange, had succumbed to the "accomplished and genial friends" of the lessees and had fought to defeat the bill abrogating the lease. In response to the charges, Lang said he was not trying to protect Ward-Dewey, but was interested only in "having some twenty or thirty convicts" to work his place. See *Galveston Daily News,* June 8, Dec. 19, 1876.

[107] J. S. Duncan, "Richard Bennett Hubbard and State Resumption of the Penitentiary, 1876–1878," *Texana* 8, no. 1 (1976): 47–55.

[108] Ibid., p. 48.

roads of the state. They continued to be voiced during the administration of Governor Davis, after the lessees took charge of the prison. Indeed, charges of cruelty toward prisoners would be characteristic of all leases made subsequent to Ward-Dewey. The fundamental conflict of interest in the leasing arrangement between the state and the lessees made abuse and neglect of prisoners a more than likely eventuality. The only way such mistreatment could have been reduced significantly would have been for the state to end all leasing of prisoners, a proposition state officials did not seem willing to entertain seriously in 1877.

It could be argued that the state terminated the lease for financial reasons. Certainly the lease contract did not generate the amount of money state legislators had originally hoped it would. Ward-Dewey admitted difficulties in this regard. Even though the state did not make the kind of money contemplated in the lease agreement, however, neither did it have to spend much. Even during their worst financial periods, Ward-Dewey continued to maintain the prison without an appropriation from the state legislature. The state only expended monies during the lease for some of the sheriffs' charges for transporting prisoners to Huntsville. Neither prisoner mistreatment nor finances would seem to have been reasonable causes for ending the lease, and so the answer must lie elsewhere and state politics appears to be a more fruitful area of inquiry.

The same political factors and conditions that had motivated Governor Coke to convene a constitutional convention in 1875 also influenced penitentiary affairs. The Republican administration of Governor Davis had been voted out of office. The reemergence of the state Democratic party by 1873 and its subsequent capture of the governorship had ushered in, as Coke suggested, a movement to rewrite the Republican laws and alter state government along lines more acceptable to the majority of Texas citizens. Just as the Democratic leaders had disliked the Republican constitution of 1868, they also opposed the prison lease made under Davis to a company with strong Republican ties. Political partisanship seems to offer a reasonable explanation for the abrupt, almost astonishing, change of attitude toward the lessees by state officials in late spring, 1875. The contract with Ward-Dewey became simply another part of the Republican legislative legacy that was to be swept away by the resurgent Democrats.

Additional evidence for the political aspect of resumption of administration came several years after Hubbard's actions. In March, 1883, Sen. A. W. Terrell addressed his Senate colleagues on the subject of renewing a lease with the firm of Cunningham and Ellis, to whom the state had awarded the prison in 1878 in the first long-term arrangement following the passing of Ward-Dewey. Terrell, who opposed all leasing of prisoners, remarked that signing the initial lease with Cunningham and Ellis in 1878 had come about, at least in part, as a result of efforts to "chrystallize" political majorities. He also mentioned financial gain for the state as a consideration, but the political factor, to Terrell, seemed quite clear.[109]

The lease made with Ward, Dewey, and Company reflected the desperate condition of affairs in state government in the first decade or so following the Civil War. A disrupted economy, bankrupt treasury, and growing criminal population pressed state financial resources to the limit. Elected leaders, when confronted with the enormous problems before them, chose to lease the prison in the hope that in addition to providing for the prisoners, the lessees also would make regular payments to the state.

On balance, the lease cannot be considered to have been a success. Lessees encountered serious financial difficulties and had to default on their payments. In addition, the manner in which the prisoners were treated aroused public anger and hostility. For these reasons, especially the prisoner treatment, state officials said they had no choice but to revoke the lease and resume administration of the prison.

Other factors also came into play in the state's decision to end the lease. It appears that political partisanship played a prominent role. The Ward-Dewey lease had been made during the administration of the Republican Edmund J. Davis. Shortly after the Democrats regained political preeminence in the state, they began to find serious fault with the Republican lease and ended it in the spring of 1877. The Democrats then had the responsibility for making a new lease or taking other steps to handle a prison population that exceeded the capacity of the prison.

[109] *Texas Siftings,* 2, no. 47 (Mar. 32, 1883): 6.

CHAPTER III

THE SUCCESSFUL LEASE, 1878–1883

The termination of the Ward-Dewey lease presented an opportunity to make a fresh start in the prison system. Upon resuming control of the prisons, state officials negotiated a temporary, six-month lease to gain time to prepare for a much longer and more profitable arrangement. Ultimately, the prison passed into the hands of a South Texas company led by E. H. Cunningham and L. A. Ellis, both of whom had extensive land holdings and other business interests. The Cunningham and Ellis lease proved to be very profitable for both the state and the lessees. In fact, the profits eventually led a number of state leaders to argue against an extension of the lease in 1883 so that the state could resume control and keep all the money generated by prisoner labor.

When the state resumed control of the prison in 1877, general economic conditions, though somewhat improved, remained a source of concern. Farming and ranching had rebounded a little from the lows of the immediate postwar period, but the state continued to struggle with financial difficulties. The heavy indebtedness of earlier years could not be retired with a system of taxation that, owing to the ease of evasion, yielded little revenue. State leaders found their options for managing state institutions limited by shortages of money in the general revenue fund.[1]

Governor Hubbard had anticipated the financial problems involved in managing the prison and had interpreted liberally the provision in the resumption bill that authorized him to resume in any manner he deemed "necessary or expedient." Hubbard reasoned that before the state could solicit bids for a new long-term lease, it first would have to complete a full appraisal of all prison property, decide the terms under which a lease would be made, make public notice of bidding procedures, and allow a sufficient amount of time for interested persons to consider the state's offer. The governor believed it could easily take several months before all the preparations for a new lease could be completed and during that time the state would have to bear the expense of supporting the prison.[2]

[1]Edmund T. Miller, *A Financial History of Texas,* pp. 196–239.

To relieve the taxpayers of such a burden, Hubbard decided to accept the offer of a Galveston firm, Burnett and Kilpatrick, for a temporary lease of the prison. This company had contacted the governor earlier and offered to enter into a short-term agreement in which it would pay all expenses of the prison plus additional monthly payments at the rate of $20,000 per year. In return for their money, Burnett and Kilpatrick would employ the prisoners and retain the profits for themselves. Hubbard believed that the temporary lease "was the best thing that could be done under the circumstances." To administer the state's interests under the new lease Hubbard appointed Judge James E. Shepard of Travis County, I. T. Gaines of Lamar County, and H. K. White, the former inspector, of Ellis County, to serve as directors. Thomas J. Goree of Huntsville joined these three as superintendent appointed by Hubbard.[3]

In awarding the temporary lease to Burnett and Kilpatrick, Governor Hubbard provoked a controversy that ultimately hurt him in his bid for reelection. A few months after the lease was made, a leading newspaper in the state published an article charging that Hubbard gave the prison to Burnett and Kilpatrick in return for certain financial favors. The publicity surrounding the disclosure forced Hubbard to respond publicly to the accusations.[4]

The governor stated that he had awarded the lease to Burnett and Kilpatrick "partly" because he had done business before with one of the lessees, J. H. Burnett. Hubbard explained that Burnett owned a cotton commission house in Galveston and that for several years this house had marketed the cotton grown on Hubbard's 700-acre farm in Smith County. The governor denied that he had profited from the lease and pointed out that the firm of Burnett and Kilpatrick was different from

[2] *Governors' Messages, Coke to Ross, 1874–1891,* edited by and for the Archive and History Department of the Texas State Library, pp. 727–28.

[3] Ibid., p. 728; Gov. Richard Hubbard to Thomas J. Goree, Mar. 22, 1877; Hubbard to Burnett and Kilpatrick, Mar. 24, 1877; Hubbard to Messrs. Shepard, Gaines, and White, Mar. 26, 1877; Hubbard Letterpress Books, Texas State Library and Archives, Austin.

Perhaps because the Burnett and Kilpatrick lease was of a temporary nature, not much descriptive evidence has been found. In the 1878 biennial report, Superintendent Goree mentioned that the lease went well for the first four months, with "very few complaints, and none . . . grounded." During later months, however, there were numerous criticisms in regard to lack of proper food and clothing. Goree specifically attempted to absolve the lessees of any guilt in these matters, saying that "whatever their [Burnett and Kilpatrick] delinquencies may have been, they were due to other causes rather than to lack of disposition to comply with their contract and with the rules of the prison." Unfortunately, the superintendent failed to offer any explanation of the problems. See *Biennial Report,* 1878, p. 5.

[4] J. S. Duncan, "Richard Bennett Hubbard and State Resumption of the Penitentiary, 1876–78," *Texana,* 12, no. 1 (1974): 53.

the Burnett cotton commission business even though J. H. Burnett was a principal in both companies. As his ultimate rebuttal, Hubbard asserted that had he been in a position, and of a disposition, to profit personally from the lease, he would not have made it a temporary arrangement.[5]

Because the Burnett and Kilpatrick lease was destined to last only a few months, state officials prepared for a long-term contract in the fall of 1877. Governor Hubbard decided that the new lease should begin on January 1, 1878, and should run for five years. Advertisements announcing the state's intentions and soliciting bids were published "in a large number of the leading newspapers in and outside the State." To guard against possible charges of favoritism or political chicanery in the bidding process, the governor directed that all bids were to be mailed in sealed envelopes and addressed to the secretary of state. The bids would be opened by the secretary in the presence of the governor, the attorney-general, and "all such bidders or their representatives as desired to attend." After receiving a total of nine bids, the governor, in December, 1877, awarded the prison to Ed H. Cunningham of Guadalupe County, who was the "highest and best bidder." Shortly thereafter, and with the permission of Governor Hubbard, L. A. Ellis of Jefferson, Texas, became associated in the lease with Cunningham. Cunningham and Ellis agreed to pay the state $3.01 per month per prisoner for the lease of the prison.[6]

Ed H. Cunningham and L. A. Ellis were both men of some wealth and prominence in late nineteenth-century Texas. Cunningham, originally from Arkansas, had come to Texas in 1856. When the Civil War broke out, he organized a company of troops that later became part of the Fourth Texas Regiment. Cunningham ultimately attained the rank of colonel in the regiment and completed his military service as inspector general under Gen. John Bell Hood.[7]

L. A. Ellis, a native of Mississippi, came to Texas in 1859 and opened a mercantile business in Jefferson. He too had served with the Confederate forces during the war. After the war, Ellis began purchasing farmland in Fort Bend County, where he also engaged in merchandizing. Both men committed much of their land to the extensive cultivation of sugarcane.[8]

The lease agreement drawn up between the state and Cunningham

[5] Ibid.; Dallas *Herald,* Jan. 5, 1878, p. 3; George R. Nielsen, "Richard Bennett Hubbard, 'The Demosthenes of Texas,'" pp. 53–59.

[6] *Governors' Messages, Coke to Ross,* pp. 730–31; Duncan, "Hubbard," p. 53.

[7] *San Antonio Express,* Aug. 28, 1912, p. 2.

[8] Rosenberg *Herald Coaster,* June 2, 1972.

and Ellis contained many features that had appeared earlier in the Ward-Dewey contract. Other parts of the agreement, however, sought to correct some of the problems that had developed in the previous lease. The comparative success of the Cunningham and Ellis venture may, in part, have been the result of additional provisions in the lease agreement itself.

Cunningham and Ellis leased the prison for a period of five years, commencing January 1, 1878. Specifically, the contract gave them the "state penitentiary at Huntsville, together with all the property . . . real, personal and mixed, pertaining or incident thereto, whether within or without the prison walls, and the labor of all the convicts now belonging or hereafter to be sent. . . ."[9] The lessees were prohibited from subletting the lease, or any part of it, without the written consent of the governor.[10]

The contract required the lessees to keep all prison buildings and property in good repair and to feed, clothe, and work the prisoners in accordance with the rules and bylaws of the prison system. They were further obligated to hire good, reliable guards and to dismiss any guard when requested in writing to do so by the superintendent or one of the directors. This provision quite obviously sought to prevent the kinds of conflicts that had arisen between the state and Ward-Dewey involving brutal or incompetent guards.[11]

Cunningham and Ellis also agreed to pay the salaries of all state prison officials. The method of payment differed from that of the Ward-Dewey contract and was instituted specifically to permit state employees to feel much greater freedom of action as they went about their duties. Instead of having salary payments made directly by the lessees, the money was to be paid into the state treasury where checks would then be issued to prison officials. The lessees were to pay $730 per month for the combined salaries of the directors, superintendent, physician, and chaplain.[12]

Further requirements placed on the lessees included providing office space and stationery for the superintendent and directors as well as sufficient paper and postage for the prisoners to write one letter per week. Upon completion of their term of incarceration, prisoners were to receive from the lessees a suit of plain civilian clothes, a pair of shoes, a hat, and $20 in cash. Finally, the lessees had to make bond in the amount of $100,000 as a protection for the state.[13]

[9]"Bond of Lessees of Texas State Penitentiary, under Lease made January 1, 1878" (unpublished manuscript in Penitentiary Papers, Texas State Library and Archives, Austin), p. 1.

[10]Ibid.

[11]Ibid., p. 3.

[12]Ibid.

[13]Ibid., pp. 1, 3.

When the prison was turned over to Cunningham and Ellis, it had an appraised value of $239,002.86. This included the main prison at Huntsville along with all lands, machinery, tools, and supplies. The lessees invested much time and effort constructing new facilities and improving existing structures. By the end of the lease period, they returned to the state a prison system of considerably greater value.[14]

The first major evaluation of the prison under Cunningham and Ellis came in early December, 1878. Superintendent Goree reported that the lessees were providing "active and energetic" leadership to make their lease a success. Both men were described as being "kind hearted and humane." They did not force prisoners to labor unduly hard, nor did they permit any abuse of prison inmates.[15]

In Goree's opinion, Cunningham and Ellis "always evince a willing and ready compliance with the rules." The lessees provided good medical care for the inmates and more clothing than had ever been the case before, though there were problems with some items of winter clothing. Satisfaction with the food, the superintendent observed, exceeded anything he had seen in his four years with the prison system.[16]

All punishment inside the prison at Huntsville came under the jurisdiction of Goree. Authority to discipline outside work forces lay within the purview of the board of directors. Within the prison, the usual forms of punishment included the stocks, the dark cell, the ball and chain, and "occasionally whipping," which was administered only on orders from the board of directors and only under the direct supervision of the superintendent. Goree reported that there had been relatively little punishment during the early period of the Cunningham and Ellis lease. Most inmates were amenable to a light reprimand, or the withholding of some minor privilege, as punishment for an infraction of the rules. Prisoners felt that the days of the arbitrary and excessive reprisals on the part of the guards were over, "that no unnecessarily harsh or cruel punishments will be inflicted, and that all punishments are for just causes."[17]

On the topic of discipline, Superintendent Goree demonstrated most clearly his preeminence among the many superintendents of the prison system during the period of this study. He continually evinced considerable concern over the objectives of punishment and, of equal importance, the best way to achieve those objectives. Goree admitted that he had much to learn about discipline and the best means of ob-

[14] *Biennial Report,* 1882, p. 15.
[15] *Biennial Report,* 1878, pp. 5–6.
[16] Ibid.
[17] Ibid., p. 7.

taining it. He requested that higher state officials also give this matter some thought and consider making available a small sum of money to enable Texas prison officials to visit and observe similar institutions around the country. He hoped to learn from what others were doing and incorporate what he learned into his management of the Texas prison.[18]

Goree further recommended that a commutation or "good time" law be requested of the legislature. He had in mind a legislative enactment that would permit a reduction in sentence for prisoners who manifested good conduct during their period of incarceration. Goree reported that such laws were already in effect in most other states and that all reports indicated their "good effects upon the discipline of the prison and conduct of the prisoners."[19]

With regard to working prisoners in camps outside the main prison, the superintendent recognized its necessity and the likelihood that the situation would not change in the foreseeable future. The greatest objection he saw to such an arrangement was "the temptation offered to convicts to escape, and the great number of escapes which occur." This proved especially true of white prisoners working in the railroad construction camps, in saw mills, and chopping wood. The largest percentage of escapes came from the small camps scattered about the countryside, whereas in the larger outside forces escapes were relatively rare. Goree thus recommended that white prisoners be worked with the spur, or shackles, and that "the lessees be requested not to hire out forces in less numbers than twenty, and to give preference to such hirers, other things being equal, who will take the largest number not exceeding sixty."[20]

Goree reported that he had established procedures for keeping records in the various prison departments, many of which had not kept records before. There had been problems of long standing—for example, in getting accurate reports from outside work camps. As a result, during the latter part of the Ward-Dewey lease, Inspector Campbell had shown 184 prisoners unaccounted for. Goree had begun requiring the sergeants in charge of outside camps to send him a monthly written report showing the name and number of every prisoner in their care, along with information on the numbers of deaths, escapes, and punish-

[18]Ibid.

[19]Ibid.

[20]Ibid., p. 8. The spur was a tight-fitting metal collar placed around the ankle. There were prongs pointing downward toward the foot. The prisoner wearing the spur was not prevented from walking or working, but running was impossible. See *Galveston Daily News,* July 5, 1879, p. 1.

ment. With the new reporting system, Goree had reduced to forty-four the number of inmates whose whereabouts were unknown.[21]

Dr. Thomas W. Markham, the prison physician, also spoke favorably of the new lessees. Nothing "conducive to local sanitation has been overlooked or neglected." The prisoners had been properly clothed, "plentifully supplied with wholesome, nutritious food, and an abundance of pure cistern water." The new hospital rooms, which had been moved from over the kitchen, were "commodious, well-ventilated and well-supplied with all needed appliances for the comfort and welfare of the sick." There had been but one recent epidemic in the prison and that was of a "mild type of measles." Dr. Markham urged legislative action to remove the criminally insane prisoners incarcerated at Huntsville. According to the doctor, there was no way to treat such persons properly in the main prison among the general inmate population. He recommended "the erection of a suitable building, near the Lunatic Asylum at Austin, where the patient could be placed under the care of physicians who make the treatment of diseases of the mind a specialty."[22] The presence of the criminally insane among the general inmate population generated much complaint from prison officials. Little relief was forthcoming, however, and throughout the period of this study the more violently insane remained within the prison walls.

As of December 1, 1878, there were 1,738 persons serving sentences in the Texas prison system. This figure showed an increase of 150 individuals over the 1,588 incarcerated at the time Ward-Dewey surrendered their lease. Cunningham and Ellis employed the prisoners in the following manner:[23]

Railroad construction crews	182
Wood chopping	299
Saw mill	18
Sugar and cotton plantations	916
Wheelwright, blacksmith, chair, paint, shoe, broom, and cabinet shops and in the cotton factory, all within the prison proper	323
TOTAL	1,738

For the period from January through November, 1878, the state earned a total of $56,718.98 from the Cunningham and Ellis lease. The monthly

[21] *Biennial Report,* 1878, p. 9.
[22] Ibid., pp. 26, 10–11.
[23] Ibid., p. 13.

amounts owed to the state by the lessees varied with the fluctuating prison population, from the lowest figure, $4,706.23, in January, 1878, to the greatest monthly amount, $5,621.97, paid in November.[24] Governor Hubbard reported that the Cunningham and Ellis lease had paid more "actual cash" into the state treasury during the first year than had been received in the entire history of the institution prior to that time, and "for the first time in the history of this institution does it yield a clear profit."[25]

The report on the first year of the new lease came as very welcome news to public officials who had watched almost helplessly as the prison system declined steadily and floundered amid seemingly insurmountable burdens. Cunningham and Ellis had tackled problems forthrightly and seemed to be making progress toward establishing the system on a sound economic footing. The superintendent had instituted new procedures designed to improve the overall administration of the system so that it would ultimately become a more efficient, competent agency of state government. In addition, he had begun to think about various reforms that would enable the prison to function more smoothly and therefore better serve the interests of the individuals imprisoned and of the state.

The sixteenth legislature, meeting in the spring of 1879, reacted to the new professionalism in the prison by responding favorably to the requests made. In a bill passed in March, state lawmakers formalized the administrative structure of the prison by amending certain parts of the state penal code and the Cunningham and Ellis lease agreement. The new law brought together in one document the policies and regulations regarding prison management that had evolved separately in a somewhat haphazard manner over several years. The nature and limits of the authority and responsibility of each prison official were carefully delineated and new policies concerning prison inmates and their care were defined.[26]

The new law required the governor to appoint three persons, subject to Senate confirmation, to act as directors of the prison. The directors would serve two-year terms and their duties included responsibility for establishing all rules and regulations of the prison. They could set up any policies they deemed "proper and necessary" and all such policies would be binding upon all prison employees. Directors were to meet in formal session at least three times per month to confer on matters relating to the prison and its management, and were to submit to the governor a written report of their meetings.[27]

[24] Ibid.
[25] *Governors' Messages, Coke to Ross,* p. 732.
[26] Gammel, *Laws of Texas,* VIII, 1347–57.
[27] Ibid., pp. 1347–48, 1354.

The directors were also required to inspect the prison at least three times per month and to investigate all complaints made by prisoners. They were authorized to "administer oaths, summon, and examine witnesses" as part of their effort to settle disputes and correct abuses. They were to report to the governor for his action any complaints or allegations of improper conduct on the part of the superindentent or lessees.[28]

The superintendent, as the chief executive officer of the prison, received responsibility for carrying out the rules and regulations established by the board of directors. He was to be appointed by the governor, with the consent of the Senate, and would serve for two years. The superintendent would have "general supervision and control" over all prisoners and guards, and could remove any of the latter for failure to perform their prescribed duties in a satisfactory manner. Additional duties of the superintendent included responsibility for the maintenance of discipline in the prison; frequent visits with prisoners to make certain they were "humanely and properly treated"; and keeping accurate records of all prisoners and their behavior. Furthermore, the superintendent should report monthly in writing to the governor, "showing the management of the penitentiary and the character of the treatment and discipline of the prisoners." He should also maintain all prison books and accounts to show the amount of money coming into and leaving the prison.[29]

The decision to have the directors and superintendent serve two-year terms proved to be unfortunate. Inasmuch as the governor also served for two years, it meant that chief executives would appoint their own men and they generally would be chosen because of their loyalty and previous service to the governor. The positions would become important parts of the patronage that fell within the governors' purview. Had the appointments been conferred for longer periods of time—say, four or six years—prison officials would have had more time to learn and practice the business of running a prison. More importantly, they would have had an opportunity to expand beyond the confines of a patronage system, thereby enabling them to direct their attention primarily to prison affairs rather than political matters.

Besides appointing the directors and the superintendent, the governor was required to name an assistant superintendent whose job it would be to oversee the outside camps where prisoners were employed. He was to visit the camps at least once each month to determine the care the prisoners were receiving and prepare a written report giving complete

[28]Ibid., pp. 1347–48.
[29]Ibid., pp. 1348–50.

information on each of the camps. The reports had to include the names and number of prisoners in the camps, the nature of their care, and full details of escapes and deaths.[30]

Individuals hired as guards would be selected by the directors upon nomination by the superintendent and would be compensated "for their services as the directors may prescribe." All guards would receive their pay from the state and could be dismissed from state service by the superintendent "on account of inefficiency or misconduct." The law listed no qualifications for guards save that they had to be qualified voters of the state.[31]

On the topics of prison discipline and prisoner treatment, the new law made its most drastic departure from the preceding statutes. The state appeared intent on correcting some of the more obvious areas of neglect and mistreatment of the past. Prisoners would have a broader range of opportunities available to them provided their conduct comported with prison regulations.

After making the usual acknowledgments as to the state's responsibility for providing suitable clothing and food, the law outlined the new policies respecting the treatment of prisoners. Inmates were to be treated with "humanity, and a distinction made in their treatment, so as to extend to such as are orderly, industrious and obedient, comforts and privileges according to their deserts." Prisoners would not be forced to do more labor than their "physical health and strength may render proper," and no work would be required of those persons deemed medically unfit by the prison physician. Finally, no prisoner would be forced to labor on Sunday, unless it was "absolutely necessary."[32]

The law also attempted to make available to prison inmates opportunities for self-improvement hitherto unavailable. Those who were unable to read and write when admitted to the penitentiary would be permitted to receive instruction during the study period, "under such regulations as the directors may prescribe." The directors were authorized to hire a teacher to instruct the prisoners.[33]

On the subject of punishment, the new law listed the means by which refractory conduct could be controlled. Prisoners disobeying regulations would be subjected to "closer imprisonment, confinement in irons, deprivation of privileges, and other punishments of like character," except that no prisoner would be denied food at regular meal times. Whipping would be the punishment of last resort and could be carried out only

[30]Ibid., p. 1350.
[31]Ibid., p. 1352.
[32]Ibid., p. 1352.
[33]Ibid.

"upon the special order of the directors in particular cases." The law further stipulated that a prisoner's head could not be shaved.[34]

In addition to prescribing punishment for those guilty of breaking the rules, the law provided rewards for those who "evince a purpose of reformation and a disposition to obey the rules of discipline." Good conduct could result in the commutation of the sentence being served. Prisoners who obeyed the rules could earn a specified number of days off their sentence for each month "in which no charge of misconduct is sustained." For their first year prisoners could earn two days per month off their sentence. This number would increase at the rate of an additional day per month up to the maximum of fifteen days per month for any period of good behavior longer than nine years. For every sustained charge of misconduct, however, the prisoner would lose one month's time of that year, and all commutation time would be lost in the event the inmate participated in a mutiny, conspiracy, or escape attempt.[35]

Lessees would have the right to employ prisoners either within or without the prison, "but no convict shall be hired or put to labor outside the walls when his labor can be utilized within the walls." The superintendent and directors could, if they chose, decide which classes of prisoners could be worked outside the prison and could formulate any other policies in this regard that they deemed proper and useful. In conclusion, the legislature stipulated that by January 1, 1880, "or as soon thereafter as possible," all prisoners should be confined at work inside one of the penitentiaries.[36]

The reorganization of the prison system under the 1879 law represented a substantial step forward for the state. Serious problems of all the usual varieties would continue to plague prison administrators for a good many years. But by assigning specific responsibilities to individual state officers, a sense of order and stability was introduced. The state was maturing as a political entity and one sign of it was the effort to foster greater competence and efficiency in the administration of state agencies. The provision in the 1879 law that called for all prisoners to be within the walls by January 1 or as soon thereafter as possible, proved to be an illusion. It could have been achieved only had the state been willing to embark upon an enormously expensive construction program to build additional prisons. Once the prisons had been completed, additional expenditures would have been necessary to establish industries and put them on a profitable basis. The state had begun

[34] Ibid., p. 1354.
[35] Ibid., pp. 1353–54.
[36] Ibid., p. 1355.

only recently to enjoy the financial fruits of a successful lease. It was too much to expect, given prevailing attitudes, that state officials would have reversed their course and ended an arrangement that was proving to be so profitable.

The stated intention to work prisoners within the walls represented a response on the part of lawmakers to a growing public concern over placing prisoners in outside work camps. During the last year of his administration Governor Hubbard had received several petitions from citizens' groups upset and angry that prisoners were being put to work in their counties, taking jobs from local workers. A group of 313 residents of Longview wrote the governor asking him to "stay the avaricious hand of the monopolists" who were bringing prisoners into Gregg County and taking the means of livelihood from local citizens. A group of 124 residents of Harrison County, one of them the county attorney, protested the use of prison labor to cut cross ties for the Texas and Pacific Railroad in their county. The petitioners estimated that such work could provide employment for 500 of their fellow citizens. From 695 persons in Bowie County came protests of a recent contract that had enabled Cunningham and Ellis to use prisoners in cutting fuel wood for the railroads. The lease contract had deprived approximately 500 Bowie County residents of employment and had given the jobs to men "upon whom the state has passed condemnation."[37]

Concern over the growing public resistance to the use of prisoners in outside labor forces continued to be manifested by Hubbard's successor, Oran M. Roberts, who had been elected governor in November, 1878. Late in his second term, Roberts wrote to the prison superintendent expressing his fear that the public outrage on this subject was "getting strong and widespread." Roberts anticipated a storm of public protest unless state officials took some action to mollify the critics. The governor admitted to the superintendent that no part of the state government had caused him such "constant uneasiness and apprenhensions" as the prison system and especially the treatment afforded prisoners in outside camps.[38]

The sections of the prison reorganization bill that sought to guarantee humane treatment and care for prisoners proved to be as difficult to enforce as such provisions had been in earlier legislation. State officials had to be vigilant to detect mistreatment. Once abuse or neglect

[37]Citizens of Gregg County to Governor Richard Hubbard, April 24, 1878; Citizens of Harrison County to Governor Hubbard, April 30, 1878; Citizens of Bowie County to Governor Hubbard (no date), Hubbard Papers, Governor's Letters Received.

[38]Gov. O. M. Roberts to Superintendent T. J. Goree, Dec. 13, 1881, Roberts Letterpress Books, Texas State Library and Archives, Austin.

was reported, it had to be attested to by witnesses whose testimony would be accepted in a court of law. But they were not always available. Nor was it always possible to believe those persons who came forth to speak against the lease and the practice of working prisoners in outside camps.

Very early in the Roberts administration, reports came in of severe abuse of prisoners working in a wood-cutting camp near Mineola. Governor Roberts responded by ordering the superintendent and assistant superintendent to undertake a complete investigation of the matter. The investigation and its findings are worth examining in some detail, although this was neither a typical investigation nor one of the more thorough ones. It is worth examining because it demonstrates quite clearly the complex of conflicting opinions and statements that had to be sifted thoroughly to get at the truth.

The incident first came to the governor's attention in late June, 1879. He recounted to Goree the information he had heard, and told the superintendent to investigate the matter thoroughly. He recommended that Goree have the assistant superintendent, D. M. Short, go to Mineola and mix with the people to see what could be learned of public feeling regarding the alleged mistreatment.[39] In a subsequent letter to Short, Roberts again repeated his desire that the investigation be as thorough and complete as possible. He specifically told Short to search out and make contact with Senator Buchanan, who represented the area in the state Senate. According to Roberts, Buchanan was a reliable man who could be of great help.[40]

Shortly before the investigation began, the Wood County *Flag* ran a special edition describing the prison camp in the area and the treatment given the inmates. The newspaper charged that the prisoners were completely at the mercy of guards who were "heartless brutes in the shape of men," and who were guilty of "unnecessary cruelty, brutish treatment, and outrageous conduct toward the convicts." It recounted stories of numerous unmarked convict graves near the camp, of convicts being whipped to death, and of guards unnecessarily and deliberately shooting and killing men who attempted to escape. The paper called for an immediate investigation to determine the truth in all the rumors and charges made against the camp administration.[41]

Shortly after publication of the *Flag* extra edition, the *Galveston Daily*

[39]Gov. Roberts to Goree, June 27, 1879, Roberts Letterpress Books.
[40]Gov. Roberts to D. M. Short, July 15, 1879, Roberts Letterpress Books.
[41]Wood County *Flag,* Extra, June 28, 1879, p. 1.

News ran a similar article. It detailed stories of brutal treatment of state prisoners under the care of the lessees. One prisoner, Ed Johnson, had attempted to escape but had been recaptured quickly near the camp because the metal spur bound to his foot had made it impossible for him to run. The two guards who had chased him simply shot and killed him rather than take him back to camp. According to the newspaper, there was evidence to indicate that Johnson had been killed after he was already in the guards' custody. The reporter pointed out that a large percentage of citizens in and around Mineola resented having the prison camp in their midst and that this hostility might lie at the bottom of much of the criticism of the prison officials. Local citizens were angry that the work being done by the convicts denied jobs to free citizens in the area. To them the camp appeared to exist solely for the profit of the lessees, with no thought being given either to the reformation of the prisoners or to the safety of residents near the camp.[42]

The newspaper quoted the attorney for the lessees, a Mr. Giles, who argued that the reasons underlying the criticism of the lessees in Wood County were primarily economic in origin. Local citizens resented seeing prisoners do work that county residents could perform. Giles further pointed out that there had been no demonstrations of public outrage regarding treatment of prisoners as long as local citizens had been able to supply the prison camp with needed goods and commodities. But when Cunningham and Ellis began contracting for supplies outside the area, local citizens became upset and began complaining of abuse of prisoners.[43]

Superintendent Goree and Assistant Superintendent Short, with the aid of Senator Buchanan, conducted the official investigation between July 15 and July 18, 1879. They focused on the alleged abuse and mistreatment of prisoners in a work camp at Lake Fork, near Mineola. The camp housed approximately eighty prisoners (the number fluctuated owing to escapes, discharges, and deaths) who were engaged in cutting wood for the Texas and Pacific Railroad. The camp was supervised by a sergeant and as many guards, usually eleven, as were necessary to control the men and keep them at their work.[44]

Twenty-nine persons appeared before the investigating committee. All testified under oath and signed written transcripts of their testimony. The inquiry focused most sharply on the period from September 1 to

[42] *Galveston Daily News,* July 5, 1879, p. 1.
[43] Ibid.
[44] Ibid.

December 24, 1878, when the camp had been supervised by Sgt. J. H. Randle. During this period most of the alleged abuse and neglect of prisoners had taken place.[45]

Only eight witnesses could offer solid, eyewitness testimony of mistreatment. The others could only repeat rumors they had heard from friends and acquaintances around town. Two of the witnesses, O. C. Reeves, a bookkeeper, and B. F. Read, a merchant in Mineola, had signed a petition calling for an investigation of the camp even though they had not personally seen any mistreatment of convicts. As justification for their actions, they argued that ever since it had become known that an investigation would be made, there had been no further reports of bad treatment of prisoners. This led them to believe that they had been correct in their actions and that the rumors had had at least some element of truth in them.[46]

The investigating committee called as its first eyewitness Willie Donahue, seventeen years old, who had worked as a guard for Sergeant Randle. Donahue had been paid $18 per month while working as a guard. He stated that he had once seen Sergeant Randle kick an Indian prisoner two or three times because the Indian had said he was sick and could not work. Randle forced the prisoner to go to work anyway and he died later that day. No doctor was called to attend the man before his death. Donahue further testified that he had seen Randle place men in the stocks and whip them with limbs from persimmon trees when they said they were too sick for work. He mentioned that the convicts were required to cut a specified amount of cordwood each day. White prisoners were to cut three-fourths of a cord, whereas black convicts had to cut one full cord.[47]

The next witness, James Long, aged forty-nine, stated he had seen Randle leave a man in the stocks for over six hours. The stocks, as described by Long, were made of wood with holes for the convict's neck and arms. Sergeant Randle would place the men in the stocks and raise them off the floor. The prisoners would just be able to reach a small stake in the ground with their toes to relieve some of the pressure on their neck and arms.[48]

Long went on to describe some of the incidents he had witnessed. He said he had seen Sergeant Randle use dogs to chase men who were attempting to escape. He would permit the dogs to attack the prisoners

[45]The report of this investigation is found in an unpublished, untitled, handwritten synopsis of testimony, Penitentiary Papers, Texas State Archives and Library, Austin.

[46]Ibid., pp. 17–22.

[47]Ibid., pp. 1–2.

[48]Ibid., p. 4.

after recapture. Long said he personally had seen two men whose bodies were badly torn and chewed by the dogs. He had seen two other prisoners each of whom had cut off one hand to keep from having to work, but they were forced to continue working anyway. He did not mention any medical attention the two men might have received. Long concluded his testimony by stating that the men seemed to be well fed, both in terms of the quality and quantity of food, but were housed in filthy quarters.[49]

Dr. A. L. Patton, a physician in Wood County, confirmed much of Long's testimony. He said that the men were greatly neglected during illness and that he often had seen Randle force the men to work when they obviously were unable to and should have been given medical treatment. Dr. Patton testified that during the fall of 1878 there had been a great deal of sickness and disease throughout the entire county. In spite of this, Randle had not taken any extra measures to provide the kind of medical treatment needed to protect the camp inmates.[50]

Two of the witnesses, J. W. Richardson, Jr., and W. A. Kennon, had worked as guards at the camp. They said they had often seen men vomit and soil themselves while hanging in the stocks. Kennon testified that he had seen Randle place a man in the stocks shortly after the man had been shot in the back while trying to escape. Both men agreed that conditions in the camp had improved considerably since Sergeant Randle had been relieved of duty.[51]

At one point in the proceedings Superintendent Goree took the stand to testify regarding his actions in the matter. Goree stated that he had first heard of the abuse of convicts at Lake Fork in December, 1878. He then had contacted several prominent citizens in Mineola to ask what they knew. At the same time, he had ordered some of the guards from a nearby camp to look into the matter as well. When their reports confirmed the rumors, Goree asked I. T. Gaines, a commissioner of the prison system living in Paris, Texas, to go to Mineola and make a full report with recommendations for further action. Gaines's report charged Sergeant Randle and one of his guards, F. P. Bounds, with "gross violations of the rules." Gaines recommended that Superintendent Goree ask the lessees to relieve the two men from duty and appoint a new sergeant to command the camp. When this had been done, Goree ordered the new sergeant to make a complete report of all violations of the rules with a copy going to a local magistrate for possible criminal prosecution. According to Goree, the sergeant's report confirmed all

[49] Ibid., pp. 4–5.
[50] Ibid., pp. 5–6.
[51] Ibid., pp. 33–41.

the instances of abuse and neglect that had been testified to before the investigating committee, as well as many others not mentioned. Goree concluded by saying that he had done all he could have in the matter; he did not at that time have the authority either to appoint or remove sergeants and guards.[52]

Several of the witnesses who could not testify to mistreatment of the convicts by guards did offer evidence as to the mood of the people of Mineola regarding the camp. T. F. McDaniel, deputy sheriff of Wood County, said that virtually everyone he knew objected to permitting the convicts to work outside the main prison and that most believed that convict labor took work away from local workers. D. C. Williams, editor of the Wood County *Flag,* agreed with McDaniel's assessment. Williams said that as far as he knew, fully nine-tenths of the residents in the county opposed having the camp near them. He further stated that he had used his paper to try as best he could to represent that sentiment.[53]

At the conclusion of the investigative hearings, Goree and Short filed a report of their findings with Governor Roberts. They concluded that all the publicity given the Lake Fork camp had developed out of deep-seated and widespread hostility to convict labor on the part of local citizens who desired to use the example of gross mismanagement under Sergeant Randle to discredit and destroy the entire leasing system. They did not deny that much abuse and cruelty had attended Randle's tenure as sergeant, but defended their actions in having him removed as soon as they had verified that he had misused his authority. Goree did mention that the inspector who normally visited camps in the area had been ill through much of the fall, 1878. Thus he had not been able to keep a close watch on operations. He also informed the governor that Senator Buchanan had spoken at some length with local prosecutors who believed there was not enough solid evidence upon which to base an indictment or conviction for any of the parties involved in prisoner abuse. Strictly speaking, because no eyewitnesses testified to having seen Randle or any of the guards actually kill a prisoner, the prosecutors could do very little. There had been testimony to certify abuse and neglect but only as part of the accepted means of disciplining prisoners. The testimony indicated violations of prison procedures but not the penal code. And Randle had been discharged, the proper course of action under the prison rules and regulations.[54]

Shortly after Goree and Short filed their report, Cunningham and

[52]Ibid., pp. 28–31.
[53]Ibid., pp. 7–11.
[54]Superintendent Goree to Governor Roberts, July 19, 1879, Roberts Papers.

Ellis prepared one of their own. In essence, they wanted the governor to use his influence to prevent further harassment of their employees, the sergeants and guards, who, they contended, were simply doing their jobs. They admitted that they had been deceived by Sergeant Randle, whom they referred to as a "cruel and unprincipled man." But they argued that they had acted responsibly by dismissing him as soon as they had become aware of his activities. They further explained that every time one of their guards was accused of mistreating convicts, it had proved to be very costly. The charges had to be investigated, the convicts had to be locked up and kept from working while the investigation was under way, and traveling costs and attorney fees had to be paid.[55]

The lessees reported that they had encountered considerable hostility along the entire line of the Texas and Pacific Railroad. The opposition, in their view, came primarily from ex-convicts, former guards, private wood-cutting contractors, and relatives of persons in the lease camps. These persons, all with narrow personal or selfish motives, eagerly talked to the press and related all manner of outrageous stories with little regard for the truth. The tone of the report from the lessees implied that if some form of relief was not immediately forthcoming from the governor's office, they might have to consider terminating the lease. This would force the state to resume control of the convicts and find housing and work for them.[56]

The investigation at Mineola seems to have satisfied no one. It did not silence the critics of the lease system. It did not bring an end to the practice of working prisoners outside the prison, nor did it result in any indictments or convictions. It embarrassed the state and the prison officials, and demonstrated quite convincingly that mistreatment of prisoners in remote work camps was virtually impossible to prevent, notwithstanding all the legislation designed to accomplish that end.

Governor Roberts, by demanding a full investigation of the Wood County matter, maintained his determination to see that the rules and regulations of the prison system were fully obeyed. On at least three other occasions, the governor ordered the prison superintendent to check into complaints made regarding the treatment of prisoners. In one of the incidents, a thirteen-year-old black youth had been sent to the prison for theft. Upon his arrival, he was told by the officer in charge that he did not "want no children here, it won't pay." Whereupon the boy was whipped and sent back home. Roberts instructed Goree to investigate the matter and prepare a report of his findings.[57]

[55]Cunningham and Ellis to Governor Roberts, July 24, 1879, Roberts Papers.
[56]Ibid.
[57]Governor Roberts to Superintendent Goree, Apr. 22, 1880, Roberts Letterpress Books.

On another occasion, the governor ordered Goree to check into possible abuse of prisoners working on the International and Great Northern Railroad near Grapeland. Roberts wanted the truth of the allegations determined and instructed the superintendent to take charge of the investigation. In the event Goree could not go, he was to send Assistant Superintendent Short, who, like Goree, was also an attorney.[58]

In a matter involving possible mistreatment of prisoners in some of the coastal counties, Governor Roberts not only ordered a thorough investigation, he even suggested the manner in which it should be conducted. Roberts wrote Goree telling him that several citizens alleged brutal treatment of prisoners in the camps in Brazoria, Matagorda, and Fort Bend counties. According to the governor's information, prisoners were whipped severely, were not fed an adequate diet, and were subjected to generally abusive treatment by the guards. Roberts suggested that Goree have the camps inspected and then, about a week later, arrange for another surprise inspection to see if anything was amiss. The superintendent was instructed to hire private investigators, if necessary, to determine the truth of the charges.[59]

Continued mistreatment of prisoners, especially those working outside the prison, made a virtual mockery of the legislation designed to protect inmates. The laws were only as effective as the officials in charge of the camps chose to make them. The superintendent, working with the lessees, was able from time to time to bring about some improvement. But the situation represented a dilemma: despite all the effort expended, some abuse could not be prevented.

Recognition of the problems in the outside camps occasioned some of the few negative comments about the Cunningham and Ellis lease. Superintendent Goree reported in 1880 that the lessees had cooperated with him when he attempted to enforce compliance with regulations, but that much remained to be done to bring the camps up to the desired level. Apart from this, however, the superintendent offered much to please state officials.

The prison directors—S. R. Smith, J. W. Carey, and J. M. Wynne—believed that considerable progress in the management of prison affairs had been made during the first two years of the lease. The lessees had completed a number of construction projects to improve the main prison at Huntsville, including the building of a strong wall to surround the entire facility. The brick wall formed a rectangle 500 feet by 778 feet

[58] Governor Roberts to Superintendent Goree, Dec. 4, 1881, Roberts Letterpress Books.
[59] Governor Roberts to Superintendent Goree, Dec. 2, 1881, Roberts Letterpress Books.

in length, had a foundation of four feet, was 32 inches thick, and varied in height from 18 feet to 26 feet above the ground. There also had been improvements made in the cell buildings, the dining room, and the guard houses, and a residence had been built for the superintendent, who was required by law to live in the prison. The total cost of all the improvements came to approximately $52,000. The directors recommended that the superintendent's salary be increased from $1,500 to $2,000 per year and that some provision be made to establish the position independent "of political changes and party bias of every kind." This request represented not only a tribute to Goree, whom the directors considered to have "few if any equals as a prison executive in any state," but was also a policy that had been adopted in "several older states" and had produced satisfactory results.[60]

Goree revealed that the state was doing very well financially from the lease. The net proceeds for the period from December 1, 1878, to November 1, 1880, totaled $186,910.97. In addition, Cunningham and Ellis had made permanent improvements to the prison buildings and structures in the amount of $224,331.11, including $120,000 for the construction of the East Texas penitentiary at Rusk. The lessees had paid an additional $47,029.18 for the recapture of escaped prisoners, salaries of prison officials, and money and transportation for inmates discharged from the prison.[61]

The proven profitability of the lease may go far toward explaining why state officials felt such concern over the treatment given prisoners in outside camps. Humanitarian considerations aside (and these were not inconsiderable), the state realized the importance of seeing to it that prisoners were not treated cruelly or permitted to escape and terrorize the countryside. Horror stories of guard brutality and mistreatment of prisoners, or frequent escapes, could stir up public opinion against the lease system and force elected officials to end it and have to resort to taxation to support the prisons.

The prison population as of November 1, 1880, totaled 2,157, an increase in twenty-three months of 419. The prisoners were employed in the following manner:

[60] *Biennial Report,* 1880, pp. 5–9. There had been a wall around part of the Huntsville facility prior to the construction of the new one by Cunningham and Ellis. The architect who designed the new wall, J. Larmour of Austin, examined the existing wall and decided it was substandard and that security consideration demanded a new one. The accuracy of his assessment became obvious to everyone when, as the workmen began demolishing the old wall, "it fell nearly the whole length, the workmen barely having time to escape from under it."

[61] Ibid., pp. 10–11.

In Huntsville prison proper	342
Constructing Rusk prison	256
On railroad construction crews	156
Cutting wood	215
At Kelly's Ironfurnace—Marion County	104
On farms	1,045
Miscellaneous	39
TOTAL	2,157

Prisoners confined within the prison proper at Huntsville included men with over fifteen years to serve, those with work skills, those considered "notoriously bad," and those judged to be physically unfit for outside labor.[62]

The prison industries continued to be modestly successful, especially the furniture, wheelwright, shoe, and harness shops. These four produced the most goods and the work was of high quality. The prison cloth factory still had not been modernized; it continued to turn out a fabric "for which there is but little demand." Goree explained that the lessees had not invested much money in the cloth factory because "the term of lease is too short, and the uncertainty of legislation too great to justify the cost."[63]

Discipline and punishment occupied a large part of the superintendent's attention, a reflection, no doubt, of official concern over the seemingly unsolvable nature of these problems. Goree said he was pleased with the state of discipline in the Huntsville unit. Punishment, when necessary, was inflicted strictly according to regulations. He expressed less satisfaction, however, with disciplinary procedures in outside forces, suspecting that a good bit of illegal or unauthorized punishment was meted out by guards without the knowledge of prison officials. Because of illegal punishment, "several sergeants and a great number of guards" had been relieved of duty. Although Goree saw room for much improvement, he believed that conditions in the outside camps had become more tolerable over the previous year.[64]

In response to public criticism of using prisoners in work forces outside the prison, an "opposition manifested . . . throughout the country," Superintendent Goree explained the necessity for such practices. He noted that instances of mistreatment of prisoners in outside camps had been reduced considerably since the state had begun to demand

[62]Ibid., pp. 11–12, 51–52.
[63]Ibid.
[64]Ibid., p. 13.

that lessees discharge their obligations to care for the prisoners. State officials inspected the camps regularly and removed officers when cases of abuse could be documented. State vigilance had led to the result that mistreatment was becoming the exception rather than the rule. The prisoners, according to the superintendent, were "well clad, well fed, and, as a rule, well treated." He did agree, however, with those who charged that the lease system left much to be desired: "No one will attempt to deny that the system is an evil, the true reason of which is because of the large mortality attending, the facilities afforded for escapes, and because under it there is little or no chance for reform. It can only be defended on two grounds: necessity, and because it is a source of revenue."[65]

Goree believed that the "principal opposition" to the use of outside convict forces arose from the belief that such use of prisoners came into competition with free labor and, therefore, should be ended. He responded that if that were, in fact, true, "the same objection can be urged *with equal if not greater force* to the labor of convicts in the walls." No matter where, or in what manner, prisoners were worked, they would, to some degree, compete with free labor. Almost everyone agreed, the superintendent continued, that prisoners should work and that the work done should be profitable, "so that the convict may earn the expenses attendant upon his incarceration." Therefore, the dilemma could be solved logically only by placing prisoners in the kind of work that would compete least with free workers. Goree argued that farm work was ideal, given "the great scarcity of farm labor" in Texas. He preferred to see outside forces placed on large farms where better facilities could be built and more frequent inspection made possible.[66]

The superintendent made additional recommendations designed to improve prison discipline. He requested that the legislature amend the commutation law to guarantee reenfranchisement for prisoners who completed their sentence with no sustained charges of misconduct. He also recommended that any person sentenced to a term exceeding thirty years be eligible for release after serving thirty years, provided there were no misconduct charges after the first five years of the incarceration period.[67]

In keeping with the superintendent's suggestions, Governor Roberts, early in 1881, addressed a special session of the seventeenth legislature, a session necessitated in part by the need "to make further improvements and regulations for the State penitentiaries." Roberts commended the

[65] Ibid., p. 21.
[66] Ibid., pp. 21–24.
[67] Ibid., pp. 14, 18–19.

superintendent and the prison board for the hard work they had done in the area of improving prisoner care. He informed the lawmakers that the policy of his administration was to place "as many convicts as can be used to any profit" within the penitentiaries at Huntsville and Rusk. The remainder were to be put on large farms:[68]

> By working . . . the convicts in large bodies on farms, they can be taken care of better, and will be more healthy, there will be fewer escapes, and fewer of them will be wounded and killed in the effort to prevent escapes; they can be made equally as profitable to the State in that way; and a portion of them might be employed in the erection of another penitentiary in the western portion of the state.[69]

Roberts sought from the legislature an appropriation large enough "to fit up the two . . . penitentiaries with new and improved machinery" to make them attractive to any potential lessee. He also wanted the state to commit itself as to the number of prisoners it would make available to work in prison industries. The governor believed that only a total effort by the state could ensure "that the experiment of such labor within the walls can be tested."[70]

The legislature responded to the governor's remarks, passing a bill to bring about another reorganization of the prison administration. The lawmakers were concerned, not only about the nature of any lease that might supersede the Cunningham and Ellis contract, but also that the Rusk penitentiary be organized properly and put on a sound administrative footing. To accomplish these objectives, the governor received much greater responsibility for determining prison policy.[71] The new law abolished the board of directors and created a new penitentiary board. The new body would be composed of the governor, the state treasurer, and the prison superintendent, and would have the ultimate responsibility for all prison matters, including the making and revoking of lease agreements, subject to the approval of the legislature. The penitentiary board received the authority to construct buildings, and to purchase land, equipment, tools, and other materials "to the end that the largest number of State convicts that can be profitably employed and comfortably accommodated, therein, may be confined and worked within the walls as soon as practicable."[72]

The superintendent became the chief executive officer of the prison

[68] *Governors' Messages, Coke to Ross,* pp. 387–88, 395.
[69] Ibid., p. 396.
[70] Ibid., pp. 395–96.
[71] Gammel, *Laws,* IX, 130–42.
[72] Ibid., pp. 130–32.

system. He was responsible for overseeing every aspect of penitentiary management and was to prepare monthly reports to the governor. The law also required the superintendent to visit each penitentiary at least once a month and each outside camp twice a year.[73]

The governor was to appoint an assistant superintendent to manage each penitentiary. The assistant superintendents would have full control and responsibility for their institutions. They would prepare monthly reports covering convict care, costs, and receipts, for submission to the superintendent.[74]

Two inspectors received the assignment to supervise the outside work camps. Each of the inspectors would be responsible for half the camps. The camps were to be visited at least once a month and a written report made to the superintendent. Inspectors would have the right to remove any officials under their supervision if charges of incompetence or mistreatment of prisoners could be sustained.[75]

The provisions in the law regarding treatment of prisoners remained much as the existing laws already provided. Prisoners were not to be whipped except by written order of the superintendent, assistant superintendent, or inspector, and all whipping was to be carefully supervised. There was to be no use of the stocks or "horse" under any circumstances. The commutation statutes remained in effect with only minor changes and the new law also left intact the provision for basic education for those inmates who needed it.[76]

On April 14, 1881, the new penitentiary board met for the first time. It announced its principal raison d'être to be the part of the reorganization bill that "requires that on the first day of January, 1882 or as soon thereafter as practicable," there should be confined within the walls of the penitentiaries "as many convicts as can be comfortably accommodated and profitably employed." The board also denied a request by Cunningham and Ellis to extend their lease beyond the expiration date of January 1, 1883, as "impolitic . . . for reasons not necessary to enumerate."[77]

In late December, 1881, the lessees again asked the board for an early renewal of their lease. As an extra inducement, they offered to build a railroad east and west out of Huntsville to connect with major rail lines. The board again refused, however, saying that such an agree-

[73] Ibid., pp. 132–33, 139.

[74] Ibid., pp. 134–35, 139.

[75] Ibid., pp. 135–36; 139.

[76] Ibid., pp. 138–39.

[77] "Minutes of the State Penitentiary Board from April 14, 1881 to April 28, 1885," Penitentiary Papers, pp. 1–3.

ment would be "impolitic and inconsistent with the best interests of the state."[78]

The board never revealed the specific reasons for refusing to consider an extension of the Cunningham and Ellis lease. Presumably, board members believed they could comply with the provisions of the 1881 reorganization by having as many prisoners as possible within the walls by January 1, 1882, or they believed they could enter a lease agreement with other parties under terms more advantageous to the state. As the date for the termination of the Cunningham and Ellis lease drew nearer, however, the board discovered that the kind of arrangement it sought was not attractive to potential lessees.

On June 30, 1882, the penitentiary board made formal preparations to advertise for bids to lease the state prisons beginning January 1, 1883. Uppermost in the minds of board members was their desire to place within the walls of both prisons as many inmates as could be comfortably housed and profitably employed. Furthermore, they wanted to see this done as soon as possible, "without the imposition of a heavy tax upon the people of the State."[79]

In preparing the advertisements, board members decided not to seek another lease of the same type held by Cunningham and Ellis. They wanted, instead, to solicit bids for two separate and quite different contractual arrangements. Their decision to depart from customary practice in this instance resulted from the observation that under the previous leases of the prison, the lessees had neglected developing the industries inside the prison in favor of employing more and more prisoners at outside labor. According to the board: "Outside labor can be operated without any investment of capital, and is the most profitable. The policy of the State is to increase the inside force at the expense of the outside, while every effort of the lessee is to build up the outside, because it is to his interest to do so."[80]

With this realization in mind, board members decided to seek separate bids for inside and outside labor. First of all, they wanted to make a lease for each penitentiary, Huntsville and Rusk. Lessees would have no part whatsoever in any outside labor. The only way such leases could be profitable would be for the lessees to devote all their attention and effort toward successfully establishing industries within the prison.[81]

The board would also accept bids for prisoners to work on farms

[78]Ibid., p. 19.
[79]Ibid., p. 25.
[80]Ibid.; *Biennial Report,* 1882, p. 7.
[81]*Biennial Report,* 1882, p. 7.

away from the prisons. The outside labor would be contracted for directly from the state—without going through a lessee. The board announced that preferential consideration would be given those bidders who desired to hire large numbers of prisoners, preferably in groups of at least sixty or more. By keeping the convicts in large groups, they could be guarded more easily, and would likely be better housed and fed, and could be watched over more carefully by inspectors.[82]

Having decided upon the kinds of bids it was willing to accept, the board placed advertisements in newspapers in Galveston, Dallas, Austin, and San Antonio. Additional notices appeared in New York, Chicago, Louisville, and St. Louis. The ads ran for eight weeks in the Texas newspapers and for four weeks in the out-of-state papers. Bids for outside labor were received until August 15, 1882, and until September 15, 1882, for the lease of the prisons.[83]

The board opened the bids for outside labor on August 15 and awarded contracts for a total of 1,040 prisoners. The contractors agreed to pay the state $15 per month per prisoner hired. They further agreed to furnish housing for the convicts, and to feed the prisoners and the guards. In return, they were entitled to ten hours' labor per day from the prisoners. The state agreed to employ the pay guards, and to take care of any "other expenses." Board members estimated that the expenses assumed by the state would total $9 per month per convict, leaving a net profit of $6 per month per convict.[84]

The state did not have the same success in the attempt to lease the two prisons. On September 15, the penitentiary board met and discovered that no acceptable bids had been submitted. It then decided to extend the date for receiving bids until November 1, 1882, and ran newspaper ads announcing the extension. On November 1, there were, once again, no acceptable bids, so the date was extended to November 20; the same results were obtained. Finally, on November 21, Cunningham and Ellis, along with Gen. W. R. Hamby of Tennessee, met with the board and "were invited to make propositions for lease of [the] penitentiaries."[85]

Following the state's invitation, Cunningham, Ellis, and General Hamby submitted proposals that the board found unacceptable. All parties then began lengthy negotiations that lasted just over one week. An agreement was ultimately reached: the state leased the Huntsville peni-

[82]Ibid., pp. 7–8; "Minutes of Penitentiary Board," pp. 28–29.
[83]"Minutes of Penitentiary Board," p. 27; *Biennial Report,* 1882, pp. 7–8.
[84]*Biennial Report,* 1882, p. 8.
[85]Ibid.; "Minutes of Penitentiary Board," p. 41.

tentiary to Cunningham and Ellis, and the Rusk penitentiary to General Hamby and his two associates Cherry and Morrow, "two of the lessees of the Tennessee Penitentiary."[86]

State officials believed the agreements reached with the lessees were "not bad." The new contracts would not generate as much revenue as earlier agreements had, but "better provision is made for the security and comfort of the convicts." In the end, the state agreed to accept a little less than it wanted from the lessees because the only other choice was to have the state operate the prisons. Apparently no one on the prison board thought it would work financially:[87] "It has failed elsewhere, where there were better facilities for success, and would be apt to fail here. It would seem that the lease system is the only one left us."[88]

The prison board signed the new contract leasing the prisons on December 18, 1882, and accepted the required bonds on January 11, 1883.[89] The terms agreed to by the lessees differed somewhat from the earlier leases. Among the major provisions, the state agreed to lease each penitentiary for fifteen years and to assign half of the prisoners to each institution. The lessees agreed to "carry out in good faith" the contracts for farm labor that had been made on August 15, 1882, and to pay all expenses associated with the prisons that the state would have had to pay had no leases been made. The lessees would have full use of all prison property, which they agreed to keep in good condition. The state would place three hundred prisoners in the Rusk penitentiary on January 1, 1883, and increase the number annually so that by the end of the third year, a total of eight hundred persons would be incarcerated in the East Texas facility. Similarly, the Huntsville unit would house four hundred prisoners as of January 1, 1883, and the total would increase to six hundred by the end of the third year. The lessees agreed to pay the state $10,000 per year for each penitentiary. The state would employ and pay all guards. Finally, the state reserved the right to remove boys from the prison population if the legislature authorized the establishment of a reformatory for juvenile offenders.[90]

[86]"Minutes of Penitentiary Board," pp. 42–44.

[87]*Biennial Report,* 1882, p. 9.

[88]Ibid., p. 10.

[89]"Minutes of Penitentiary Board," pp. 44–45.

[90]*Biennial Report,* 1882, p. 9. On Nov. 10, 1888, construction was completed on the first juvenile reformatory in the South, located on 696 acres near Gatesville, Coryell County, Texas. The young men sentenced to the reformatory worked on the juvenile farm but were not hired out to private parties. See *Governors' Messages, Coke to Ross,* pp. 632–34; Hilda Jane Zimmerman, "The Penal Reform Movement in the South during the Progressive Era, 1900–1917," *Journal of Southern History* 17 (Nov., 1951): 476–82.

Shortly after the leases were signed, the new governor, John Ireland, presented them to the eighteenth legislature for ratification. The members of the prison board apparently believed legislative approval would be a mere formality. Events, however, proved them wrong. On February 18, 1883, Superintendent Goree appeared before a joint session of the House and Senate penitentiary committees to review the leases and clarify the actions of the prison board in making them. He explained that his presence before the committees came as a result of criticism made "by some of the newspapers of the state, as well as by a few individuals." Goree defended the new contracts as being the best arrangement the state could make under the circumstances.[91]

After detailing all the steps taken by the board to obtain satisfactory leases, the superintendent argued that the contracts for the two prisons would enable the state to recognize a profit and at the same time ensure that the majority of prisoners would be housed within the prison walls at the end of three years. To those critics who charged that the terms of the final lease agreements differed substantially from those presented in the advertisements seeking bids, Goree pointed out that no one seemed to have wanted the prisons under the original terms of the state. With the end of the Cunningham and Ellis lease drawing near, the prison board had decided to alter its position and accept something less than it had sought initially, "rather than to have the State resume on the 1st of January."[92]

The superintendent admitted that the state would make less money from the new leases than it had under the recently expired contract, but explained that the demands placed on the lessees under the agreements dictated that the state receive less cash in the immediate future in return for other long-term benefits. By agreeing to place the majority of the prisoners inside the prisons by the end of three years, the lessees had committed themselves, in the process, to the enormous cost of building up the prison industries. There would be eventually less of the profitable outside labor and more of the relatively unprofitable inside work. In the end, however, the new agreements, if they worked as planned, would leave the state with firmly established, economically viable industries inside the prisons. Goree reminded the lawmakers that the law authorizing leases of the prisons did not require that the state derive "any large revenue" from them. There was a requirement, however, "that

[91] *Address of T. J. Goree, Superintendent of Penitentiaries, on the Penitentiary Leases, Delivered before the Penitentiary Committees of the Senate and House of Representatives, Eighteenth Legislature, in Joint Session, February 14, 1883* (Austin: E. W. Swindells, State Printer, 1883), pp. 3–14.

[92] Ibid., pp. 3–4.

the [Prison] Board shall provide as soon as possible for the confinement of as many convicts within the walls as can be comfortably accommodated and profitably employed."[93]

In early March, the state Senate ratified the new leases by a vote of sixteen to fifteen. Those voting in the affirmative included ten members of the twelve-member penitentiary committee. Shortly after the Senate vote, one source commented that Governor Ireland had lobbied actively for ratification of the lease and was chiefly responsible for the favorable result.[94]

When the bill reached the House, that body also seemed to be well on its way to granting approval. The penitentiary committee, on March 15, voted to ratify the lease. Eight members favored ratification, four opposed it, and one member abstained. Once again, Governor Ireland brought his influence to bear in favor of ratification.[95] Before the House as a whole voted, however, events came to light that embarrassed House members and caused many to reverse themselves on the lease contracts. In late March, *Texas Siftings,* an Austin newspaper, published articles in which it described attempts by the lessees to pressure the legislature into approving the leases. The charges made by the newspaper angered legislators, who subsequently voted 85 to 7 to set up a special commission to investigate the allegations. The investigative findings indicated that the lessees had devoted considerable time and money to the task of influencing lawmakers to favor lease ratification.[96]

In the course of the investigation, a good many individuals were questioned. Although several refused to name names, all asserted that the lessees had indeed attempted to influence individual legislators to favor approving the lease. The lessees had maintained private rooms in Austin and had invited members of the legislature to partake of the free hospitality, which included good liquor and cigars. One witness explained that because it was considered "vulgar and ungentlemanly" to give cash directly to elected officials, legislators were allowed to win at poker. The newspaper asserted that the eighteenth legislature would forever be known as "the poker Legislature."[97]

[93] Ibid., pp. 4–6.

[94] *Journal of the Senate of Texas Being the Regular Session of the 18th Legislature Begun and Held at the City of Austin, January 9, 1883* (Austin: E. W. Swindells, State Printer, 1883), p. 6; *The Daily Post* (Houston), Mar. 8, 1883, p. 1; Mar. 18, 1883, p. 2 (quoting the Marlin *Ball*).

[95] *The Daily Post* (Houston), Mar. 16, 1883, p. 1; Mar. 18, 1883, p. 2 (quoting the Sherman *Courier*).

[96] Ibid., Mar. 31, 1883, p. 1; *Texas Siftings,* 2, no. 47 (Mar. 31, 1885): 6; 2, no. 49 (Apr. 14, 1883): 8.

[97] *Texas Siftings,* 2, no. 49 (Apr. 14, 1883); 8.

Further accusations against the lessees came from two Austin saloon-keepers. They revealed that since the legislature had convened, the lessees had spent in the neighborhood of $250 to $400 each in their saloons treating state legislators. The purpose of the generosity, of course, was to secure approval of the lease.[98]

Texas Siftings charged additionally that the lessees' efforts had been most effective. The newspaper stated that fully nine-tenths of the people of Texas opposed the lease and that as a result, at the beginning of the legislative session, very few of the legislators had spoken in support of it. As the session wore on, however, and as more members succumbed to the blandishments of the lessees, support for the lease had increased.[99]

It is impossible to measure the impact that the information revealed in *Texas Siftings* had on feelings regarding the lease. Certainly the newspaper angered the legislature. Whether the legislators were upset at the truth of the charges or were simply reacting to the fact that their honor had been inpugned is unclear. From the furor that accompanied publication of the articles, however, the lessees sensed that the contracts were doomed. On March 30, 1883, Cunningham and Ellis, along with Morrow, Hamby, and others, wrote Governor Ireland, asking to surrender their leases. They stated that it had become apparent the legislature would refuse to ratify the contracts and that they, therefore, wished to be relieved of all responsibility regarding the prisons. One day later, the House voted 65 to 21 to revoke the leases.[100]

The House vote in late March ended forever this type of leasing system in Texas. The state would never again permit the control and management of its penitentiaries to pass into private hands. With the resumption of state control, prison officials faced the twin tasks of making the prisons self-sustaining financially and caring for the prison inmates in such a way that the abuses of the lease system could be either eliminated altogether or reduced to publicly acceptable levels.

The passing of the Cunningham and Ellis lease brought to an end a period of great prosperity for the prison system. During the life of the lease the state had earned roughly $358,000, in addition to the permanent improvements made to the prison facilities. The lessees themselves, according to one source, had made a "clear profit" of over $500,000.[101]

Given the proven profitability of the Cunningham and Ellis lease, it becomes important to determine why the state chose to end it and,

[98]Ibid.
[99]Ibid.
[100]*The Daily Post* (Houston), Mar. 31, 1883, p. 1.
[101]Galveston *Daily News,* Apr. 11, 1883, p. 2.

by doing so, deprive itself of a substantial source of revenue. By any economic measure, the spring of 1883 appears to have been a most uncertain time for the state to have embarked on a new course in penitentiary management. The prison population was continuing to grow, straining the available housing space. The industries in the Huntsville prison had not yet been established on a long-term, self-sustaining basis, and there was every indication that large amounts of money and expertise would be needed to do so. The new Rusk prison faced a difficult future. Yet the elected officials of the state, fully aware of the gravity of their decision, chose to revoke the leases and resume possession of the penitentiaries.

In taking such action, state legislators responded to a variety of public pressures. There is no way of measuring with any accuracy the true depth of the public hostility toward the lease. Nor is there any way to determine all the reasons why Texans opposed the system. But there is no denying that such feelings existed. Governor Roberts himself had acknowledged their presence and had spoken of his personal concern that public feelings on this matter not be further aggravated. In the letters and petitions the governor received, as well as the findings of investigations conducted under his aegis, it had been demonstrated quite convincingly that a growing percentage of Texans did not approve of the way the prisoners were treated by the lessees and resented the convicts taking jobs that law-abiding citizens should have.

Further evidence of the public anxiety regarding lease came from some of the legislators themselves. Representative J. Q. Chenoweth of Fannin County, speaking in favor of ratification of the lease contracts in 1883, mentioned the great discussion and debate concerning lease that was taking place "throughout the entire State." Representative A. K. Swan of Clay County, who also supported the lease, stated that he was doing so even though he recognized that "public sentiment is largely against the ratification of the lease."[102]

Some measure of opposition to leasing derived from the belief that the state could work its prisoners as the lessees had done and keep the profits. In essence, the state could eliminate the intermediary, the lessees, and earn even greater revenues. Several members of the legislature admitted the existence of such opinions and further proof appeared in some of the newspapers around the state. The *Courier* (in Sherman), for example, argued that "If there are fortunes in it [lease] for the les-

[102] *The Penitentiary Leases. Speeches delivered in the House favoring their Ratification by Hon. J. Q. Chenoweth, Hon. H. J. Labatt, Hon. R. R. Hazlewood, Hon. A. K. Swan, Hon. W. F. Upton, and Hon. A. J. Chambers, March, 1883* (Austin: Press of Deffenbaugh and Co., 1883), pp. 3, 12.

sees, or at least 'big money,' why not the state derive the benefit?" A source in Marshall reported that the lease did not meet with the approval of local citizens, who felt that "a great wrong has been inflicted upon the state in a pecuniary way." One of the larger newspapers in the state, the *Galveston Daily News,* also supported state resumption of the penitentiaries and urged state leaders to appoint a "known first-class businessman" to serve as financial agent of the prison system. The newspaper editorialized that "properly managed by competent men, the penitentiaries can be made to yield an immense revenue to the state."[103] With such expressions of optimism, the state prison system thus entered the next phase of development.

Ironically, the public haste and clamor to abrogate the leases in the spring of 1883 destroyed the single most promising opportunity to get all the inmates back within the walls of the prisons and working in prison industries, the admitted goal of the prison reformers. The lessees had demonstrated something of their administrative abilities with their success in their earlier lease. They had agreed, furthermore, to accept the terms of the new contract, which called for the gradual elimination of the more profitable outside labor in favor of strengthening the industries within the walls so that inmates could be transferred back from contract farms. If one may assume that they would have brought to the second lease the same skill, talent, and dedication that had led to their success with the first (and they had committed themselves to do so), it is not unreasonable to think they might have succeeded again and the prison industries would have enjoyed more sanguine prospects of surviving and flourishing.

The demise of the Cunningham and Ellis lease in a sense marked the end of an unfortunate era of Texas history. The financial distress and political turmoil that had led state officials to make the contract in 1878 had eased considerably. The lessees had improved substantially the permanent penitentiary facilities and structures. At the same time, they made money for themselves and for the state treasury. More importantly, their successful management of the prison had convinced the state that it could do the same and, in so doing, assert a greater measure of public responsibility for the care of state prisoners.

[103] Ibid., pp. 2–23; *The Daily Post* (Houston), Mar. 15, 1883, p. 1; Mar. 18, 1883, p. 1; *Galveston Daily News,* Apr. 11, 1883, p. 2.

CHAPTER IV
THE STATE AS LESSOR, 1883–1912

The legislative decision to terminate the leases with Cunningham and Ellis, and with Morrow, Hamby, and Company, did not bring an end to all leasing, as some of the critics might have hoped. Instead it marked the beginning of a thirty-year period during which the state attempted to run the system like the former lessees had. The prison system continued to grow, in terms of inmate population and the acquisition of additional lands and permanent penitentiary structures. Thus, by the end of the first decade of the twentieth century, the foundation for the modern penal system in Texas had been laid.

Even though state government remained financially feeble in early 1883, considerable progress in the way of economic recovery had taken place since the advent of leasing. The severe financial distress of the late 1860s and early 1870s had been eased substantially by the sometimes extreme retrenchment policies of Democratic governors Coke, Hubbard, and Roberts, who served during the 1870s and early 1880s. Governor Roberts, the quintessential Texas Bourbon, embarked on a program to rid the state entirely of its long-standing debt by drastically cutting state expenditures beyond anything Coke and Hubbard had done, while selling off public lands at fifty cents an acre to any and all purchasers. Roberts additionally committed state government to a "pay as you go" philosophy in public spending and saw it become an article of faith among his successors.[1]

By the time Roberts left office in the spring of 1883, he had managed to retire a sizable portion of the indebtedness. In addition, he had renegotiated the remainder to reduce the annual interest payments to levels that could be managed with reserves from the general revenue fund. The Roberts policies, by lifting much of the burden on the state treasury, permitted state officials the luxury of some flexibility in the management of state institutions, such as the prison system.[2]

Most of the operating expenses for the penal system throughout the

[1] Edmund T. Miller, *A Financial History of Texas,* p. 240; Frank Edgar Norton, "The Major Administrative Policies of Oran Milo Roberts, with an Introduction to His Life," pp. 49–85.

[2] Miller, *Financial History,* pp. 229–39.

post-1883 period came from the labor of prisoners hired out to private individuals. The state acted as the hiring agent and derived the financial benefit that had previously gone to lessees. State officials, in both the executive and legislative branches, continued to act from the belief that the cost of operating the penitentiaries should come from the proceeds of prisoner labor and not from the taxpayers of the state.

Unfortunately, and in spite of what appears to have been closer state supervision, abuses of prisoners in outside work camps continued to be a major problem. Additional rules and regulations, plus the hiring of inspectors to enforce them, simply could not guarantee full protection against arbitrary and capricious conduct by guards. In the end, the treatment of prisoners in outside camps figured prominently in the movement to end forever the practice of hiring out prisoners to private individuals in Texas.

At the time the former lessees made known their intention of surrendering the lease, in 1883, Governor Ireland sent a very pointed message to the legislature asking the membership to decide the course of action to be taken upon state resumption of control. Specifically, he wanted the state lawmakers to offer guidance to the prison board so that prison policies would be in complete conformity with legislative intentions and feelings. Ireland wanted to know, for example, if the decision to terminate the leases of Cunningham and Ellis, and Morrow, Hamby, and Company, precluded any further leases. Also, if prisoners were not be to leased, the governor wanted to know what disposition to make of them. He cautioned that if the legislature sought to have all inmates within the walls of the prison at once, at least $500,000 would be required to maintain them during the approaching biennium. If on the other hand the legislature authorized the prison board to hire out prisoners to private parties, it needed to indicate for whom the prisoners could work and the types of labor they could perform.[3]

The governor further requested that the legislature consider removing the prison superintendent from the prison board. As chief executive officer of the institution and, concurrently, a member of the governing board, the superintendent found himself in the administratively anomalous position of having to pass judgment on his own job performance. Ireland believed the best interests of all concerned would be served much better by relieving the superintendent of all duties save those of running the prison.[4]

Acting on the governor's requests, the legislature reorganized the ad-

[3]The *Daily Post,* (Houston) Mar. 31, 1883, p. 1; *Governors' Messages, Coke to Ross,* p. 486.

[4]*Governors' Messages, Coke to Ross,* edited by and for the Archive and History Department of the Texas State Library, p. 480.

ministrative structure of the state prison system. In a bill passed on April 18, 1883, the restructured prison board included the governor and two commissioners of penitentiaries who would be appointed by the chief executive and approved by the Senate. The new prison board would appoint an individual to serve as financial agent of the penitentiaries with ultimate responsibility for prison fiscal matters.[5]

The new law prohibited leasing the prisons and charged the prison board with the responsibility of confining all inmates within the walls of the penitentiaries "as soon as suitable prisons can be provided for their confinement and employment in such manner that they will be self-supporting." The board was authorized to employ prisoners on state account, at contract labor, or both, depending on prevailing circumstances. Prisoners were not to be employed on public works projects other than the building of additional prisons, nor were they to perform any "mechanical labor outside of the walls, in any city or town." Should it become necessary, the board could purchase prison farms to work those convicts "not self-supporting" at other labors.[6]

Shortly after passage of the prison reorganization bill, Governor Ireland appointed I. G. Searcy and Walter Tips, both of Austin, to serve as the prison commissioners. The two men received no salary for their duties but were paid $5 per day "while in attendance on the meetings of the board." The law specified that the commissioners would hold office for two years or "until the appointment and qualification of their successors."[7]

As one of its first actions, the prison board drew up new rules and regulations to reflect the return to state management of the penitentiary. Many of the specific duties assigned to the various prison officers remained similar to the responsibilities listed in previous reorganizations. One significant exception, however, concerned the increase in authority given officials to enforce rules and regulations. The superintendent, assistant superintendents, and inspectors could dismiss any lower officers, such as sergeants and guards, who were found to be acting in violation of prison procedures.[8]

[5] H. P. N. Gammel, comp., *The Laws of Texas, 1822–1897,* IX, 422–23. On Mar. 31, 1885, the prison board was altered by the addition of a third commissioner to take the place of the governor, who removed himself from the day-to-day operation of prison affairs. Inasmuch as the contract system had functioned smoothly from its beginning, in 1883, the chief executive did not need to give prison matters such close attention. See Gammel, *Laws,* IX, 707–708.

[6] Ibid., pp. 422–23.

[7] Ibid.; *Rules, Regulations and By-Laws for the Government and Discipline of the Texas State Penitentiaries, at Huntsville and Rusk, Texas* (Austin: E. W. Swindells, State Printer, 1883), p. 54.

[8] *Rules, Regulations and By-Laws,* 1883, pp. 3–12.

The listing of specific duties and responsibilities for the financial agent were the most extensive—a reflection, no doubt, of the importance of this position in the eyes of the board members. The financial agent was dubbed the principal "purchasing, selling and disbursing agent for the State Penitentiaries." He would receive all monies appropriated for penitentiary use and would supervise the purchase of all goods necessary to operate the facility. He would handle the payroll of all prison officials and, working with the superintendent, would make all contracts and receive all monies due the state from inmate labor or the sale of convict-made goods. Although the financial agent served under the superintendent, he reported directly to the prison board.[9]

On April 20, 1883, the board considered the applications for financial agent. A total of four persons had expressed interest in the position. After reviewing the qualifications of each applicant, the board members, upon the recommendation of commissioner Tips, unanimously selected Haywood Brahan, who had previously worked as "cashier and general business manager" for Cunningham and Ellis. According to Governor Ireland, Brahan was chosen because of his experience in prison financial matters, an expertise badly needed by the state.[10]

The board recognized very quickly that the two prisons could not accommodate all the prisoners sentenced there. Hiring out some of them to private parties, therefore, became a necessity. In considering this option, the state levied certain specific demands of those wishing to work prison inmates. Among other requirements, private contractors should provide "a secure and commodious prison house" for the inmates. The building should be heated in winter and well ventilated in summer. There should be within the structure at least 250 cubic feet of living space for each prisoner as well as two and one-half feet of window ventilation for each occupant. There should also be separate quarters for the detention and care of sick prisoners.[11]

Contractors also had to provide all the food for both prisoners and guards. Each inmate was to have a bunk with bedding, as well as a cup, a plate, a soup pan, a knife, a fork, and a spoon. Prisoners' clothes

[9] Ibid., pp. 5–7. The position of financial agent and the duties assigned to the individual who served in that capacity were not new in 1883. The criminal code adopted by the state in 1858 had provided for a financial agent for the penitentiary. The position was done away with, however, during the years the prisons had been leased to private parties. See George W. Paschal, *A Digest of the Laws of Texas: Containing Laws in Force, and the Repealed Laws on Which Rights Rest,* p. 405.

[10] Dallas *Weekly Herald,* Apr. 25, 1883, p. 1: "Minutes of State Penitentiary Board from April 14, 1881 to April 28, 1885," Penitentiary Papers, Texas State Library and Archives, Austin, p. 59; *Biennial Report,* 1884, p. 38.

[11] *Rules, Regulations and By-Laws,* 1883, pp. 35–36.

were to be washed weekly and the bedding "as often as necessary."[12]

On matters of working conditions, the board stipulated that prisoners were not to leave their quarters to begin work until daylight and were to cease their labors in time to return to the prison house by dark. Contractors could not work the prisoners on Sunday or in inclement weather unless such work was "absolutely necessary to prevent great loss." In the event Sunday work became necessary, the prisoners were to be paid fifty cents per day by the contractor.[13]

In establishing the rules for hiring out the prison labor, the board recalled past problems in the outside camps and sought to lay down ground rules to prevent their recurrence. The outside forces, for example, were to be "consolidated as much as practicable," and situated in areas "most accessible . . . by railroad." Such placement would enable inspectors to visit the camps regularly, thereby bringing a greater measure of state supervision to the prisoners working away from the prison. In addition, as part of the effort to reduce the number of escapes, the board set the minimum number of prisoners to be sent to any outside camp at forty, with preference to be given to those persons wishing to hire even larger numbers. By congregating prisoners in relatively large groups, the board believed that contractors and guards, cognizant of their responsibilities for such a sizable force, would go to greater lengths to design facilities and establish supervision procedures in such a way as to minimize opportunities for escape.[14]

A further guarantee against potential trouble came in the ruling that only the sergeants of outside camps were authorized to discipline prisoners. Neither guards nor private contractors could inflict punishment for any reason or under any circumstance. The board restricted the types of punishment allowed at the contract camp to confinement in the dark cell not exceeding seven days at one time, confinement in irons, and use of the ball and chain, shackles, or spike on the ankle. It further allowed deprivation of privileges, forfeiture of commutation time, and whipping, "but only by special order, in writing, of [the] Superintendent, Assistant Superintendent or Inspector in particular cases."[15]

The rules and regulations drawn up in 1883 remained in effect, with

[12]Ibid. Beginning in early 1898, the state began feeding contract forces. See *Biennial Report,* 1898, p. 7.

[13]Ibid.

[14]Ibid., pp. 37–38.

[15]Ibid., p. 41. An amendment to the rules and regulations adopted in 1893 established the maximum number of licks a prisoner could receive at one time at thirty-nine. See *Rules, Regulations and By-Laws for the Government and Discipline of the Texas State Penitentiaries and the Convicts Belonging Thereto at Huntsville and Rusk and at Outside Camps* (Austin: Ben C. Jones and Company, State Printers, 1893), p. 27.

minor changes, throughout the thirty-year period the prisons operated under the state contract system. Prison officials, anxious to prevent the mistakes and abuses of the past, sought to extend state supervision and control over every level of prisoner activity. The degree to which the new regulations were effective, however, depended, as in the past, on whether the individuals charged with enforcement performed their duties. Regrettably, the resumption of control of the penitentiaries by the state did not bring an end to the mistreatment of prisoners by private contractors seeking only personal gain.

As far as the individual prisoner was affected, the reorganization of the prison system and the promulgation of new rules and regulations made little difference. The provisions designed to improve living and working conditions represented little more than paper reforms, despite the good intentions that might have prompted them. In another sense, however, that of generating income, the overhauling of prison management policies ushered in a period of great prosperity for the state.

At the time the state resumed possession of its prisons, their value stood at slightly over $700,000. All the improvements made by Cunningham and Ellis at the Huntsville facility had increased its value from approximately $240,000 to $450,000. Monies expended in the construction and equipping of the Rusk prison had totaled $276,356.50.[16] Physical improvements notwithstanding, the two institutions remained a drain on state revenues. Prison officials thus faced the immediate necessity of taking steps to establish industries inside the prisons so that as soon as possible they could be made to turn a profit.[17]

On May 5, 1883, the prison board authorized the publication of advertisements seeking bids to operate the prison shops. The announcements appeared daily for two weeks in newspapers in Galveston, San Antonio, Dallas, Louisville, New York City, Nashville, and St. Louis. Bids were received until July 16, 1883.[18]

A total of five firms responded to the state's offer. After a great deal of negotiation, bordering at times on haggling, the prison board entered into agreements with three of the companies. The Wiggin-Simpson Company contracted for "machine and boiler shops and foundry" in the Huntsville unit. Also at Huntsville, the firm of H. C. Still and Brother used inmate labor to manufacture "saddle-trees, stirrups, and girths." the most substantial of the three agreements went to the firm of Comer

[16]*Biennial Report,* 1882, pp. 4, 15.

[17]*Biennial Report,* 1884, pp. 7, 16.

[18]"Minutes of the State Penitentiary Board from April 1881 to April 28, 1885," Penitentiary Papers, p. 70.

and Fairris, which received a thousand prisoners to operate the various parts of the iron industry at the Rusk prison.[19]

The state would have preferred to see a larger response to its offer for outside contractors to work the convicts within the prison. Quite obviously, the greater the variety of industry pursued within the prisons, the greater likelihood of financial profit for the state. Moreover, healthy, profitable industries within the prisons would enable prison officials to place larger numbers of convicts within the walls. An "exceedingly anxious" Superintendent Goree hoped to see the three contractors succeed "because their success may induce others to contract for labor and shops."[20]

Unfortunately, Goree did not realize his expectations. None of the contracts worked out as planned and within a very few years, the state was forced to cancel the agreements and operate the industries on the state account system.[21] The reasons surrounding the failure of the three private firms merit examining at some depth for the information they reveal concerning the difficulties of establishing prison industries and the state's handling of the problems.

The contracts with Wiggin-Simpson and H. C. Still and Brother failed primarily because of undercapitalization of the two firms, coupled with a general "stagnation of business" that set in shortly after the agreements were signed. Wiggin-Simpson had received seventy-five convicts for which they agreed to pay sixty cents per day per man. The company made a good faith effort in behalf of its contract, but by January, 1885, found itself unable to make the monthly payments to the state. The company asked for and received an extension on its labor payment, but by early summer its financial situation had not improved measurably. So on June 10, 1885, the Wiggin-Simpson Company surrendered its contract and ceased operations in the prison.[22]

H. C. Still and Brother originally had contracted for a total of thirty-five prisoners, twenty-five at sixty cents per day and ten at fifty cents per day. This company fell victim to the same difficulties that had plagued Wiggin-Simpson but found itself able to hold on a little longer. It re-

[19] *Biennial Report,* 1884, pp. 8–11.

[20] Ibid., p. 8.

[21] *Biennial Report,* 1888, p. 12.

[22] *Biennial Report,* 1884, p. 8; 1886, pp. 10–11, 71–72. The official report on the demise of the Wiggin-Simpson contract is somewhat confusing in the chronology of the company's financial problems. In one part of the 1886 biennial report, both the superintendent and financial agent mention that the contract ended on June 10, 1885. In another part of the report, however, the financial agent states that the company did not begin to experience financial difficulties until December, 1885, several months after it had terminated its contractual agreement with the prison system.

ceived several extensions from the prison board on labor payments, but by late May, 1887, it too had exhausted all sources of financial assistance and terminated its contract with the state.[23] Following the collapse of the two firms operating in the Huntsville prison, the board decided to hire outside managers and operate the prison shops on state account.[24]

The problems that beset the private contractors in the Huntsville prison also visited the shops run by the state. Prison officials put much hope in the manufacture of farm wagons, an enterprise that no private contractor could be persuaded to undertake, but their hopes were not to be gratified. As early as 1888, it was discovered that the preferred wood for the construction of wagons (white oak) could not be found in sufficient quantity or quality in Texas, the nearest supply point being St. Louis. The cost of shipping the raw wood to Texas, plus the time lost as the wood seasoned fifteen to twenty-four months, caused a considerable delay before a finished wagon could be shipped to retailers. Hefty appropriations from the legislature were needed to make the initial purchase of the timber, and additional monies were required to operate and maintain the wagon shop until the wood matured and fabrication could begin.[25]

Once the wagons were completed and offered for sale, additional problems arose. Some potential customers refused to buy the wagons, charging they had been built by unskilled prisoners. Other wagon manufacturers, in an effort to sell their products, exploited the fact that the prison wagons were convict-made, thus appealing to those persons who resented prison inmates taking work from free citizens. All the problems tempted prison officials to abandon altogether the manufacture of wagons. Such a course was not taken, however, because the work kept a certain number of prisoners busy and made use of expensive machinery that was suited only for the wagon industry.[26]

The general failure of the Huntsville industries was duplicated, if not exceeded, at the East Texas penitentiary in Rusk. The legislature appropriated enormous sums of money to exploit and develop an iron industry from the abundant ore supplies in the northeastern part of the state. But mismanagement and administrative neglect, in conjunction with all the usual economic vagaries, eventually induced state officials to cease their efforts.[27]

[23] *Biennial Report,* 1884, p. 8; 1886, pp. 10, 72–73.

[24] *Biennial Report,* 1884, p. 8; 1888, pp. 10–12.

[25] *Biennial Report,* 1884, pp. 43–45; 1886, pp. 72–75; 1888, pp. 10–12.

[26] *Biennial Report,* 1888, pp. 10–12.

[27] For an account of the financial difficulties at the Rusk prison, see Billy Martin Birmingham, "An Historical Account of the East Texas Prison at Rusk" (M.A. thesis, In-

The Rusk prison became operational in the spring of 1883, coinciding with the end of the Cunningham and Ellis lease. In July, Comer and Fairris made their contract with the prison board and officially took over the management of the facility on January 1, 1884. Almost from the beginning, serious disputes arose between prison officials and the contractors.[28]

The agreement drawn up between the state and Comer-Fairris stipulated that the contractors were to receive a thousand prisoners who would be divided into three classes. No mention was made as to the criteria for classification, but the agreement did specify that the state was to receive $100 per year for each first-class prisoner, $75 per year for second-class inmates, and $50 per year for those designated as third-class.[29] Given the different types of work that would be needed to develop the iron industry at Rusk (miners, furnace operators, machinists, and so forth), it is reasonable to surmise that the prisoner classification system was based on relative skill levels of the inmates.

The contract sought to have as many of the thousand prisoners as possible at work inside the prison and specifically enjoined Comer and Fairris from working inmates outside the penitentiary except for "such number . . . as might be necessary to cut wood, dig ore, burn coal, get lime rock, saw lumber and make provisions and forage for the necessary operation of the furnace and penitentiary." Before the agreement was signed, prison officials estimated that about three hundred prisoners could take care of all the outside work. Superintendent Goree insisted that the contractors strictly limit the number of inmates working outside, for the state paid the guards, and the larger the number of prisoners outside the prison, the greater the size of the force necessary to watch over them.[30]

One of the first disagreements between the state and Comer-Fairris resulted over the interpretation of the outside work "to make provisions and forage" to support the prison. The contractors interpreted this clause to mean that they had "the right" to use as many prisoners as they wanted to raise cotton, presumably to sell at a profit. When the superintendent, backed by the prison board, refused to permit such use to be made of the prisoners, the contractors asked that their contract be modified so that they would receive and be responsible for only five hundred inmates.[31]

---

stitute of Contemporary Corrections and the Behavioral Sciences at Sam Houston State University, 1979).

[28] *Biennial Report,* 1884, pp. 10–11.

[29] Ibid.

[30] Ibid., p. 11.

[31] Ibid., pp. 11–12.

The size of the work force Comer and Fairris had expected to use raising cotton—five hundred prisoners—leads to the conclusion that their interest in making iron was secondary at best. Had they been allowed to proceed with their original plan, cotton would likely have become their major source of income, at least in the short term, and would have received most of their attention and effort. Members of the prison board had every reason to question the degree of commitment on the part of the contractors to carry out in good faith the primary objective of developing the East Texas industry. In spite of the obvious anxieties they must have felt, prison board members approved the reduction in the Rusk work force as requested. Other problems would not be solved so easily.

The original furnace installed at Rusk had a twenty-five-ton production capacity.[32] It went into blast in the latter part of February, 1884, but failed to perform up to expectations. Instead of producing twenty-five to thirty tons of iron per day as expected, it yielded only eight to ten tons, much of which was of substandard quality. The poor performance was attributed to faulty design. Thus after two months of operation, "it was blown out" and the necessary structural changes made.[33]

The modified furnace went back into blast in early June and production increased although at levels still below those originally anticipated. This, along with other problems, led prison officials to bank the fires once again in early September. Within a few days of the second shutdown, Comer and Fairris contacted the prison board and surrendered their contract.[34]

The problems encountered by Wiggin-Simpson and H. C. Still and Brother at Huntsville also seem to have plagued the Rusk contractors. Comer and Fairris faced insurmountable difficulties in marketing their products and had to delay labor payments to the state. The prison board demonstrated a willingness to work with them through the difficult early months of operation, but by September the contractors sought to be relieved of their responsibilities and obligations toward the prison system and to settle with the state.[35]

The initial setbacks in establishing the iron industry at Rusk did not deter Superintendent Goree from his belief in the ultimate success of the venture. He believed that the poor production and other problems that had attended the first few months of the furnace operation had emanated from a lack of leadership and business skill on the part of

[32] *Biennial Report,* 1882, p. 5.
[33] *Biennial Report,* 1884, p. 12.
[34] Ibid., pp. 12–13.
[35] Ibid.

the contractors: "The furnace plant is a good one as originally constructed; the iron ore is convenient, abundant and of fine quality, there is plenty of good wood accessible for charcoal. Lime rock is inconvenient, and transportation for it high, but it can be procured, and in my opinion the only thing that is needed to make good iron, and a plenty of it, is good management."[36]

Goree went on to recomment that a professional furnace operator be hired and the iron industry at Rusk be developed on the state account system. He envisioned using the iron to make railroad car wheels, stoves, plows, water pipe, and hollowware, all of which could find a ready market in Texas, adjoining states, and Mexico. Operation of the furnace alone would require the labor of 250 prisoners, and more could be brought into the walls as ancillary industries developed.[37]

The nineteenth legislature appropriated $50,000 to establish the Rusk iron industry on state account. As the first order of business, a Philadelphia consultant and expert in the making of iron, John Birkenbine, traveled to Texas to examine the operation at Rusk and make suitable suggestions and recommendations to state officials. Birkenbine, quite impressed with what he found, stated that the prospects of an iron industry at Rusk were comparable to, if not better than, most other places in the country.[38]

Following the submission of the consultant's report, the state acted quickly. R. A. Barrett, the St. Louis furnace expert who had supervised the initial construction of the Rusk furnace, agreed to serve as furnace superintendent. Under Barrett's management, furnace production rose sharply; "the output was seldom less than 25 tons per day, and frequently over 30 tons per day." By November, 1886, the furnace, under Barrett's supervision, had been in blast slightly over six months. Production for this period totaled 4,113 tons of iron, which was worth approximately $65,808.[39]

At about the time that the prison board had decided to hire professional managers to operate Rusk on state account, a fortuitous opportunity to stimulate iron production presented itself. Shortly after the capitol building in Austin burned in November, 1881, the state decided to proceed with the construction of a new state capitol. The contract for erecting the new building went to an Illinois firm that agreed to accept three million acres of public land as payment for the construction. The prison board moved quickly to provide the cast iron work for the

[36]Ibid., p. 13.
[37]Ibid., pp. 13–14.
[38]*Biennial Report,* 1886, p. 12.
[39]Ibid., pp. 12–13.

building. Specifically, state prisoners would fabricate the "columns, with their pedestals, bases and caps, and the castings for the dome of the building." It was estimated that some two million pounds of cast iron would be needed, thereby netting the Rusk prison approximately $67,500. In addition to the money to be earned, prison officials believed the contract to be a good one: it would provide for the consumption of the furnace products, keep a relatively large number of prisoners at work within the walls of the Rusk facility, enable "a large number of convicts" to be trained as molders, and display the products of the Rusk furnace for all to see.[40]

The original plans for the building called for a "superstructure of limestone upon a base of two courses of granite." But when the cost of importing the limestone from outside the state proved to be prohibitive, a decision was made to use red granite from quarries in Burnet, Texas, for the outer walls. A relatively smaller amount of limestone available from quarries near Oatmanville, Texas, would be used for the inner walls.[41]

The decision to use local granite rather than limestone as the principal construction material prompted Governor Ireland to recommend the use of state prisoners to quarry the stone. Prison inmates also could build a railroad needed to move the granite from the quarry in Burnet to Austin. The prison board, in July, 1885, adopted the governor's recommendations and made available to the capitol contractors approximately five hundred prisoners. The terms of the agreement stipulated that the state provide guards, housing, and food for the inmates in return for a labor charge of sixty-five cents per day for each prison worker.[42]

The contracts for quarrying stone also proved to be profitable for the state. The prisoners at Oatmanville completed their work on May 1, 1887, earning a clear profit for the state of $1,720.64. The force at Burnet finished its work one month later and yielded a profit of $5,178.08. The state thus earned nearly $7,000 over and above all costs to maintain the prisoners.[43]

The use of prison labor in conjunction with the construction of the new capitol pleased legislators and prison board members whose responsibility it was to keep the prisoners at remunerative employment.

[40]Ibid., p. 14. Ruth Allen, *Chapters in the History of Organized Labor in Texas,* pp. 45–88; Records of the Capitol Building Commission, p. 1, Texas State Library and Archives, Austin.

[41]Allen, *Chapters,* pp. 45–46; *Biennial Report,* 1888, p. 69.

[42]*Biennial Report,* 1886, pp. 19–20; *Governors' Messages, Coke to Ross,* p. 536.

[43]*Biennial Report,* 1888, p. 69, and Exhibit F, p. 8.

They no doubt would have been satisfied had the earnings from the inmate labor only covered expenses. That a profit was recognized as well simply made the effort that much better.

The enthusiasm of state officials, however, was not shared universally. The decision to use prison inmates to quarry the stone for the capitol building aroused the ire of the Granite Cutters' National Union, which discouraged its members from working on the job and training prisoners. The union argued that if a few journeymen granite cutters trained convicts, those convicts, in turn, would train others and soon there would be no need for the higher-salaried free granite cutters.[44]

The call for a boycott of the capitol project proved to be so successful that the contractors had to import granite cutters from Scotland to supervise the work. This prompted a lawsuit filed in Austin against the contractors for violation of an 1885 federal law that prohibited the importation of foreigners under contract to perform labor in the United States. After considerable delay and legal maneuvering, the case came to trial in August, 1889, and the contractors were found guilty. They were held liable for fines and court costs totaling $65,000. After the granting of executive clemency by President Harrison, the amount was reduced to $9,000.[45] The enthusiasm the granite cutters demonstrated in their opposition to the use of prison labor and the national notoriety focused on the Texas case generated a lengthy discourse by state prison officials on the rationale for working prisoners and the proper disposition to be made of convict labor.

Superintendent Goree noted that the issue had aroused considerable feelings in Texas as well as the rest of the nation and was "the most difficult of solution of any pertaining to political economy." All the efforts made to devise a compromise acceptable to the greatest majority had failed; "the question of what to do with convicts is further from solution than ever."[46]

Goree believed "that the working of convicts outside the walls is an evil, because of the mortality and escapes attendant on the system." He noted additionally, however, that existing state law provided that convicts be kept within the walls only if they could be employed "in such manner that they will be self supporting. However much any penitentiary management may desire to work convicts within the walls, they have to be governed by the requirements of the law while in force."[47]

The population of the Texas prison system late in 1886, when Goree

[44] Allen, *Chapters,* pp. 46–48.
[45] Ibid., pp. 48–53.
[46] *Biennial Report,* 1886, p. 22; 1888, p. 24.
[47] *Biennial Report,* 1886, p. 23.

made his remarks, stood at "nearly 3,000." Cell capacity of the Huntsville and Rusk prisons was only sixteen hundred. According to the superintendent, "even now if we were to fill the prisons to their full capacity, it would be impossible to find employment to render them self supporting." Furthermore, there existed, according to Goree, "a very large class of convicts in Texas . . . who are totally unfit for skilled labor, and cannot be profitably employed in the walls."[48]

The only way to solve the problem, he believed, would be to recognize that the different types of prisoners required different types of work to keep them busy and earning their keep. Provide the necessary work, the superintendent argued, and be prepared to deflect as well as possible the inevitable criticism:

> The true policy would seem to be to confine as many convicts as can possibly be made self sustaining within the walls, and to provide additional prisons and equip them for as many of that class as can be so made self sustaining. Those convicts who cannot possibly be made self sustaining in the walls should be worked at some remunerative employment on the outside, either on state account or otherwise, as may be deemed best. Let them be placed at such labor as is least detrimental to health, where they can be most securely kept, and where they are least likely to antagonize, or come in real competition with free labor.[49]

Ideally, Goree's suggestions would seem to have been the least objectionable way to deal with a most difficult problem. By placing prisoners in the kind of work for which they were best suited, they would have been productive and the income from the labor would have gone to help maintain the prisons. Unfortunately, as the system evolved over the years, the balance the superintendent had envisioned did not develop. The industries inside the two prisons languished because of a number of difficulties, and even though they continued to provide jobs for some inmates, they never became profitable. The outside forces, on the other hand, flourished and paid handsome dividends. Inevitably, the profits from hiring the prisoners to work outside the prison led to larger and larger numbers being so employed, with a corresponding neglect of the inside industries.

For well over a year following resumption of control, the prison board made contracts with outside parties seeking to hire state prisoners. By November, 1884, a total of 1,148 inmates worked for private individuals on farms scattered through the southern and eastern parts of the state. In addition, 176 state prisoners worked on construction crews for four

[48] Ibid.
[49] Ibid., p. 24.

railroads, the Galveston, Houston, and San Antonio; the Houston and Texas Central; the International and Great Northern; and the Texas Central.[50]

Over the years, the railroad contracts proved to be more lucrative than was farm labor. In 1884, for example, the state received $1.25 per prisoner per day for those working for the railroads. The price declined a few cents during the hard economic times of the mid-1880s and remained at only slightly over $1 until the early years of the twentieth century, when it climbed, once again, to $1.15 per day.[51]

In areas other than the relative profitability, however, the railroad forces proved to be far less attractive. The railroads never made use of more than a small minority of the total convict population. During the year 1892, for example, the various railroads employed the largest number of state prisoners, 588, of any year in which prisoners were put to such use. Yet the total convict population that year stood at 3,575, leaving 2,987 prisoners to be placed elsewhere.[52]

Another drawback to the large-scale placement of convicts at work for the railroads lay in the tenuous nature of the contractual arrangements the state was able to obtain from the companies. The railroads refused to obligate themselves for extended periods of time. They hired prison labor with the understanding that they reserved to themselves "the right of returning it at any time on short notice." Prison officials had to face the fact that at the first sign of economic troubles, the railroads could return the prisoners to the penitentiaries, thereby placing impossible demands on the state's resources. Superintendent Goree admitted candidly in 1890 that if the railroads suddenly returned the convicts then under contract, the prison system would be unable to house them or find anything for them to do.[53]

The outside farm labor, though it yielded less in earnings per prisoner, provided greater stability than did railroad work. State officials could be reasonably certain that farm forces would be kept in place for the life of the contract. On those few occasions when private farmers realized they could not honor fully their agreements with the state, prison officials encountered few difficulties in either negotiating a new contract or placing the prisoners on other farms. Throughout the entire period of state contract management, outside farm labor brought in net profits

[50] *Biennial Report,* 1884, p. 29; 1888, p. 19.

[51] *Biennial Report,* 1884, pp. 39–40; 1886, p. 67; 1908, p. 10.

[52] *Biennial Report,* 1892, p. 29; The figures given represent totals during the state contract period only, 1883–1912. The year when the largest number of state prisoners worked for the railroads was 1882, during the Cunningham and Ellis lease. See *Biennial Report,* 1882, pp. 36–37.

[53] *Biennial Report,* 1890, p. 115.

of $3,423,087.63, making it the largest single source of prison revenue for the period.[54]

The profitability of prisoner work on private farms represented only one of the attractions for the state. Such arrangements also provided a virtually limitless means of placing individuals for whom there was no space in the prisons. Also, prison officials discovered that a large percentage of prisoners possessed no formal skills or trades, so that farm work became the one type of employment in which such persons could be made productive. Superintendent Goree recognized quite clearly the value of farm labor for certain prisoners. He noted that a "large majority" of the prison population in Texas had been raised either on farms or on the prairies "branding 'mavericks.'" They had no marketable industrial skills and, if placed at labor inside the prison, "would be a clog upon good discipline, and . . . would be a constant strain upon the industry of the competent convicts." According to Goree, "The only plan to pursue with this class of convicts, white and colored, will be to place them at suitable labor on the outside, which I think should be *farm* labor."[55]

Goree's opinions and suggestions, expressed on several occasions, made an impression on the prison board and the elected leaders of the state. Every year between 1884 and 1910, at least a thousand prisoners worked on outside farms. For the first nine years following resumption, the number hovered at the thousand mark. Between 1892 and 1894, however, during the administration of Governor Hogg, it surged dramatically from 1,039 to 1,739. It increased to over two thousand by 1896 and reached its peak, 2,363, in 1902. From that point, the number began a steady decline until, by 1910, it had fallen to 1,692.[56]

As the numbers of prisoners on farms increased, so did the price of their labor. The low price of $15 per month was charged those contractors who received prisoners in the fall of 1882 and renewed their contracts in 1887. By 1892, the state had structured the labor price according to the types of crop raised. The more valuable the crop, the higher the labor charge. Those prisoners, for example, working on farms where sugar was the exclusive crop brought the state $17 per month per worker. The amount of $16.50 per month was charged those planters who raised

[54] *Biennial Report,* 1884, pp. 60–61; 1886, pp. 91–92; 1888, pp. 7–9 in Exhibits Section; 1890, pp. 128–32; 1898, pp. 89–92; 1900, pp. 100–101; 1902, pp. 120–24; 1906, pp. 103–105; 1908, pp. 109–10.

[55] *Biennial Report,* 1880, p. 23.

[56] *Biennial Report,* 1884, p. 18; 1886, p. 9; 1888, p. 28, Exhibit 9; 1890, p. 56; 1892, p. 29; 1894, p. 32; 1896, p. 39; 1898, p. 29; 1900, p. 29; 1902, p. 38; 1904, p. 38; 1906, p. 27–28; 1908, p. 31; 1910, p. 35.

both sugar and cotton, and the lowest charge, $15.50 per month, was levied against farmers who raised cotton and corn.[57]

Labor charges dropped slightly during 1894 and 1896, but by 1898 prices were on the rise once again. There appeared also in 1898 an additional classification of workers, this time into first- and second-class hands. The labor charge for first-class hands on farms raising both cotton and sugar was $19.50 per month per prisoner. First-class hands on farms where cotton alone was grown brought $18 per month, and second-class workers brought $16.50 per month.[58] The separation of the prisoners into first- and second-class categories had to do with their physical abilities to perform labor wherein age and general health figured prominently.

By 1904, the state could command $21 per month for first-class hands and $18 per month for second-class workers.[59] Sometime during the period from 1904 to 1906 a decision was made to hire out only first-class hands to private contractors for $21 per month.[60] This price was short-lived for by 1908 labor costs for state prisoners to work farms had reached their highest point, $31 per month for first-class black prisoners and $29 per month for first-class white prisoners.[61] This price continued until the contract system ended in 1912.

The rather rapid increase in the cost of prison labor during the late 1890s and the first decade of the twentieth century appears to have been little more than an attempt by the state to earn as much revenue as possible from its prisoners. Texas farms remained essentially without mechanized equipment during this time, so state officials could feel free to raise the price of the prison labor with little fear that private contractors, almost wholly dependent on human and animal labor, would look elsewhere for workers. It was not until the 1930s that agricultural mechanization began to become commonplace on Texas farms, displacing the more traditional forms of labor.[62]

[57] *Biennial Report,* 1882, p. 8; 1888, p. 19; 1892, p. 9.

[58] *Biennial Report,* 1894, p. 11; 1896, pp. 10–11; 1898, p. 12.

[59] *Biennial Report,* 1904, p. 15.

[60] *Biennial Report,* 1906, p. 11.

[61] *Biennial Report,* 1908, p. 10. No specific reason could be found for the price differential between black and white prisoners. Very likely, the higher charge for black labor stemmed from the fact that black prisoners were used almost exclusively on the sugar farms, where labor charges traditionally had been higher. As well as could be determined, the prices charged for prison labor, especially during the early years of the twentieth century, were only slightly less than the wages of free working similarly employed. The obvious advantage to hiring prison inmates lay in the fact that the state guaranteed a work force of a determined size, kept the prisoners at their assigned tasks, and freed contractors of any responsibility for involving themselves in labor matters. See John Stricklin Spratt, *The Road to Spindletop. Economic Change in Texas, 1875–1901,* pp. 229–31.

[62] Farm mechanization did not begin to arrive in Texas until the prosperity of the World

In addition to hiring out prisoners to railroads and private farmers, the state agreed to furnish a limited number of prisoners for more specialized kinds of work. In 1906, forty-nine state prisoners mined coal for the Consumers Lignite Company in Alba, Wood County, Texas. The contractors paid $35 per month for each prisoner.[63] By 1908 the contract with the Wood County company had been replaced by a similar arrangement with the S. W. Fuel and Manufacturing Company, which had prisoners working in coal mines near Calvert in Robertson County. The state received $44 per month per inmate employed in the Calvert mines.[64] By 1908, the Texas Turpentine Company in Jasper employed 833 prisoners at a cost of $45 per month for each convict.[65] Both the mining and turpentine forces were short-lived and came to an end by the fall of 1910.[66]

Considering both the necessity of placing some prisoners outside the walls of the penitentiaries and the money that could be made from their labor, it is easy to understand the flexibility the state demonstrated in dealing with private hiring parties. Contractual arrangements that initially appeared less advantageous financially nevertheless received careful consideration from state officials who knew they had to find something for the prisoners to do. One questionable financial arrangement presented to the state during the recession of the mid-1880s ultimately proved to be very profitable for the prison system.

General business prostration struck Texas during 1883 and 1884. Money was tight, manufactured goods as well as farm crops were difficult to sell for ready cash, and there was a "general decline in both the passenger and freight traffic of the different railroads in the State." The economic difficulties forced the railroads to return to prison many of the inmates they had hired earlier. The state thus held many prisoners for whom it had no work. Prison officials searched anxiously for some type of employment that would make the prisoners at least self-sustaining.[67]

War I years increased significantly the income of the state's farmers. Low prices for agricultural products during the late 1920s blunted the trend somewhat, but by the 1930s, the replacement of human and animal labor with machines had made substantial progress. The most extensive use of machinery occurred in the Panhandle and along the coastal areas of the state, with relatively less in Central and East Texas and inland on "the river bottom plantations." See Ralph W. Steen, *Twentieth Century Texas,* pp. 36–37.

[63] *Biennial Report,* 1906, pp. 11, 27.

[64] *Biennial Report,* 1908, pp. 10, 31.

[65] Ibid. The principal reason state officials disliked hiring prisoners out to turpentine companies derived from the "unusually hazardous" nature of the work. See "Minutes of the Penitentiary Board Meeting, July 10, 1907," Thomas M. Campbell Papers.

[66] *Biennial Report,* 1910, pp. 35, 88.

[67] *Biennial Report,* 1884, pp. 50–51.

A way out of the predicament came when prison officials entered into contracts with several farmers to use prison labor on their farms and share the proceeds of the crop with the state. Just as the crops would be shared, so would the effort to produce them. Farmers would furnish the land, free of rent, tools, wagons, forage for the work animals, and housing. They also would pay to transport the prisoners from Huntsville to their respective farms. The state, in return, obligated itself to provide "the convict labor and guards, clothe and feed them, and pay all expenses incident to the guards and convicts." The crops grown on the share farms would be equally divided between the state and the farmers.[68]

The hesitation of state officials to enter the share agreements primarily stemmed from the realization that all profits were tied to the crops produced and their fluctuating values. A poor crop year would mean no profits, even though the prisoners would be kept busy. As it turned out, however, the share farms did reasonably well. Beginning with two contracts in 1884, the state added two more in 1885 and, by 1886, had a total of seven share farms. The state's earnings in these ventures totalled $26,810.84.[69] Not all the farms earned a healthy profit, but enough did to result in good overall earnings, even in times when some of the farms individually might have shown a net loss. For the period from 1886 through 1908, the state earned a clear profit of slightly over $660,000 from prisoners working share farms.[70]

The profits made in the share agreements were not the only benefit that went to the state. As time passed, and as the farms prospered, prison officials came to realize that substantial sums of money could be earned from farming despite the unpredictable factors affecting yearly production and prices. There would be enough good years to offset and compensate for the times when crops were poor or prices low. Having come to this conclusion, prison officials worked actively to convince the legislature it should buy state farms on which to work prisoners.

The state acquired its first sizable farm at the time it abrogated the lease with Cunningham and Ellis. As part of the final settlement, state officials purchased the Wynne farm, located about two and one-half miles from Huntsville, for $21,000. The farm comprised approximately

[68] Ibid.

[69] Ibid.; 1886, p. 92.

[70] By 1910, the state was demanding of the share farm owners a 60/40 percent division of the crop with the state getting the larger percentage. See *Biennial Report,* 1886, p. 92; 1888, Exhibit H, p. 9; 1890, p. 132; 1892, p. 109; 1894, p. 95; 1896, p. 98; 1898, p. 92; 1902, p. 124; 1904, p. 133; 1906, p. 103; 1908, p. 109; 1910, p. 15.

nineteen hundred acres, with good fencing, a prison house, and was "well stocked with teams and farming implements." Financial agent Brahan admitted that the soil of the farm, "like most of that in Walker County," was not of the highest quality, but the property was valuable to the prison system nonetheless. Because of its proximity to the main unit in Huntsville, prison officials could employ on the farm those prisoners who, as a result of broken health or some other infirmity, could not be placed at the more physically demanding contract labor. Such prisoners otherwise would have been a "dead weight" on the system.[71]

Within a few months of its purchase, the Wynne farm began paying handsome dividends. It produced enough cotton, corn, vegetables, and animal fodder to supply all its own needs with enough left over to supply the Huntsville unit. Much of the cotton from the farm went into the manufacture of prison clothing, although some was made into "lowells and duck" for sale on the open market.[72]

The success of the Wynne farm strengthened the arguments of those promoting state ownership of prison farms. Financial agent Brahan urged state legislators to stop thinking of building additional prisons and consider, instead, purchasing farms, "in different sections of the State, where lands are rich and productive." Prisoners could improve the lands and construct all necessary buildings so that if, at some future time, the state wished to sell the property, it would not be difficult to recoup the original investment. Brahan expressed particular interest in acquiring farms on which to work the "surplus short time convicts," who had no skills and whose length of sentence precluded learning any profitable trade.[73]

The vigorous endorsement of state farms as a solution to some of the prison problems began rather quickly to bring results. In September, 1886, the state bought the Harlem plantation for $25,000. The farm, containing twenty-five hundred acres, lay "in the Brazos [River] bottom," on Oyster Creek near the town of Richmond in Fort Bend County. At the time of purchase, Harlem had a brick sugarhouse, a sugar mill, several tenant houses, livestock, and direct access to the Galveston, Houston, and San Antonio Railroad. The land was considered "as rich as any on Oyster Creek."[74]

Shortly after the purchase of the Harlem farm, the state invested additional monies to buy smaller tracts of land adjoining the property. Further outlays were made for equipment for the sugar mill and mate-

[71] *Biennial Report,* 1884, pp. 7, 41–42.
[72] Ibid., pp. 41–42.
[73] Ibid., p. 55.
[74] *Biennial Report,* 1886, p. 20.

rials needed to install permanent ditching and bridges.[75] In all, the state spent slightly over $122,000 improving the Harlem facility.[76]

The financial returns on the investment came almost immediately. In 1887, Harlem yielded a net profit to the state of $10,502.67. By the end of 1890, the farm had earned profits in excess of $167,000, approximately $20,000 more than the combined cost of the land and all improvements. Prison officials found themselves with a piece of property owned entirely by the state and valued at $200,000.[77]

Despite the relative ease and speed with which the Harlem farm established itself and began returning healthy profits, the state did not rush to buy additional farm property. L. A. Whatley, who became superintendent in 1891 under Gov. James Hogg and served through the 1890s, repeatedly urged state leaders to adopt the plan for working convicts on state farms. He pointed to the successes at Harlem as proof of the wisdom of his suggestions.[78] Whatley's words were echoed by the two financial agents during the decade, R. W. Finley and J. S. Rice. Both men expressed dissatisfaction with the outside contract system and advocated state farms as the preferred method of penal management for Texas.[79]

The pleas of the prison officials failed to bring about any substantive change. Even though the prison population during the 1890s increased from 3,199 to 4,109, state leaders permitted more and more prisoners to be consigned to contract camps rather than purchase additional state farms to hold them.[80] Governor Hogg halfheartedly attempted to make available to the prison system $300,000 from the general school fund to purchase farmland, but Attorney-General Charles Culberson deemed the transfer in violation of the state constitution. When a constitutional amendment to approve the action was presented to the voters in November, 1896, it failed. Edward M. House, confidant of both Governor Hogg and Attorney-General Culberson, wrote a few years after the electoral defeat that the amendment failed in large part from "sheer lack of attention." No one in state government felt strongly enough about the amendment or had the political clout necessary to conduct an active public campaign on its behalf.[81] Not until three years after the voters rejected using school funds did the state make additional money available to invest in farmland.

[75] *Biennial Report,* 1888, pp. 15–18.
[76] *Biennial Report,* 1890, p. 24.
[77] Ibid., pp. 24–25.
[78] *Biennial Report,* 1892, pp. 14–15; 1896, p. 11; 1898, p. 16.
[79] *Biennial Report,* 1892, p. 98; 1894, p. 81; 1896, p. 87; 1898, p. 81.
[80] *Biennial Report,* 1890, p. 56; 1900, p. 8.
[81] *Biennial Report,* 1896, p. 18; E. M. House to T. S. Henderson, 1898, Box 2R42, House Papers, Barker Texas History Center.

On December 9, 1899, the state purchased 5,527 acres of land in Brazoria County. The property, which would become known as the William Clemens farm, in honor of the chairman of the prison board, lay between the Brazos and San Bernard rivers about nine miles north of the town of Velasco. The soil was considered to be "exceptionally fertile," in an area that had long been known as the "Sugar Bowl District of Brazoria county." Two and one-half miles of the property fronted directly on the Brazos River.[82]

Under the purchase agreement, the state paid $44,216 for the property ($8 per acre). At the same time, state officials leased the adjoining Lowood plantation consisting of 2,685.47 acres. The lease terms stipulated that the rental price would be $2 an acre with the state having an option to buy the land later for $12.31 an acre. The option to buy was exercised almost immediately so that within a few months, the Clemens farm comprised 8,212.47 acres, for which $77,261.40 had been paid. Prison officials estimated that the Brazoria County property could provide employment for up to four hundred prisoners.[83]

Shortly after the purchase of the Clemens farm, the state invested heavily in a new large-capacity sugar mill that could "grind 900 tons of sugar cane every twenty-four hours." The cost came to $268,500. Prison officials then had a railroad built from the sugarhouse to the landing on the Brazos River. The expense of these improvements left the Clemens property under heavy debt for several years.[84]

Following the successful establishment of the farm in Brazoria County, state officials demonstrated a greater degree of enthusiasm for the idea of state-owned and -operated farmland. During 1908, three farms were purchased. Two of them, known as Imperial and Ramsey, were to be operated as individual agricultural units; a third, the Riddick farm, became part of the Harlem plantation. The prison board bought all three pieces of property by pledging to the former owners 40 percent of the crop at 6 percent interest until the total purchase price had been paid.[85]

The Imperial farm, located in Fort Bend County, consisted of 5,235 acres of land. The Sartartia plantation, which had originally belonged to L. A. Ellis, formed the bulk of the property. Following Ellis's death the property passed into the hands of the Imperial Sugar Company, whose directors sold it to the state for $160,000 plus interest. According

[82]*Biennial Report,* 1900, p. 12; 1902, p. 21; William Clemens was chairman of the penitentiary board at the time the farm was purchased.

[83]Ibid.

[84]*Biennial Report,* 1902, p. 21; 1904, p. 4; 1906, p. 14.

[85]*Biennial Report,* 1908, p. 15; 1910, pp. 17–18.

to J. A. Herring, superintendent of prisons at the time the farm was purchased, the price included all livestock as well as lands and structures. The farm was paid in full in two years at a total price, including interest of $165,000.[86]

The Ramsey farm, 7,762 acres along Oyster Creek in Brazoria County, also included several former plantations—Waverly, Drayton, Quarl, Smith, and Palo Alto. The state acquired it for $13.75 per acre from Bassett Blakeley, a vice-president of the Imperial Sugar Company and a former contractor of prison labor. He had purchased the land in 1905 for $5 per acre but justified selling it at $13.75 an acre because, in the three years he had owned it, he had made many improvements at his own expense. Superintendent Herring acknowledged the farm to be "one of the best tracts of land in the State, and will, when properly developed, be decidedly the most valuable property the State owns."[87]

Herring also considered the Riddick place to be of excellent quality. C. W. Riddick had used prisoners for several years on his land, which was near Sartartia in Fort Bend County. The 957 acres were sold to the state for $40 per acre. The addition of the Riddick property enlarged the Harlem prison farm to 3,740 acres.[88]

The acquisition of the farm property in 1908 constituted a major investment for the state in terms other than merely financial. Elected officials and prison administrators expressed in concrete terms their preference for working prisoners on state account rather than exclusively under contract to outside individuals. From 338 prisoners on state farms in 1906, the number jumped dramatically to 1,064 by the end of 1908.[89] The overwhelming dependence on contract labor that had been the hallmark of state prison management for twenty-five years gave way to a mixed system that sought to strike a balance between prisoners working for the state and those hired out to private parties.

Unfortunately, it turned out that prisoners working in the state-owned

[86] *Biennial Report,* 1908, p. 15; 1910, pp. 17–18; *Report of the Penitentiary Investigating Committee Including All Exhibits and Testimony Taken by the Committee* (published by order of the House of Representatives, August, 1910), pp. 692–97; *A Record of Evidence and Statements before the Penitentiary Investigating Committee Appointed by the Thirty-third Legislature of Texas* (Austin: A. C. Baldwin and Sons, 1913), pp. 71–72.

[87] *Biennial Report,* 1908, p. 15; 1910, p. 17; *Report of Evidence before Penitentiary Investigating Committee, 1913,* p. 226; Abner J. Strobel, *The Old Plantations and Their Owners of Brazoria County, Texas* (Houston: Union National Bank, 1930 [1926]), pp. 36–37; "Report of Meeting of Penitentiary Board, July 10, 1907," Campbell Papers. By Jan. 11, 1911, the Ramsey farm had been paid in full. See *Message of Governor T. M. Campbell to the Thirty-second Legislature of Texas* (Austin: Austin Printing Company, 1910), p. 32.

[88] *Biennial Report,* 1902, p. 38; 1904, p. 38; 1906, p. 28; 1908, p. 15; 1910, p. 17.

[89] *Biennial Report,* 1906, p. 28; 1908, p. 31.

camps fared little better than those in other locations away from the main prisons. The desire to reap rich returns from prison labor and make the state camps as profitable as possible led managers of the state farms to exact as much labor as they could from their charges yet return little to them in the way of adequate food, medical care, or proper living quarters. This would have breathed life into the hopes of state officials who believed state-run farms offered an acceptable solution to the difficult problems encountered in keeping inmates productively employed. Not until a major scandal and a subsequent legislative investigation in 1910 (to be discussed in chapter VII, below), did the state act decisively to end outside leasing completely and improve conditions on the state farms.

The decision to begin placing more of the prison inmates on large state-owned agricultural holdings marked the beginning of a transitional period that led ultimately to having all prisoners under state control. Just as the earlier leases of the entire prison had given way to greater state control in 1883, the acquisition of state farms further enhanced public control of prison inmates. Relatively speaking, the state had established a good position from which to make an excellent start at state farming. The farms that had been acquired since the end of leasing in 1883, especially those in the Brazos River bottoms, had very rich, productive soils and good drainage. They had made money for their former owners, had shown excellent initial profits for the state, and under proper management could continue to be good investments.

Guard force, with dogs, for the prisoners working at Burnet, Texas, 1887. Courtesy Archives Division, Texas State Library, Austin, Texas. *Below:* Prisoners quarrying granite in Burnet for the new state capitol, 1887. Courtesy Archives Division, Texas State Library, Austin, Texas.

The fifty-ton blast furnace, "Sam Lanham," at the Rusk penitentiary, 1908. Courtesy Archives Division, Texas State Library, Austin, Texas. *Below:* Interior view of the Rusk prison, 1908. Courtesy Archives Division, Texas State Library, Austin, Texas.

Prison inmates, with mounted guard, working the sugarcane fields southwest of Houston, ca. 1910. Courtesy Archives, Texas Department of Corrections, Huntsville, Texas.

Prisoner with some of the mules used to haul the cane on the farms southwest of Houston, ca. 1910. Courtesy Archives, Texas Department of Corrections, Huntsville, Texas.

Thomas J. Goree, superintendent of the Texas penitentiary, 1877–91. Courtesy Archives, Newton Gresham Library, Sam Houston State University, Huntsville, Texas.

Interior view of Huntsville prison, ca. 1877. Courtesy Archives, Newton Gresham Library, Sam Houston State University, Huntsville, Texas.

Fourth of July meal at the Huntsville prison, 1911. Governor O. B. Colquitt in inset photo. Courtesy Archives, Texas Department of Corrections, Huntsville, Texas.

Edward M. House, advisor to four governors and employer of prison labor. Courtesy Barker Texas History Center, University of Texas, Austin, Texas.

Thomas M. Campbell, governor of Texas, 1907–11. Courtesy Barker Texas History Center, University of Texas, Austin, Texas.

Oscar B. Colquitt, governor of Texas, 1911–15. Courtesy Barker Texas History Center, University of Texas, Austin, Texas.

CHAPTER V

THE PRISONER'S LOT

The efforts by state officials to establish and maintain a prison system during the last half of the nineteenth century represented only one side of a multifaceted story. The growth of the prisons demonstrated considerable progress, albeit with many persistent problems, and presented a record of achievement that kindled the optimism of those who wished to see the system eventually become a large-scale industrial and agricultural enterprise operated efficiently by and for the benefit of the state. By 1913 the production potential at the main unit at Huntsville, at the penitentiary at Rusk, and on the several state farms gave state leaders the flexibility to embark upon new economic ventures in the prisons with a reasonable chance of success. Such assurance had not been so obvious in 1883 when the leases of the prisons had been terminated.

In areas other than the acquisition of land, structures, and property, however, the prison system record of achievement during the late nineteenth and early twentieth centuries was considerably less successful. In such things as prisoner care and treatment—amenities that figured prominently in the reform aspect of incarceration—the situation did not change much from 1871 to 1913. Some improvement occurred in a few areas of prisoner management, but the inmates in 1913 generally found themselves subject to the same sorts of abuse and neglect that their predecessors had endured many years earlier.

Tables 1 through 7 document statistically the changing prison population for the period from 1870 through 1912. The average inmate was a nonwhite male, in his twenties, born in Texas. He was serving a first-term sentence of less than five years for the nonviolent crime of theft or burglary. Furthermore, he had no particular skill or profession and little or no formal schooling when he entered prison.[1]

[1] Information on the personal characteristics of the prisoners appeared in the biennial reports published in the late fall of the even-numbered years. All the reports for the years 1870 through 1912 listed the population of the prison at the time. Frequently, however, the reports for the 1870s were incomplete and contained contradictory data. Not until the 1880 report, the first for which Thomas Goree bore full responsibility, did a more complete picture of inmates emerge. For that reason, with the exception of Table 1, all the statistical exhibits are drawn only from the reports for 1880 through 1912.

Table 1

Prison Population, 1870–1912

Year	*Total Number of Prisoners*
1870	489
1872	944
1874	1,453
1876	1,723
1878	1,738
1880	2,157
1882	2,278
1884	2,539
1886	2,859
1888	3,302
1890	3,199
1892	3,575
1894	4,125
1896	4,421
1898	4,474
1900	4,109
1902	3,865
1904	3,975
1906	3,864
1908	3,466
1910	3,578
1912	3,471

The figures shown in Table 1 reveal an increase in the prison population of approximately 700 percent in the space of just over one generation.[2] Population figures for the entire state for the same period reflect an increase of only about 500 percent. The disparity in the two growth patterns derives from several sources, including better and more vigorous enforcement of laws, concomitant to the reestablishment of public order and the growth of urbanization in the last quarter of the nineteenth century. During this period also the state government extended its influence into the more remote western portion of the state, thus bringing to that region the legal structure of civil government that held lawbreakers accountable for their crimes.

[2] *Report of the State Penitentiary, 1870,* p. 43; *1871–72,* p. 66; *1873–4,* p. 5; *1874–5–6,* p. 74; *1878,* p. 13; *1880,* p. 23; *1882,* p. 22; *1884,* p. 15; *1886,* p. 9; *1888,* p. 4; *1890,* p.6; *1892,* p. 4; *1894,* p. 6; *1896,* p. 6; *1898,* p. 8; *1900,* p. 8; *1902,* p. 15; *1904,* p. 11; *1906,* p. 6, *1908,* p. 5; *1910,* p. 9; *Annual Report of the Officials of the Texas Prison System for the Year Ending December 31, 1911* (Austin: Von Boeckmann-Jones Co., Printers, 1912), p. 20.

Table 2

Prison Population by Race or Ethnic/Nationality Group, 1880–1912

Year	White	Percent of Total	Black	Percent of Total	Hispanic	Percent of Total	Indian	Other
1880	720	33	1,233	57	184	8	4	*
1882	918	40	1,183	52	175	8	2	
1884	1,020	40	1,317	52	200	8	1	1 Chinese
1886	1,122	39	1,470	51	264	9	3	
1888	1,316	40	1,620	49	363	11	3	
1890	1,273	40	1,536	48	386	12	3	1 Chinese
1892	1,431	40	1,688	47	452	13	2	2 Chinese
1894	1,593	39	1,956	47	572	14	2	2 Chinese
1896	1,729	39	2,141	48	549	12	1	1 Chinese
1898	1,630	36	2,323	52	518	12	3	
1900	1,421	35	2,226	54	460	11	2	
1902	1,224	32	2,192	57	448	11	1	
1904	1,253	32	2,314	58	405	10	3	
1906	1,240	32	2,209	57	413	11	2	
1908	1,094	32	1,987	57	383	11	2	
1910	1,119	31	2,095	59	363	10	1	
1912	1,011	29	2,071	60	388	11	1	

*Racial/ethnic background not given for sixteen prisoners.

The racial composition of the prison system (as shown in Table 2) also provides clues to help explain the extraordinary increase in the prison population.[3] The large number of blacks serving time throughout the entire period of this study exceeded by a considerable margin their percentage of the population as a whole. In 1870 the federal census counted 253,475 blacks living in Texas. By 1910 the number had grown to 690,049. Notwithstanding this increase in the total number, however, the percentage of the population listed as black declined from 31 percent to 18 percent in relation to the majority population, which grew from 564,700 to 3,204,848 over the same period. Yet blacks seldom accounted for less than 50 percent of the prison population and frequently approached 60 percent.[4]

[3] *Biennial Report,* 1880, p. 49; 1882, p. 23; 1884, p. 32; 1886, p. 35; 1888, p. 27; 1890, p. 55; 1892, p. 28; 1894, p. 31; 1896, p. 30; 1898, p. 28; 1900, p. 28; 1902, p. 36; 1904, p. 36; 1906, p. 26; 1908, p. 30; 1910, p. 34; *Annual Report,* 1911, p. 31.

[4] Department of the Interior, *The Statistics of the Population of the United States, Embracing the Tables of Race, Nationality, Selected Ages, and Occupations, Ninth Census* (Washington, D.C.: Government Printing Office, 1872), I, x–xvii; Department of Commerce, Bureau of the Census, *Thirteenth Census of the United States Taken in the Year 1910, vol. 3, Population* (Washington, D.C.: Government Printing Office, 1913), p. 804.

The principal explanation for the preponderance of blacks among the inmate population in this period can be found by examining their status in Texas society at the time. With regard to the legal system, black Texans existed essentially outside the protections of law. For the most part, their straitened financial circumstances rendered them unable to avail themselves of legal counsel to defend their interests in court. They became, in effect, passive participants in any legal matters in which they were involved; the laws acted upon them rather than the reverse. In addition, the majority policies of systematically excluding blacks from jury service and of discounting their testimony further removed them from any active role in judicial matters. The threats and intimidation vented against black voters by county-level all-white political organizations, which began to appear in the latter decades of the nineteenth century, and the poll tax, which was adopted early in the twentieth century, effectively closed to this minority segment of the population political avenues to redress grievances.[5]

The contention that special laws were enacted during the post–Civil War period to ensnare blacks and feed them into the state prison system simply cannot be supported by the available evidence. According to the entrapment argument, the Democrats, who returned to power in the early 1870s passed what were known as "pig laws," which made theft of small farm animals (supposedly a favorite target of blacks), a felony punishable by confinement in the penitentiary. Records of committals to the prison, however, indicate otherwise. Table 8, showing the major crimes committed, reveals that the theft of hogs, goats, and sheep remained a minor category of offense throughout the lease period. In 1898, the year in which the most persons, 191, were incarcerated for such crimes, the total represented only 4 percent of the entire prison population. An examination of the laws of the period also refutes the entrapment position.

The pre–Civil War state penal code adopted by the legislature in 1856, to take effect early in 1857, listed specific penalties for the theft of farm animals. Conviction for stealing "any horse, gelding, mare, colt, ass, or mule" carried a punishment of not less than five or more than fifteen years in the state penitentiary. Theft of beef cattle, sheep, goats, or hogs carried a penalty of penitentiary confinement for at least two but no more than five years. These statutes, passed over a decade before Reconstruction, were to be enforced regardless of the monetary view of the animals.

[5] Alwyn Barr, *Black Texans: A History of Negroes in Texas, 1528-1971,* pp. 83–84; Lawrence D. Rice, *The Negro in Texas, 1874–1900,* pp. 113–39, 240–57.

In November, 1866, the first codification of penal statutes following the end of the Civil War brought a reduction in sentence for those convicted of stealing cattle, sheep, goats, or hogs. The new penalties called for penitentiary sentencing only if the value of the stolen animal came to at least $20, and in such cases, the punishment would be two to five years of confinement. If the value of the animal were less than $20, the sentence would take the form of up to two years in the county jail, or a fine of not more than $100. In the 1879 codification of state criminal statutes, adopted following the return to power of the Democratic party and the ratification of the 1875 constitution, the penalties for larger animals, such as horses, remained the same as in the antebellum code. The statutes regarding cattle, however, were changed to provide for a prison sentence of two to five years regardless of the value of the animal. Theft of hogs, goats, or sheep remained punishable by a prison sentence of two to five years only if the value of the animal came to at least $20. The parts of the 1879 penal code dealing with farm animals remained unchanged until March, 1893, when the legislature made theft of hogs a felony equal to that of cattle regardless of the value of the animal, but decreased the penalty for conviction to two years to four years in the state penitentiary. A few years later, the penalty for horse theft was reduced to two to ten years in prison.

A major part of the reason for cattle and hog theft becoming such a serious matter late in the nineteenth century had to do with their relative value as compared with the other common types of livestock in the state. In 1900, for example, beef cattle and hogs, along with horses, formed the three most valuable categories of farm animals in Texas. Over the thirty-year period from 1870 to 1900, the number of cattle in the state increased from approximately 3 million to just under 6.5 million. The total value of the cattle grew from $21,350,000 to $77,736,000, an increase of over 360 percent. During the same time, the number of hogs grew from slightly over 1.2 million to well over 2.6 million. The monetary value of the animals jumped from $2,681,000 to $10,612,000, an increase of 390 percent. The increasing value of the animals to the state's agricultural system dictated that they receive greater protection under the penal statutes.[6]

[6]William E. Blatner, "Some Aspects of the Convict Lease System in the Southern States," p. 19; Thomas Michael Parrish, "This Species of Slave Labor: The Convict Lease System in Texas 1871–1914," p. 18; George W. Paschal, *A Digest of the Laws of Texas: Containing Laws in Force, and the Repealed Laws on Which Rights Rest,* pp. 465–66a; *The Penal Code of the State of Texas passed by the Sixteenth Legislature, February 21, 1879* (Austin: State Printing Office, 1887), p. 97; H. P. N. Gammel, comp., *The Laws of Texas,* 1822–1897, X, 455, 1137; Joseph Stricklin Spratt, *The Road to Spindletop. Economic Change in Texas, 1875–1901,* p. 298.

Table 3

Prison Population by Age, 1880–1912

Year	*Under 15*	*15–19*	*20–24*	*25–29*	*30–34*	*35–39*	*Over 40*
1880	11	487	621	542	196	132	159[a]
1882	14	495	623	573	219	153	193[b]
1884	31	409	907	566	253	152	221
1886	55	456	983	603	327	162	273
	Under 16	*16–19*	*20–24*	*25–29*	*30–34*	*35–39*	*Over 40*
1888[c]	55	576	1,086	700	377	209	299
1890	0	487	1,100	697	403	207	295
1892	0	578	1,196	742	460	248	350
1894	10	711	1,394	824	262	262	422
1896	3	756	1,465	838	606	293	440
1898	2	760	1,413	931	586	294	491
1900	17	757	1,209	824	549	264	489
1902	31	677	1,128	763	537	245	484
1904	40	711	1,116	806	536	242	524
1906	30	740	1,035	785	540	256	478
1908	15	654	929	696	498	228	446
1910	11	685	928	769	499	238	448
1912	23	660	876	722	483	251	399

[a] Age not stated for nine prisoners.
[b] Age not stated for eight prisoners.
[c] After 1888, prisoners below age sixteen were placed in the juvenile house of correction at Gatesville.

The information in Tables 3, 4, and 5 demonstrates that the majority of the prisoners were between the ages of fifteen and twenty-nine, were male, and had had little education. It has proven to be impossible to determine the criteria used to measure the educational level of the prisoners. In the absence of any conflicting evidence, however, it seems reasonable to assume that the "limited-common" designation included all prisoners who had received the basics of an education—namely, the ability to read and write, and do simple arithmetic. Any education above this level would have fallen in the "fine-good" category, whereas anything less would have been termed "illiterate." It is striking that at no time during the years covered did the portion of prisoners described as having had a good education rise above 9 percent.[7]

[7] *Biennial Report,* 1880, pp. 40,46, 49; 1882, pp. 23, 30, 34; 1884, pp. 32, 36; 1886, pp. 34–35; 1888, pp. 26–27; 1890, pp. 54–55; 1892, pp. 27–28; 1894, pp. 30–31; 1896, pp. 29–30; 1898, pp. 27–28; 1900, pp. 27–28, 31; 1902, p. 36; 1904, pp. 36–37; 1906, pp. 26–27; 1908, pp. 29–30; 1910, pp. 33–34; *Annual Report,* 1911, pp. 30–31.

Table 4

Classification of Prison Population by Sex, 1880–1912

Year	*Male*	*Female*
1880	2,121	36
1882	2,253	25
1884	2,506	33
1886	2,814	45
1888	3,271	31
1890	3,152	47
1892	3,522	53
1894	4,057	68
1896	4,364	57
1898	4,385	89
1900	4,030	79
1902	3,756	109
1904	3,861	114
1906	3,781	83
1908	3,395	71
1910	3,520	58
1912	3,413	58

Table 5

Educational Level of Prison Population, 1880–1912

Year	*Fine-Good*	*Percent of Total*	*Limited-Common*	*Percent of Total*	*Illiterate*	*Percent of Total*
1880	72	3	1,317	61	768	36
1882	67	3	460	20	1,751	77
1884	130	5	1,048	41	1,361	54
1886	121	4	1,024	36	1,714	60
1888	116	4	1,126	34	2,060	62
1890	181	6	1,026	32	1,998	62
1892	324	9	1,312	37	1,939	54
1894	298	7	1,776	43	2,051	50
1896	297	7	1,877	42	2,247	51
1898	68	2	2,219	50	2,187	48
1900	60	1	2,110	51	1,939	48
1902	0		1,950	50	1,915	50
1904	298	8	1,826	46	1,851	46
1906	320	8	1,742	45	1,802	47
1908	220	6	1,586	46	1,660	48
1910	176	5	1,775	50	1,627	45
1912	64	2	1,821	52	1,586	46

Table 6

Percentage of Prison Population Born in Texas, 1880–1912

Year	*Number*	*Percent of Total*
1880	538	25
1882	700	31
1884	1,070	42
1886	1,213	42
1888	1,348	41
1890	1,274	40
1892	1,516	42
1894	1,848	45
1896	2,190	50
1898	2,374	53
1900	2,240	55
1902	2,155	56
1904	2,264	57
1906	2,259	58
1908	2,022	58
1910	2,100	59
1912	2,012	58

The information regarding the birthplace and skill level of prisoners, in Tables 6 and 7, respectively, illustrates, to a degree, the changing nature of the state population during the late nineteenth century. Prior to 1896 the majority of state prisoners had been born outside Texas. Of this majority, most came from the other states of the former Confederacy, particularly Alabama, Arkansas, Louisiana, and Mississippi. Such findings coincide precisely with the immigration pattern into Texas in the years following the end of the Civil War and Reconstruction.[8]

The decline in the number of prisoners having no skill or professional training (Table 7) can be interpreted as a reflection of the changing nature of the Texas economy during the period. The state was moving away from an overwhelmingly agricultural orientation to one that included manufacturing, lumbering, oil processing, and incipient industrialization, all of which required a work force with some degree of specialization. The growing urban centers also demanded a myriad of skills

[8] *Biennial Report,* 1880, pp. 47–48; 1882, pp. 31–33; 1884, pp. 33–34; 1886, pp. 31–32; 1888, pp. 21–23; 1890, pp. 49, 55; 1892, pp. 23–25; 1894, pp. 25–28; 1896, pp. 25–26; 1898, pp. 23–25; 1900, pp. 23–25; 1902, pp. 30–33; 1904, pp. 29–30, 32–33; 1906, pp. 22–23; 1908, pp. 24–27; 1910, pp. 28–32; *Annual Report,* 1911, pp. 25–27.

Table 7

Percentage of Prison Population Listed as Having No Trade or Occupation, 1880–1912

Year	*Number*	*Percent of Total*
1880	1,753	81.0
1882	1,864	81.8
1884	2,150	85.0
1886	2,397	83.0
1888	2,729	82.6
1890	2,546	79.6
1892	2,776	78.0
1894	3,292	79.8
1896	3,585	81.0
1898	3,572	80.0
1900	3,031	73.7
1902	2,708	70.0
1904	2,666	67.0
1906	2,694	69.7
1908	2,376	68.5
1910	2,333	65.0
1912	2,284	66.0

to provide the various services necessary for a city to function.[9] Of those inmates possessing skills, barbers, cooks, carpenters, and machinists constituted the largest numbers.

An examination of the major crimes for which prisoners had been convicted (Table 8) also demonstrates the evolving nature of Texas society.[10] The marked decreases in the number of convictions for cattle and horse theft over the period can be interpreted as an accompaniment to the passing of the comparatively lawless, open-range frontier period of the state's history. Correspondingly, the dramatic increases in penitentiary committals for burglary and forgery can be viewed as characteristic of a more stable, complex society in which a sizable percentage of the population congregated in established towns. Generally, one does not think of burglary involving illegal entry into a habitation or place of business, as a serious problem for small, relatively isolated farmers and ranchers, many of whom likely would not have had items

[9] Spratt, *Road to Spindletop,* pp. 228–85.

[10] *Biennial Report,* 1880, p. 45; 1882, pp. 28–29; 1884, p. 35; 1886, p. 33; 1888, p. 24; 1890, p. 52; 1892, p. 26; 1894, p. 29; 1896, p. 28; 1898, p. 26; 1900, p. 26; 1902, p. 34; 1904, p. 34; 1906, pp. 24–25; 1908, pp. 27–28; 1910, p. 32; *Annual Report,* 1911, p. 29.

Table 8

Principal Crimes for Which Prisoners Were Convicted, 1880–1912[a]

Year	*Assault to Murder*	*Murder, 1st Degree*	*Murder, 2nd Degree*	*Rape and Attempted Rape*	*Manslaughter*	*Burglary*	*Forgery*	*Robbery*	*Theft—Cattle*	*Theft—Hogs, Goats, Sheep*	*Theft—Horses*	*Theft—Miscellaneous*	*Theft from Person*	*All Crimes against Property as % of Total*	*All Crimes against Persons as % of Total*
1880	222	136	178	83	42	213	62	66	172	39	665	236		73.4	25.0[b]
1882	204	161	181	84	27	206	75	58	196	32	650	176		67.3	29.6
1884	189	178	209	82	36	267	74	46	154	17	691	435		70.5	27.7
1886	177	216	220	92	32	439	78	67	121	21	745	413		68.0	28.0
1888	252	237	250	113	33	550	112	81	126	15	831	402		65.0	30.0
1890	206	268	273	119	49	498	144	74	113	15	766	364		64.0	32.0
1892	249	310	327	127	57	639	171	82	155	20	710	390		63.0	32.0
1894	295	338	403	150	68	783	209	125	162	77	684	478		46.0	46.0
1896	322	374	446	156	55	939	241	141	262	129	644	317		45.8	45.0
1898	298	411	459	204	61	1,039	219	148	280	191	582	257		44.6	46.6
1900	325	430	446	233	78	1,022	177	141	241	47	465	149	31	59.0	37.0
1902	288	444	469	223	77	984	163	131	128	67	350	184	71	57.0	40.0
1904	277	415	478	282	72	1,081	214	142	109	92	321	177	66	58.0	39.0
1906	255	416	470	328	76	1,042	222	140	86	79	272	185	50	56.7	40.5
1908	231	411	432	333	85	869	217	147	53	36	222	175	48	54.0	44.0
1910	247	400	438	295	103	888	218	154	61	51	253	183	56	54.0	42.0
1912	261	364	400	352	93	902	221	113	75	41	212	169	44	55.0	40.0

[a]Those with twenty or more per reporting period.

[b]Percentages for 1880 are approximations due to discrepancies in some categories affecting a total of 188 prisoners.

of great value in their homes. Cities and towns, on the other hand, represented some concentration of wealth and offered to thieves both a variety of targets as well as opportunities to conceal themselves quickly after the crime. In a similar view, forgery did not become a significant problem until Texas society had reached the point of sophistication that it began making regular use of written legal and financial instruments in conducting its commercial affairs.

The information presented in Table 9 showing the terms of confinement seriously challenges statements made by prison officials concerning the feasibility of reforming prisoners by teaching them a trade during their incarceration.[11] It suggests that little reforming of inmates took

[11]*Biennial Report,* 1880, p. 46; 1882, pp. 29–30; 1884, p. 36; 1886, p. 34; 1888, p. 25; 1890, p. 53; 1892, p. 27; 1894, p. 30; 1896, p. 29; 1898, p. 27; 1900, p. 27; 1902, p. 35; 1906, p. 25; 1908, pp. 28; 1910, p. 33; *Annual Report,* 1911, p. 30.

Table 9

Terms of Sentence, 1880–1912

Year	*1–2 years*	*2–3 years*	*3–4 years*	*4–5 years*	*5–6 years*	*6–7 years*	*7–8 years*	*8–9 years*	*9–10 years*	*10–15 years*	*15–60 years*	*Over 60 years*	*% Serving more than 4 years*
1880	5	482	178	110	604	44	159	51	18	176	166	162	69
1882	0[a]	484	135	122	626	67	166	31	31	220	190	184	73
1884	4	668	139	128	594	94	153	67	32	223	232	205	68
1886	0	742	144	156	712	108	154	81	46	228	241	248	68
1888	4	814	154	233	830	128	198	90	50	272	261	268	71
1890	1	760	153	219	764	126	194	89	44	278	269	302	71
1892	0	972	171	219	781	134	198	105	41	295	303	356	68
1894	0	1,196	196	313	873	142	203	104	48	299	353	398	66
1896	0	1,229	192	329	928	185	247	110	52	322	388	439	68
1898	2	1,356	217	335	748	184	230	100	47	325	743	487	65
1900	1	1,212	225	349	562	194	195	92	37	292	437	513	65
1902	0	1,190	186	322	465	191	154	83	30	243	465	536	64
1904	1	1,226	173	318	517	206	159	92	28	248	490	517	65
1906	1	1,135	159	277	536	195	150	103	29	267	493	522	66
1908	0	908	122	217	453	162	130	144	22	255	490	521	68
1910	6	1,175	145	186	436	134	104	98	15	272	490	517	60
1912	27	1,210	148	203	412	128	103	92	6	237	438	467	60

[a]Two prisoners were serving less than one year.

place while they were in the custody of the state. The percentage of the prison population serving terms of greater than four years duration, 60 percent or more, calls into serious question the assertions by Superintendent Goree and others that it was impractical to teach industrial skills to previously untrained prisoners who were serving relatively short sentences. Such statements had been made to justify the state's decision to commit its prison work force to outside farm contract labor at the expense of developing industries within the prisons. It would appear that a sentence of four years or more would provide ample time to train any person of average ability to operate the kinds of machinery needed in a prison industry. The fact that such training was not provided when it clearly could have been strengthens the argument that the decision to place prisoners at outside contract labor derived less from necessity and more from the desire for profit.

The decline in the number of prisoners serving a first-term sentence and the corresponding increase in those confined for a second term or more (Table 10) provides additional evidence that reforming offenders

Table 10

Commitments and Recommitments, 1880–1912

Biennium Ending	*1st Term*	*%*	*2nd Term*	*%*	*3rd Term*	*%*	*4th Term*	*%*
1880[a]	2,033	94.0	54	2.0	18	1	50	2[b]
1882[a]	2,211	97.0	48	2.0	5		4	
1884	2,454	96.6	82	3.0	3			
1886	2,697	94.0	152	5.0	10			
1888	2,994	90.6	264	8.0	44	1		
1890	2,835	88.6	297	9.0	65	2	2	
1892	3,109	86.9	392	10.9	72	2	2	
1894	3,654	88.5	390	9.0	75	2	4	
1896	3,878	87.7	462	10.4	75	2	6	
1898	3,884	86.8	494	11.0	85	2	10	
1900	3,504	85.0	511	12.0	79	2	14	
1902	3,211	83.0	561	14.5	83	2	10	
1904	3,297	82.9	564	14.0	99	2	15	
1906	3,235	83.7	526	13.6	82	2	19	
1908	2,769	79.8	587	16.9	90	2	16	
1910	2,899	81.0	583	16.0	71	2	22	
1912	2,798	81.0	579	17.0	69	2	20	

	5th Term	*6th Term*	*7th Term*	*8th Term*
1880[a]	—	—	—	—
1882[a]	—	—	—	—
1884	—	—	—	—
1886	—	—	—	—
1888	—	—	—	—
1890	—	—	—	—
1892	—	—	—	—
1894	2	—	—	—
1896	—	—	—	—
1898	1	—	—	—
1900	1	—	—	—
1902	—	—	—	—
1904	—	—	—	—
1906	1	—	1	—
1908	3	—	—	1
1910	2	—	—	1
1912	3	1	—	1

[a]Figures for this biennium are not as reliable as the totals for subsequent years. The keeping of official records was unsatisfactory, especially regarding prior commitments to the Texas prison or confinement in prisons of other states. Accuracy in reporting improved substantially following state resumption of the prisons in 1883.

[b]In all subsequent years, inmates serving a fourth term amounted to less than 1%.

did not command a high priority in the administration of the prison.[12] Had reform been the primary objective of incarceration, one would expect to see fewer second-term commitments rather than more. The increases in third- and fourth-term sentences, beginning in the 1890s, indicate that by the first decade of the twentieth century, the state was well on its way to developing a class of persons committed to a life of crime despite previous confinement in the penitentiary and the threat of future incarceration. The prison was not preparing many of its charges to lead useful, productive lives upon their release. Indeed, in the words of one inmate, the prisons were "a nurse and school" where one began the long-term commitment to criminal activity.[13]

The number of escapes and deaths over the period (Table 11) shows few signs of genuine progress.[14] There was a rather marked decline in the number of escapes following resumption of state control in 1883, yet the figures remained far above the level one might have thought acceptable. The number of deaths, the measure that spoke most forcefully of the manner in which prisoners were treated, did not decrease substantially until the biennium ending in 1910. One can assume that the major legislative investigation of 1909–10 had a positive effect in reducing the prisoner death rate even though the figures were still too high at the end of the period under study, 1912.

For the average inmate, the trip to the penitentiary began following conviction for a felony charge in one of the counties of the state. Upon completion of the court's term, the prisoners were turned over to the contractor hired to transport the guilty to the prison. Generally, prisoners traveled on public carriers, frequently by train, under careful guard throughout the trip. They were chained together by neck collars to make escape virtually impossible.[15]

One former prisoner, describing his trip to the Rusk facility, wrote that he and others recently convicted in Kaufman County left by train in the care of the contractor. The group arrived in Tyler "about 10 o'clock at night," after a day during which they had not been fed. The prisoners spent the night "on the cold, sandy floor without covering of any kind."

[12] *Biennial Report,* 1880, p. 50; 1882, p. 36; 1884, p. 32; 1886, p. 35; 1888, p. 27; 1890, p. 55; 1892, p. 28; 1894, p. 31; 1896, p. 30; 1898, p. 28; 1900, p. 38; 1902, p. 37; 1904, p. 37; 1906, p. 27; 1908, p. 30; 1910, p. 34; *Annual Report,* 1911, p. 31.

[13] J. L. Wilkinson, *The Trans-Cedar Lynching and the Texas Penitentiary,* p. 101.

[14] *Biennial Report,* 1880, p. 38; 1882, pp. 21–24; 1884, p. 29; 1886, p. 37; 1888, p. 26; 1890, pp. 46, 59; 1892, p. 19; 1894, p. 35; 1896, p. 21; 1898, pp. 27, 32; 1900, p. 27; 1902, p. 36; 1904, p. 36; 1906, pp. 26, 31; 1908, p. 29; 1910, p. 33; *Annual Report,* 1911, pp. 30, 35.

[15] Charles C. Campbell, *Hell Exploded: An Exposition of Barbarous Cruelty and Prison Horrors,* pp. 12–13.

Table 11

Number of Escapes and Deaths per Biennium, 1880–1912

Biennium Ending	*Escapes*	*Percent of Average Annual Population of the Biennium*[a]	*Deaths*	*Percent of Average Annual Population of the Biennium*[a]
1880	366	9	256	7
1882	397	9	205	5
1884	273	6	206	4
1886	236	4	221	4
1888	115	4	223	4
1890	166	3	183	3
1892	130	2	114	2
1894	166	2	150	2
1896	164	2	217	4
1898	133	2	196	2
1900	189	2	269	3
1902	152	2	164	2
1904	129	3	173	2
1906	131	3	120	3
1908	177	2	161	2
1910	175	2	90	1
1912	125	2	50	1

[a]The number of escapes and deaths as a percentage of the prison population was figured by determining the average annual population of the biennium and dividing that number into one-half the total number of escapes and deaths for the biennium. The results are rounded off to the nearest percentage point.

The next morning, still without having eaten, they were "loaded on a frosty flat car" for the last part of the trip.[16]

Upon arrival in Rusk, the group of prisoners walked the mile and a half to the prison where all their belongings were taken from them without receipt by the gate guard. They then marched to an office inside the walls where the neck collars were removed and a "convict clerk" questioned them as to their "age, nationality, occupation, habits, and the like." Once this was completed, a guard forced them to march "lock step" to a "wash shed" where they were issued the blue-striped prison garments.[17]

The group stopped next at the dining hall, a room wherein "rows and rows of wooden desk-like tables stood with their tin plates and cups." Each of the cups contained " a few swallows of warm, greasy water,"

[16]Ibid.

[17]Ibid., pp. 13–14. The "lock step" required prisoners to form a straight line and walk, one behind the other, with the right hand on the shoulder of the man in front.

that was augmented with "several pans of cold corn bread and raw, fat bacon." In spite of the unappetizing appearance of the food, the men ate heartily: it was the first food they had been given in thirty-six hours.[18]

Following the meal, the new arrivals marched to the barber shop where all beards were shaved off. The barbers also cut the men's hair so that it resembled a "winding stairway around the head." Thus dressed, fed, and shorn, the prisoners were ready to proceed to their respective work assignments.[19]

All evidence indicates that the desire for profits formed the major consideration in determining the type of work the individual prisoners would do. The private contracting parties wanted healthy, ablebodied persons in return for their labor payments to the state. Therefore, prison officials separated the prisoners accordingly and retained within the walls those individuals whose physical condition would not bear up to the strenuous working regimen in the outside camps. There seems to have been little regularity in making assignments to specific camps. Generally, black prisoners were sent to the farms in river bottoms, including the sugarcane plantations. White and Hispanic prisoners usually worked on other farms, in railroad construction crews, and in coal mines.[20]

Had they been given the choice, the inmates would have preferred to remain within the walls. In addition to a work load that was relatively light, better living conditions also prevailed. Moreover, only inside the prisons could inmates receive educational opportunities, religious instruction, use of a library, and medical care. To a significant degree, prisoners in the contract camps lived outside the pale of even the most minimal reformatory efforts.

Despite the provisions in the 1883 rules and regulations that sought to provide better care for prisoners in the outside camps, life outside the prisons remained almost unendurable. Sergeants and guards in the camps, although employed and paid by the state, succumbed frequently to the economic blandishments of contractors who promised generous pay incentives to the state personnel in return for increases in production. Generally, greater production could be accomplished only by working prisoners beyond reasonable limits. Legislative investigations in 1902 and 1909 attested to the failure of state officials to manage the prisons and supervise the camps in accordance with established policies.[21]

[18]Ibid., pp. 14–15.

[19]Ibid.

[20]See *Biennial Report,* 1886, p. 19.

[21]*Report and Proceedings of the Senate Investigating Committee, Provided for in Sen-*

The 1902 investigation by members of the legislature resulted from Senate Joint Resolution Number 1, passed in late October, 1901, during the second called session of the twenty-seventh legislature. The resolution created the State Investigating Committee and charged it with the responsibility of investigating "the various departments of the State government." Committee members were to gather information on all state agencies and prepare recommendations for the governor to present before subsequent sessions of the state lawmakers.[22]

The committee tendered its report to the governor in mid-June, 1902, following "one hundred and twenty days of incessant labor." It is impossible to determine the amount of time the committee spent with each agency. Given the size and scope of the task, however, plus the fact that the committee consisted of only five members, one can assume that the examination was perforce superficial. Further evidence that the 1902 committee did not get a complete picture of prison conditions came from one of the prisoners who, upon his release from custody several years later, wrote that prisoners were often reluctant to speak openly with the investigators for fear of reprisals by the guards once the committee had departed.[23]

Despite the limitations, the investigators managed to see enough of prison life to convince them of the venality inherent in the policy of hiring out prisoners to private individuals. They considered leasing to be "a disgrace to the State" and so "harsh, cruel, [and] inhumane" as to be "unworthy of an enlightened people":

> When men are shot down like dogs and are worked until they drop dead under this system, the people of Texas cannot hope to escape responsibility for these wrongs, and we believe that if the present condition of things were known to them, and they could be made to realize it, they would bring such pressure to bear upon the next Texas Legislature that these evils would be stopped.[24]

The investigation committee found evidence that officers in outside camps frequently accepted extra payment from contractors to coerce greater production out of the prisoners. The committee held such practices to be "wrong in principle." The state paid the men a "fair salary,"

---

ate Joint Resolution No. 1. Passed at the Second Called Session, Twenty-seventh Legislature (Austin: Von Boeckmann, Schutze and Company, State Printers, 1902), p. 325; *Report of the Penitentiary Investigating Committee,* 1910, pp. 7–29.

[22] *Proceedings of Senate Investigating Committee,* 1902, pp. 3–5.

[23] Ibid., pp. 3–4; Henry Tomlin, *Henry Tomlin. The Man Who Fought the Brutality and Oppression of the Ring in the State of Texas for Eighteen Years, and Won,* pp, 121–24, 146.

[24] *Proceedings of Senate Investigating Committee,* 1902, pp. 323–24.

and "an employee of the State ought not to receive additional pay from outside parties."[25]

The only tangible result of the 1902 investigation appeared in legislation passed in 1903. Lawmakers prohibited penitentiary employees from accepting or receiving "any salary or other compensation from any person or corporation hiring or otherwise employing State convicts." Penalties for violators included dismissal from state employment, a fine of not less than $25 or more than $100, and confinement in the county jail for at least one month but not longer than one year.[26]

In contrast to the 1902 investigation, the one in 1909 was better organized; a more accurate picture of prison conditions emerged. For one thing, the 1909 committee, made up of nine members, five from the House and four from the Senate, spent the better part of four months investigating only the prison. Having more time, committee members heard testimony from a greater number of sources and gathered corroborative evidence to confirm what they had been told. In addition, the fact that the press daily publicized the findings of the committee intimidated into inaction those prison officials who might have been tempted otherwise to threaten and coerce inmates into silence.[27] One former prisoner noted that the 1909 investigation, unlike previous efforts, constituted a genuine search to "go to the bottom of things."[28]

The investigation began in Austin on July 15, 1909, and the final report was forwarded to Governor Campbell on November 24 of the same year.[29] By way of general observations, the committee reported that the rules and regulations adopted for the government and discipline of state prisoners had "in many important respects been almost wholly ignored." Few of the sergeants and guards had any familiarity with the rules, "either as to their own duties or the rules governing the conduct of convicts." Indeed, in some instances, the committee found sergeants who disobeyed the regulations willfully and "displayed no apparent inclination" to change.[30]

The most egregious lapses from accepted policy occurred in the punishment meted out to inmates in contract camps, where whipping was the preferred method of enforcing discipline. The milder forms of pun-

[25] Ibid., p. 325.

[26] *General Laws of the State of Texas Passed at the Regular Session of the Twenty-eighth Legislature Convened at the City of Austin, January 13, 1903, and Adjourned April 1, 1903* (Austin: Von Boeckmann-Jones Company, State Printers, 1903), pp. 161–62.

[27] Wilkinson, *Trans-Cedar Lynching,* pp. 146–48.

[28] Ibid.

[29] *Report of Investigating Committee,* 1910, pp. 1–7; *Members of the Legislature of the State of Texas, 1846 to 1939* (n.p., 1939), pp. 221–28.

[30] *Report of Investigating Committee,* 1910, p. 7.

ishment, such as deprivation of privileges or confinement in the dark cell, were seldom used, if ever. The committee found prisoners, "in a great many instances," whose bodies had been scarred badly by sergeants using whips constructed according to whatever "their fancy or brutal inclinations might dictate." Seldom did officials in outside camps seek to follow procedures and secure written permission before whipping a prisoner.[31]

The committee based its findings regarding excessive and unauthorized punishment upon the sworn testimony of prisoners who either had been beaten themselves or had witnessed the beating of others. During the initial stages of the investigation, the committee members expressed skepticism over the veracity of convicted felons. As the hearings progressed, however, the doubts melted away when the same stories were recounted by prisoners in different camps with no opportunities for collusion or for knowing what previous testimony had been.

A twenty-nine-year-old Fort Worth man, H. W. Johnson, who was serving a ten-year sentence for burglary and theft, proved to be one of the most informative witnesses. Johnson had been convicted in February, 1902, and, since his entry into the prison system, had been moved a total of fifty-four times depending on the wishes of prison officials. He had spent time in both Huntsville and Rusk, both of which he preferred to outside camps:

> Well, I have nothing to say against the Walls; I have been treated fairly right here in the Walls, except the guards get it in for a convict in here and he is transferred out on to a farm, and I call those farms hard, as hard as it can be anywhere. I have been pretty near all over the U.S. and I have seen a good deal, and I don't think I have seen anything that would compare with some of those farms in the State of Texas.[32]

Johnson revealed that he had been whipped several times during his period of confinement. On one occasion, he had received twenty-seven licks for not pulling enough cotton. Although he was picking three hundred pounds a day on average, the sergeant said that was not enough. Prior to being whipped, he was stripped of his clothing and pinned on the floor as other prisoners held his feet, arms, and head. In addition to the whippings he had endured, Johnson stated that he had seen at least eight hundred other men so disciplined since he had been in the prison. When the committee expressed surprise that the figure was so

[31] Ibid., pp. 7–8. The committee report described a typical leather whipping strap as being "from four feet to more than five feet in length and from three to four inches in width" (*Report of Investigating Committee,* 1910, p. 7).

[32] Ibid., pp. 243–47.

high, he explained that a good many of the whippings administered had not been reported on the record books. If a guard lost his temper or for any other reason decided suddenly to whip a prisoner, he did it and did not bother to report it.[33]

When asked by the committee if he had ever seen the guards kill a man, Johnson replied in the affirmative and described the incidents. In one case, a prisoner on the Whatley and Herring farm had asked the guard for permission to "get on a job," that is, relieve himself. The guard gave his permission but as the man walked away and prepared to lower his trousers, the guard shot and killed him. According to the testimony, the man had not attempted to run and the guard had said nothing in the way of a warning prior to the killing. The other two deaths related by Johnson came as a result of whippings. A Mexican prisoner named Antonio and "an Irishman" named Mike Dunn, both working on the Whatley and Herring farm, received such severe whippings that they died a few hours later. The next morning they were buried on the farm after the guard forced another of the prisoners to do a dance on one of the coffins. No inquests were held in either of the killings and the cause of death was listed as sunstroke.[34]

In concluding his testimony, Johnson detailed other examples of the seemingly wanton conduct of guards. He described instances in which inmates had died after having been dragged through the fields by guards mounted on horseback. He told of prisoners being forced to work when they were sick and unable to move. To demonstrate the degree to which prisoners existed at the perverted whim of their keepers, he told of an inmate who had been forced to eat his own feces simply because the guard had instructed him to do so.[35]

The testimony given by Johnson proved typical of much that the investigating committee heard. As the investigation progressed and prisoners became convinced that the committee would take steps to protect them, they spoke freely of the conditions under which they had been forced to live. One black prisoner, John Carr, described his treatment after recapture following an unsuccessful attempt to escape from the Harlem state farm. He stated that the guard who caught him knocked him down with the butt end of a pistol, then turned the dogs loose on him. Upon his return to camp, Carr also received a severe whipping. He mentioned that it was not unusual for the guards to turn the dogs

[33] Ibid.
[34] Ibid., pp. 250–54.
[35] Ibid., pp. 243–57.

on recaptured prisoners and that he "never saw a man come back here with all his clothes on."[36]

Prisoner Eugene Lee, convicted in 1898 of murder in Ellis County, told the committee that he had seen close to two hundred men whipped since he had been in the Texas prison system. On one occasion, Lee himself had received seventy-one licks for failure to perform his work in a manner satisfactory to the sergeant. In the course of the whipping, many of the blows fell on Lee's lower back, damaging his kidneys. As a result, he passed blood for several days and had never regained full control of his bladder. He also described for the committee the punishment known as "hanging them in the window." Prisoners were forced to grab the bars high up in the window, then pull their feet as close to the hands as possible and hang there holding their entire weight. When they fell from exhaustion, usually after five to ten minutes, they had to repeat the ordeal. Lee recounted an instance in which a prisoner named Oscar Walker was hanging in the window when the sergeant came into the room. The sergeant, a man named Mac Williamson, was "⅔ drunk." According to Lee, Williamson had the prisoner taken down from the window and whipped him a total of eighteen licks.[37]

At one point in the proceedings, the committee questioned the Reverend Jake Hodges, the former chaplain of the Huntsville unit. Hodges testified concerning two cases that affected him particularly. In one incident, a prisoner died as a result of excessive punishment by prison personnel. The other case concerned a young man who mutilated himself to escape the arduous work routine of the prison.

According to Hodges, a fifty-four-year-old prisoner named Foster had been sent to the Huntsville unit hospital to recover from a severe beating he had received on the Whatley-Herring farm. In the words of Foster, as related by Hodges: "Oh, they have nearly killed me; they have whipped me on the farm; I was too old and couldn't keep up . . . with the younger men and they stripped my britches . . . off and whipped me and then sprinkled sand on me and whipped me again and then made me climb a tree that was covered with ants and they got all over me . . . they bit me all over."

Foster died approximately one week after relating his story to the chaplain. Hodges told the committee that the sergeant who had whipped Foster had been discharged by Whatley, one of the owners of the farm, but had been hired subsequently on another contract farm in another

[36] Ibid., pp. 297–300.
[37] Ibid., pp. 285–92.

part of the state. As far as Hodges knew, the sergeant was still in state employment at the time the committee was making its investigation.[38]

The other incident related by Hodges involved a young man named Oscar Peterson, described by the chaplain as having been "not very strong mentally." Peterson had been serving his time in the Huntsville unit, but found himself scheduled to be sent to one of the outside farms. The prospect of living on the farm so terrified him that he went to one of the prison shops and cut off two of his fingers in a planing saw, thus ensuring that he would remain in Huntsville. As soon as the wounds had healed, Peterson had been whipped until he lost consciousness. According to Hodges, "it looked as if . . . the lash was turned edgeways and had cut quite a gash . . . on his back."[39]

Hodges identified the man who had whipped Peterson as Capt. R. H. Coleman, the assistant superintendent at Huntsville. When confronted with the testimony against him, Coleman replied that indeed he had whipped Peterson and that he had done so with the approval of Superintendent J. A. Herring. In Coleman's view, cutting off one's fingers to avoid work was a "violation of the rules," and "I mean to convey the idea that when a man violates the rules and knows he is violating them at the time to whip him for it."[40] Because Coleman had requested and received approval to whip Peterson, his action complied fully with established prison procedures.

By the time the committee had visited several of the camps and had heard all the testimony from the prisoners, one might assume that the legislators would have become so inured to the continuing evidence of outrages that nothing would have surprised them or moved them very deeply. Such was not the case, however. At one camp visited, new evidence presented appears to have profoundly offended every person who heard it.

On the afternoon of November 12, 1901, at the Clemens state farm, committee members discovered evidence of prisoner mistreatment unlike anything previously encountered. Andrew Walker, a prisoner from Tarrant County, told the committee that approximately eight months prior to the investigation, Capt. R. W. Grace, the assistant sergeant at the camp, had discovered two prisoners, "playing man and wife." Grace had disciplined the two men by whipping them and then forcing them to perform the act of sodomy before the other inmates in the camp. Several other prisoners supported Walker's testimony, including one of the men involved in the affair who had been ordered to humiliate him-

[38]Ibid., pp. 204–206, 585. The Whatley mentioned here was L. A. Whatley, onetime superintendent of the prison system.

[39]Ibid., pp. 208, 282–83.

[40]Ibid., pp. 591–92.

self even further by telling the other inmates how much he had enjoyed the sexual act with the other man.[41]

The shocking revelations of Walker and the other prisoners in the camp reinforced even further to members of the committee the realization that the authority of guards and sergeants over the inmates was total and absolute. State prisoners existed at the caprice of an arbitrary power that recognized few if any restraints. The nature and degree of punishment was limited only by the imagination of those whose job it was to see that the prisoners received proper care.

Despite all the testimony describing the many acts of brutality and cruelty perpetrated by sergeants and guards, it appears that none of the state personnel was punished for their actions. Rather late in the investigation, and perhaps as a reaction to public outrage at newspaper disclosures of prison conditions, Governor Campbell asked the committee to furnish him with the names of anyone guilty of breaking prison rules. Specifically, the governor wanted "the name of any officer, sergeant, guard, or other person now in the employ of the penitentiary system who has been found guilty of any violation of the law or mistreatment of convicts since January 15, 1907, the beginning of the present administration."

Campbell expressed no interest in anything that might have happened prior to his assumption of office. The committee responded by placing the matter back in the governor's hands for any action. After the final report of the investigation had been made public, the committee wrote Campbell expressing its belief that the legislation creating the investigating body did not empower it "to pass upon the guilt or innocence of any man." Campbell had a copy of the final report, he could read the testimony for himself and "determine whether there had been any violations of the law by your appointees in the penitentiary service." There is no indication the governor acted on the evidence of mistreatment unearthed by the investigating committee.[42]

In a sense, the manner in which Campbell phrased his request to the committee suggests his motives were more political than genuinely inquisitive. By limiting his inquiry to his administration, the governor implied that he bore no responsibility for anything that might have happened under earlier chief executives. To a degree, he was correct and yet, the very fact that he had appointed the prison officials in the period after January, 1907, virtually ensured that he would take no action against them. To have done so would have cast suspicion on his leadership and discredited his administration.

[41]Ibid., pp. 72, 916–30.
[42]Ibid., p. 25.

In addition to examining the manner in which prisoners were disciplined, the investigating committee sought to learn the conditions under which prisoners lived and labored. Inmates were asked to describe the work they did, the quality and quantity of food they received, and the manner in which they were clothed and housed. The findings demonstrated that although conditions in the Huntsville and Rusk units were adequate, prisoners in outside camps did not receive care that even approached the minimum contemplated by the regulations.

Prisoner Sam Tubb described for the committee a typical day's meals in Huntsville. For breakfast, the prisoners received a slice of bread, boiled meat, and molasses syrup. Lunch consisted of bacon and bread, a few vegetables, coffee, and milk, which was often sour. For dinner, there was rice, boiled meat or bacon, beans, and, usually, corn bread. All meat scraps left after a meal were collected and served in a different form later. Tubb said he was pleased with the food he was given and believed it to be "better than most of the farmers get on the outside." The only complaints he made concerned the heat and numerous mosquitoes that bothered the inmates.[43]

Another Huntsville prisoner, German-born John Lenz, confirmed much of Tubb's testimony, saying he had no major complaints as to the care and treatment in the main prison. Lenz did remark that although he received a sufficient quantity of food, the quality was not always such as he would have preferred. The bread was often "kinder musty and . . . I don't know, it don't smell good, don't taste good." Before being transferred to Huntsville, Lenz had worked on the Clemens and Imperial state farms and on the Ellis contract farm. When asked to compare life on the farms with what he had experienced within the walls, he replied that there was as much difference as "day and night." He remarked that on the Imperial state farm, prisoners were fed very little and the food they did receive was inedible. "I wouldn't feed a dog like it. I would give them more and better."[44]

When asked to elaborate on his remarks about the Imperial farm, Lenz stated that the men awoke before dawn and for breakfast were given two biscuits that "never got done—raw dough and molded," plus a half inch of coffee if they were lucky and could fight to get it. They had to run the "two or three miles" from the prison house to the work site where they were kept at their labors "until the stars were shining down." For lunch, which was eaten out in the fields in the turn rows, the men had a little meat, corn bread that was "cold and hard," and

[43]Ibid., pp. 275–76.
[44]Ibid., pp. 222–25.

black-eyed peas, also "cold and hard." The evening meal was a repeat of lunch. On some days the prisoners received no meat at all and no coffee, except that made from "little turnip greens cooked with black water," taken directly from "the field where it gathered." The men were allowed to bathe in groups of eight or ten once a week, on Saturday nights, in a "great big tank dug in the ground and bricked out." The water was partly heated. They received no changes of underwear or socks but were given a change of outer clothing once a week. Most of the prisoners, however, chose not to change clothes regularly, because very often the ones they were given were dirty. As a result, most of the men were louse-ridden.[45]

The investigating committee described the main building on the Imperial farm as being 60 feet long by 25 feet wide. It was unscreened and housed 74 men. There was about the building "a very strong, obnoxious, offensive odor." Connected to the main building was the dining room, also unscreened, which measured 60 by 14 feet. The bathing trough was located in the dining room. The bedding provided for the men was never changed; it stayed filthy. The men, exhausted from their day's labors, often did not bother to clean the mud off their clothes before falling into bed. Lice and bedbugs infested the beds, and cockroaches ran everywhere.[46]

In all the essential details, the facilities and conditions at the Imperial state farm appeared typical of the outside camps. Long, arduous workdays, poor quality food, and filthy, unsanitary living quarters were standard. Unheated bathing water on most of the farms, even during the winter, represented the only noteworthy difference. Given the conditions under which they had to live on the farms, most prisoners preferred to serve their time in Huntsville or Rusk. In the words of a Huntsville inmate, "Well, gentlemen, put me twenty-five solid years; I take that before I take six months on the farm. Give me twenty years solid here before I would get six months on the farm."[47]

Most of the outside camps, like the Imperial farm, housed male prisoners performing agricultural labor. There were two exceptions: the Eastham women's farm and the Calvert coal mining force. Because of the unique nature of these two camps, they merit examination in some detail. At the Eastham share farm in Houston County, owned by Mrs. Delha Eastham of Huntsville, the work force was divided into two camps. One camp housed approximately sixty women prisoners, over 90 percent of whom were black. By the labor division on the farm, the white

[45] Ibid., pp. 225–29.
[46] Ibid., pp. 230, 879.
[47] Ibid.

women worked inside the buildings; black women toiled in the fields. Although women formed the work force in the camp, they were guarded by men. This situation had given rise to charges of improper conduct between the two sexes. Most of the committee's questions, therefore, sought to ascertain the truth of such assertions.[48]

Of the nine women who testified before the committee, only two were white. Both of them stated that they had been treated satisfactorily while in prison. None of the guards had ever made improper remarks or suggestions to them. The seven black women who testified told a different story. One of the witnesses reported that the women were forced to work in the fields despite any physical infirmity they might be suffering. The onset of the menstrual cycle did not excuse them from work. If whipping became necessary, the guards tied the prisoners hands, took off their clothing, and whipped them "on the naked meat," in front of other guards. The prisoners recounted a number of instances when guards came for the prisoners at night and used them for their pleasure. Sometimes the women were paid for their services. On other occasions, the guards promised to use their influence to secure a pardon or early release.[49]

One black prisoner testified that she had been in prison eight years when she gave birth to a child. The father, whom she alleged to be a guard named Jerry Bowden, was the son of the man who was in charge of the camp at the time. The witness never revealed the father's identity while she was incarcerated for fear that she would have been killed.[50]

The shameful manner in which female prisoners were treated had been made known to state officials prior to the visit by the investigating committee, but nothing had been done to correct matters. As early as October, 1907, a former inmate of the women's camp had written a lengthy letter to Governor Campbell explaining in some detail the conditions under which the women lived. The letter spoke of the hard work the women had to do, the abusive language used by guards, the filthy quarters in which prisoners lived, and told of pregnant women who, being without adequate medical care, had delivered their babies in the fields where they worked. The testimony before the committee confirmed the stories related by the former prisoner.[51]

Conditions prevailing at the coal mining camp near Calvert, Texas, also differed from anything encountered elsewhere by the investigating

[48]Ibid., pp. 15, 35, 546, 575; *Biennial Report,* 1904, p. 125.

[49]*Report of Investigating Committee,* 1910, pp. 544–62, 572.

[50]Ibid., pp. 564–67.

[51]Lula Sanders to Thomas M. Campbell, Oct. 2, 1907, Letters Received, Thomas M. Campbell Papers; *Report of Investigating Committee,* 1910, pp. 514–77.

committee. The extreme filth and the severe nature of the work exceeded by a considerable degree anything the committee members might have expected. The legislators were so shocked by what they saw that they called for the immediate closing of the camp. The committee described the main prison building at Calvert as being "extremely filthy." It was 84.5 feet long and 35.5 feet wide. The dining room was slightly smaller than the main building. The 105 men assigned to the camp worked underground in the mine where water stood all the time. Every man was required to mine seven tons of coal per day. The men faced whipping if they did not make their quota. Living and working conditions at Calvert were so physically debilitating that at one point half of the men were hospitalized.[52]

Representative Bowman described one of the Calvert prisoners who appeared before the committee:

> He has on no underwear. Just two top [outer] pieces. Coat or shirt may have been washed a couple of years ago. Has no button nor button holes either in front or on the sleeves. Greasy black in appearance. All stripes obliterated by reason of the dirty grease, etc. Trousers black in appearance and dirty, greasy and smutty, without any buttons. Fastened around the waist with a horseshoe nail, without belt or suspenders. Too large in the waist by six or eight inches or more. Sleeves of the shirt without buttons and are ragged. Shirt fastened in front with a match. Both shirt and trousers decidedly filthy.

A bit later, Bowman commented on the condition of the feet of a prisoner who worked in the mine:

> They are very dirty and have scales on them like an alligator's foot. They are wrinkled, scaly and cracked and have the appearance of being painted with iodine and the bottom is as black as a negro's foot. They are brown, parched and shriveled, the skin having the appearance of dead skin and are red up to and above the ankle.[53]

The overwhelming evidence of prisoner mistreatment naturally called into question the quality of state inspection that went on in the camps. When the committee questioned the two inspectors, the interrogation revealed shocking malfeasance in this area of prison administration. Sam Hawkins and J. G. Barbee, both appointed by Governor Campbell, had been serving as inspectors since February, 1907. They were paid $2,000 per year, plus traveling expenses. Hawkins had responsibility for the out-

[52] *Report of Investigating Committee,* 1910, pp. 12–13, 607–609.
[53] Ibid., pp. 613–16.

side camps in the northern part of the state; Barbee covered those in the south.[54]

Hawkins explained that there were eleven farms in his district and that he visited each of them once a month. His duties, as he saw them, were to "superintend those camps . . . in the absence of the Superintendent." He said that on a typical inspection trip he looked into all aspects of camp life and spoke privately with each prisoner. His description of his visits must have taxed the credibility of some committee members when, in speaking of a recently completed trip to the Burleson farm, he explained that he had been in the camp from noon until 5:00 P.M. Yet in that relatively brief period of time he claimed to have inspected all facilities and spoken privately with all 127 prisoners.[55]

As for his compliance with the prison rules and regulations, Hawkins explained that he was only "somewhat familiar" with them; he had received a copy of them just a month before appearing before the committee. He stated that he kept no records of prisoner punishment and did not require the camp personnel to keep him informed of discipline problems. He assumed the sergeants were "high-toned gentlemen, [and] they know the rules better than I." He admitted that he did not inspect carefully the amount of provisions on hand in each camp. It would be futile, for he did not know how much food had been requisitioned. He also said he had no way of knowing if the bulk of the food was going to the prisoners or was being used to feed the guards' families. When asked if he ever made surprise visits to the camps to see what might be happening behind his back, Hawkins explained that he had "never done that. I am not a detective." Members of the committee reminded him that the state paid him very well to be a detective, but Hawkins remained firm in his aversion to unannounced visits: "a fellow wouldn't last long at that—to slip around losing sleep all the time."[56]

J. G. Barbee, the inspector of the southern district, exercised supervision over seventeen camps on thirteen farms. As he saw it, his duty was "to visit the camps; see that the convicts are properly fed and clothed; that they are not overworked and that they are not abused in any way, and to see that they do the work that is required of them." Like Hawkins, Barbee left punishment of the prisoners to the discretion of the camp sergeants. When the committee questioned the wisdom of relying so completely on the judgment of camp personnel in disciplinary matters, Barbee became very agitated and retorted angrily that he had done

[54] Ibid., pp. 319–29, 403–18, 428; lodging was not included in travel expenses.
[55] Ibid., pp. 319–22.
[56] Ibid., pp. 328–29.

more for the unfortunates in Texas prisons "than all of you folks [the investigating committee] put together, everyone of you." He said he would not consider refusing a sergeant's request to discipline a prisoner because, "I believe every one of them [sergeants], without a single exception, to be upright, honorable men, trying to discharge their duty."[57]

Barbee was offended that the committee would presume to question his methods of doing his job. He lost his temper a second time when he was asked if he wrote his monthly reports from his own observation or simply repeated information given to him by sergeants. His response was so acerbic that the committee chairman had to remind him to observe the proper rules of decorum in his replies to questions.[58]

The pointed interrogation of the inspectors reflected the realization that these two men, more than any other state officials, were responsible for carefully monitoring activities in the camps to see that the rules and regulations were followed. They served as the eyes and ears of those more senior prison officials who bore the overall responsibility for the system yet did not have the time to visit personally all the remote places where prisoners were kept. As events subsequently would prove, the committee's interest in the inspectors was well directed. Several witnesses provided information to indicate that very little serious inspecting took place. One witness testified that he had complained once to one of the inspectors and had been whipped every day for four months afterward. Another mentioned that he had received eighty licks for reporting abusive treatment by the guards to inspector Barbee. R. J. Ritchie, a former sergeant, told the committee that it was not uncommon for the inspectors to mail signed but blank punishment slips to the camps. The sergeants could then punish a prisoner, write the prisoner's name on one of the slips, and mail it back to the inspector for his records.[59]

Several witnesses described for the committee the manner in which the inspectors discharged their duties. One prisoner mentioned that inspector Hawkins only visited his camp every three or four months. In the absence of a personal visit, he wrote the sergeant for a report on camp activities. On those occasions when Hawkins did come and talk with the prisoners, he would address them while they were assembled in a group and ask if anyone had any complaints to make. Guards were usually present, so prisoners would not speak freely and risk punishment later. The prisoner went on to explain that even had the guards

[57] Ibid., pp. 403–408.
[58] Ibid., p. 411.
[59] Ibid., pp. 396–400, 730, 873.

not been present, most inmates would not have spoken candidly in front of their fellow prisoners for fear that, in return for special treatment, one of their number would have informed the camp authorities.[60]

The testimony of prisoners regarding the inefficacy of inspection received support from former inmates who, upon their return to free society, wrote of their imprisonment and touched on the quality of inspection. Charles Campbell described an inspection visit to a camp in which he was working. The inspector went among the men to inquire into their treatment, "and this was done in an insulting and braggadocio manner." When a man told the truth as to how the prisoners were treated, the inspector gave his name to the sergeant, who whipped him severely after the inspector had left the camp.[61]

Another former prisoner, J. L. Wilkinson, wrote that a prisoner learned very early in his confinement to keep quiet about the conduct of sergeants and guards and their treatment of prison inmates. To do otherwise was to risk "being beaten unmercifully, if not to death." Wilkinson explained that, generally, the inspectors questioned the men in front of the camp personnel in the following fashion:

> The inspector: Well, boys, how are you treated?
> All right, Colonel.
> How are you fed?
> All right.
> Is your grub well prepared?
> Yes, sir, Colonel.
> Does the sergeant whip you much?
> No, sir, Colonel.
> Do you get plenty of good clothes?
> Yes, sir, Colonel.

Pleased with the responses to his inquiries, the inspector turned in a "flowery and satisfactory" report to his superiors, even though many of the men as they responded to the questions were "stinking with sores from wounds and beatings."[62]

By far the most strident criticism of inspectors came from former prisoner John Shotwell, who described an inspection visit made to a "cotton plantation" where he had been incarcerated near Cameron, Texas. He wrote that the prisoners would have preferred to see "the devil" rather than the inspector. According to Shotwell, the inspector would line up the men and "with a contemptible smile of mockery" ask how the "thieves

[60] Ibid., pp. 389, 571.
[61] Campbell, *Hell Exploded,* pp. 29–30.
[62] Wilkinson, *Trans-Cedar Lynching,* pp. 86–87.

[were] getting treated." He would order the guards to give the men plenty of work to do, and "if any of them begin to shirk, don't spare the leather, for I find in the convict business, that the using of the leather is just as essential as feeding."[63]

When one of the prisoners made complaint about the working and living conditions on the farm, the inspector became upset and sneered at the man: "Now, look here, what do you think that you thieves deserve—the Menger hotel in San Antonio? You stuck-up cuss, I'll teach you something. Here, captain, take this man out and give him 39 lashes and maybe next time I come here he will remember me."

According to Shotwell, the complaining prisoner "at once" received a "most terrible beating." The following day, the wounds of the whipping had not closed and "the blood soaked through his shirt and the flies blowed it."[64]

The manner in which inmates in the Texas prison system were treated during the late nineteenth and early twentieth centuries constituted a source of continuing shame for the state. The growing prison population, made up chiefly of young persons from the minority segments of the populace, found itself on contract prison farms where labor became the prisoner's only asset. Working long, grueling hours, inmates had to endure any form of discipline the camp authorities chose to impose, no matter how sadistic or perverted. In addition to the demanding work routine, prisoners suffered shortages of food, clothing, medical care, and proper sleeping quarters, any one of which, had it been provided, could have helped ameliorate the otherwise hellish aspects of prison life. Legislative investigations of the prison system during this period generally made no genuine effort to uncover and correct the sordid conditions. Not until the end of the first decade of the twentieth century did an impartial and thorough examination bring to light the accumulated errors of the past and give to the citizens of the state an accurate picture of life in the Texas prison system.

The variety and abundance of evidence unearthed by the investigating committee in 1909 and 1910 formed a virtually unimpeachable indictment of prison management. Testimony of inmates and prison officials revealed shocking and unchecked violations of prison procedures going back several decades. The administrative mechanism for identify-

[63] John Shotwell, *A Victim of Revenge or Fourteen Years in Hell,* The cotton farm mentioned by Shotwell was owned by Thomas S. Henderson, longtime member of the University of Texas board of regents. See *Biennial Report,* 1906, p. 28; 1908, p. 31; 1910, p. 35.

[64] Shotwell, *Victim of Revenge,* p. 17.

ing and correcting problems, the regular inspection, was shown to have been faulty, unreliable, and negligent. That such conditions had been permitted to continue for so long a time can be blamed on those prison officials and other state leaders who viewed the purposes of the prison system as being something other than the confinement and reformation of offenders.

CHAPTER VI
THE POWERS THAT WERE: LEADERSHIP OF THE PRISON SYSTEM

The deplorable conditions that prevailed in the Texas prisons during the lease and contract periods proved to be immune to any substantive attempts at remediation. Indeed, mistreatment of prisoners and the ruthless exploitation of their labor constituted veritable hallmarks of the system at the time. Those parts of the rules and regulations that sought to guarantee inmates some consideration of their basic human needs were ignored, for the most part. As long as the system showed a clear profit, all other concerns remained secondary.

The preoccupation with profits and earnings made it easy to wink at all but the most outrageous violations of the rules. Those who managed the prison system during the period must be assigned much of the culpability for the failure to govern the institution in strict accordance with the regulations. Yet not all the prison personnel universally ignored the regulations and dealt with prisoners in any way they saw fit. The available evidence indicts with some authority a good many prison officers; but just as surely it exonerates others.

This chapter will attempt to analyze the men who managed the state prison system during the late nineteenth and early twentieth centuries. It will examine their backgrounds, their qualifications for office, and the reasons they were selected to fill their respective positions. Personal information could not be obtained on all the major prison officials of the period. Enough was available, however, to draw a reasonably accurate profile of the type of individual to whom the state entrusted the care of its convicted felons.

The prison officials to be examined will be restricted to those persons at the higher managerial levels who had a measure of broad responsibility for formulating and implementing prison policy. This group includes prison directors, superintendents, assistant superintendents, and inspectors, all of whom were appointed by a governor. Physicians and chaplains in the system will be omitted from scrutiny, for they generally were not full-time employees and, as a rule, had little influence on the shaping of policy.[1]

An attempt will be made also to identify those who hired the labor of prisoners. This description of the contractors will emphasize who they were, their status in Texas society, and the influence they had on the leasing system itself. Once again, a dearth of information precludes a detailed look at all but a relatively small number of the more prominent individuals. Nevertheless, observations and conclusions about the smaller group will have a reasonable degree of validity for all.

The highest administrative authority in prison matters during the lease and contract periods resided with the board of prison commissioners, at times referred to as directors. The governors appointed the members of the board so that each new administration brought new faces to deal with prison problems. Initially, the duties of commissioners focused closely on the daily operations of the prison. Such careful monitoring of prison activities dictated that the board members live in or near the town of Huntsville.

The growing complexity of the prison system, coupled with the resumption of state control and the addition of the Rusk penitentiary in 1883, necessitated changes in the function of the prison board. It became less involved with the daily operations of the prisons and more concerned with advising the governor and managing the business affairs of the institutions. Board members had responsibility for making all contracts for repairs and improvements to the physical facilities; for establishing factories in the prisons; for purchasing additional land and equipment; and for promulgating all rules and regulations. As a consequence of the expanded role assigned to the prison board, the seat of power in penitentiary matters shifted after 1883 from Huntsville to the capital in Austin.[2]

There is reason to suspect that despite the rather elaborate definition of their duties, prison commissioners exerted little direct influence in

[1] I could find very little biographical and personal information for prison officials who served during the 1870s and early 1880s. The focus of this chapter, therefore, must be on the individuals who served during the later years of the nineteenth century and the first decade of the twentieth century.

[2] George W. Paschal, *A Digest of the Laws of Texas: Containing Laws in Force, and the Repealed Laws on Which Rights Rest*, p. 403; *Rules, Regulations and By-Laws for the Government and Discipline of the Texas State Penitentiaries and the Convicts Belonging Thereto at Huntsville and Rusk and at Outside Camps* (Austin: Ben C. Jones and Company, State Printers, 1893), p. 37; *Rules, Regulations and By-Laws for the Government and Discipline of the Texas State Penitentiaries and the Convicts Belonging Thereto at Huntsville and Rusk and at Outside Camps* (Austin: State Printing Office, 1888), pp. 49–50.

penitentiary matters. One individual who served during the Hogg administration wrote that the commissioner appointment was "purely honorary." Further evidence to support this contention came in 1898 when Superintendent J. S. Rice proposed the names of two persons to serve as prison commissioners, urging their appointment because they would be cooperative and not get in the way. They would "at all times act strictly in line with the Governor's wishes."[3]

Generally speaking, individuals selected to serve as prison commissioners had achieved a generous measure of success in their chosen fields. Commerce and the law appear to have been the most common professions. In addition, most had held an elected office at either the state or county level and thus understood the machinations of state Democratic politics and political leaders. To obtain a more accurate picture of a typical prison commissioner, it will be useful to examine the lives of a few of them as representative examples of the entire group.

One of the commissioners who served during the early years of lease, H. K. White, was an Alabama native who came to Texas in 1841 at the age of thirteen. White grew up in Grimes County, where he served as county treasurer from 1858 to 1862. Because of a physical disability, he was exempt from military service during the Civil War. After farming in Grimes County until 1873, he moved to Ellis County. He began his service with the penitentiary when Richard Coke appointed him assistant inspector in late November, 1875. Coke's successor, Richard Hubbard, appointed White to the prison board, a position he held until the election of O. M. Roberts in 1878.[4]

Although White departed prison service upon the inauguration of the Roberts administration, his association with the institution, and with state politics, continued for many years thereafter. One of his biographers described him as a lifelong Democrat and a frequent delegate to state Democratic conventions. During the later decades of the nineteenth century, he represented Burleson and Brazos counties in the eighteenth and twenty-third legislatures, respectively, and amassed sizable land holdings in those areas. Beginning in 1880 and continuing through 1900, he leased state prisoners to work his farms.[5]

[3] P. Wooldridge Collection, Box 2L124, Barker Texas History Center; J. S. Rice to E. M. House, Dec. 23, 1898, E. M. House Papers, 1896–1911, Box 2R42, Barker Texas History Center.

[4] Scrapbook, Richard Coke Papers, Box 3L130, Barker Texas History Center; John Henry Brown, *Indian Wars and Pioneers of Texas* (Austin: L. E. Daniell, Publisher, n.d.), pp. 420–21.

[5] Brown, *Indian Wars,* pp. 420–21; *Members of the Legislature of the State of Texas from 1846 to 1939,* pp. 115, 156; *Biennial Report,* 1880, p. 51; 1882, p. 8; 1884, p. 29; 1886, p. 36; 1888, p. 19; 1890, p. 56; 1892, p. 49; 1894, p. 6; 1896, p. 6; 1898, p. 8; 1900, p. 8.

J. T. Mewshaw, appointed to the prison board during the first term of Thomas Campbell, was, like H. K. White, a "prominent Democrat" known "throughout" the state. He had come to Texas in 1877 from Missouri and had settled in Garland, where he became active in civic affairs and politics. Although he was a man of "little book learning," he managed to establish a large and prosperous blacksmithing business. Apparently, the governor appointed him as a reward for the many years he had worked on behalf of Democratic candidates of the state.[6]

Another civic leader, A. P. Wooldridge of Austin, earned his spot on the prison board through service to his community and the Democratic party. Wooldridge had been born in New Orleans in 1847. After attending Yale University and the University of Virginia, he finally settled in the Texas capital in 1872 and opened a law practice. He organized the first public school system in the city, served on the committee established to choose a site for the University of Texas, and served as the first secretary of the institution's board of regents. He was president of the City National Bank in Austin and mayor of the city from 1909 through 1919. Governor Hogg appointed Wooldridge, who remained on the board during both of Hogg's terms.[7]

The two men who served longest as commissioners of the prison followed similar careers in other ways. Both Walter Tips and William Clemens were born in Germany. They came with their families and settled near New Braunfels, Texas, in 1849. Both were veterans of the Confederate Army, had served in the state legislature, and, for many years, were business associates. Not surprisingly, the two men also became lifelong friends.[8]

Walter Tips served under four governors—Ireland, Ross, Lanham, and Campbell—for a total of twelve years. Between his years of service on the prison board, he represented Travis County in the Senate of the twenty-third and twenty-fourth legislatures and was appointed by Gov. O. B. Colquitt to serve on the State Library and Historical Commission. He established the Walter Tips Company, a hardware firm considered by contemporaries to have been "one of the leading commercial enterprises of Austin."[9]

[6] L. B. Hill, ed., *A History of Greater Dallas and Vicinity* (Chicago: Lewis Publishing Company, 1909), II, 109–10; *Biennial Report,* 1908, p. 4.

[7] Walter Prescott Webb, ed., *Handbook of Texas* (Austin: Texas State Historical Association, 1952), II, 933–34; *Biographical Encyclopedia of Texas* (New York: Southern Publishing Company, 1880), p. 239; *Biennial Report,* 1892, p. 18; 1894, p. 2.

[8] L. E. Daniell, *Personnel of the Texas State Government, with Sketches of Representative Men of Texas* (San Antonio: Maverick Printing House, 1892), pp. 193–94; *Austin Statesman,* Jan. 21, 1912, p. 1.

[9] *Austin Statesman,* Jan. 21, 1912, p. 1; *Members of the Legislature, 1846–1939,* pp.

William Clemens served a total of eight years on the prison board, under Governors Culberson and Sayers. He began his political career as an alderman in the city of New Braunfels and went on to represent Comal County in the House of Representatives of the sixteenth and twenty-first legislatures. In 1890 he represented the same area in the state Senate. While in the upper house, Clemens supported bills favoring public school improvement and the creation of a state railroad commission, and opposed the use of free railroad passes by members of state government. Both Clemens and Tips were members of the Democratic party.[10]

Because the duties of the prison board were linked so closely to the purely financial aspects of prison management, the commissioners needed no experience in actually working with the penitentiary system prior to their appointment. The kind of expertise they could bring to prison management could be obtained just as easily, if not better, in the competitive commercial atmosphere outside state service. Such was not the case, however, with the individuals chosen to manage the prisons and supervise prison personnel. The qualifications needed to fulfill the duties of superintendent, assistant superintendent, and inspector necessitated some familiarity with the manner in which prisons operated and, of equal importance, the ways inmates should be handled.

Unfortunately, the persons chosen to staff the prisons received their appointments because of faithful political service to the incumbent governor rather than for any professional experience they might have had. Some of the appointees, particularly those who served for extended periods of time and approached their tasks with diligence, acquitted themselves well in their prison jobs; others, however, performed miserably and it is to this latter group that one may attribute much of the blame for the chronic problems of the prison system.

When speaking of the major prison officials of the period from 1870 through 1912, the name of Thomas J. Goree stands clearly above all others. His preeminence derives, in part at least, from the sheer length of his service to the state. More importantly, however, Goree displayed a commitment to his tasks and a sensitivity to the purposes and objectives of confinement unparalleled in any of his associates and contemporaries. Goree began his official association with the prison in 1874 when Governor Coke appointed him to serve as one of the directors in Huntsville. At the time of his selection, he was struggling none too

---

151–60; *Biennial Report,* 1884, p. 3; 1886, p. 5; 1888, p. 3; 1890, p. 3; 1906, p. 4; 1910, p. 8.

[10]Daniell, *Personnel,* pp. 193–94; *Members of the Legislature, 1846–1939,* pp. 96, 135, 140; Brown, *Indian Wars,* pp. 330–31.

successfully to build a law practice. Born in Alabama in 1835, he came to Texas while still a young man and graduated from Baylor University in 1856. During the Civil War he served first as a scout under P. G. T. Beauregard and from July, 1861, on as an aide-de-camp to Gen. James Longstreet. No doubt his close association with the law firm that represented the interests of Ward, Dewey, and Company played a part in securing for him his initial appointment to the prison board.[11]

Following his appointment to the superintendency by Governor Hubbard in the spring of 1877, Goree went on to manage the system through the last years of lease and the early period of state control. During his tenure in office he established contact with the National Prison Association and sought to incorporate into the Texas system the newer theories of prison management espoused by the national organization. Goree's consistent support for such reforms as the indeterminate sentence and a separate institution for juvenile offenders grew out of his early contacts with persons seeking reforms in American prisons during the late nineteenth century.[12]

In the spring of 1891, the newly elected governor, James S. Hogg, refused to reappoint Goree. During the gubernatorial primary of 1890, Goree and one of his relatives, Norman G. Kittrell, a well-known attorney, had withheld their support from Hogg. For this bit of perceived disloyalty, the new governor was unforgiving, even though both men supported him in the general election. Goree became a casualty of a system in which one's competence and achievements were secondary to one's political activities.[13]

A measure of Goree's stature in the National Prison Association and the high regard in which he was held by the membership appeared in a letter to governor-elect Hogg from Frederick H. Wines, executive secretary of the organization. Wines urged the governor to retain Goree,

[11] *Reports of the Texas State Penitentiary, 1873–4*, p. 2; *Biographical Souvenir of the State of Texas, Containing Biographical Sketches of the Representative Public and Many Early Settled Families* (Chicago: F. A. Battey and Company, 1889), p. 333; *Galveston Daily News*, June 18, 1876, p. 4; Henri Gerard Nordberg, "A Young Texan Goes to War, A Collection of Personal Letters by Captain Thomas Jewett Goree, C.S.A., Aide-de-Camp to General James Longstreet," *Journal, Confederate Historical Society*, 7, no. 4 (Winter, 1969): 142–59; *Proceedings of the Annual Congress of the National Prison Association of the United States, Held at Austin, Texas, December 2–6, 1897* (Pittsburgh: Shaw Brothers, Printers, 1898), p. 131.

[12] *Proceedings of the Annual Congress of the National Prison Association of the United States, Held at Boston, July 14–19, 1888* (Chicago: Knight and Leonard Company, Printers, 1888), pp. 308–20; *Proceedings of the Annual Congress of the National Prison Association of the United States, Held at Cincinnati, September 25–30, 1890* (Pittsburgh: Shaw Brothers, Printers, 1891), p. 317.

[13] Norman Kittrell to James S. Hogg, Dec. 10, 1890, Governor's Letters Received, James S. Hogg Papers, Barker Texas History Center.

for he was recognized as one of the more distinguished prison officials in the country. He was a man of "strength, good sense [and] integrity." The Texas prison system, under Goree's management, had built an enviable record that would surely be destroyed if he was not reappointed:

> I voice the sentiments of every leading member of the National Prison Association when I say that the removal of Mr. Goree for any but causes affecting his personal or official character or conduct would be regarded by them generally as a misfortune to the cause of prison reform in the United States against which they would protest if they had the opportunity to do so and were sure that their protest would be received in the spirit in which it is offered.[14]

Goree's successor, Lucius A. Whatley, served under both Governor Hogg and his successor, Charles A. Culberson, for a total of eight years. Whatley was a native of Cass County, Texas, and had represented the area in the House of Representatives in the twentieth and twenty-first legislatures. He won election to the state Senate in 1890 but resigned to accept the appointment as superintendent of the prison system.[15]

Whatley's governance of the prison was, in a word, undistinguished. Like all the men who served as superintendent after 1891, his thoughts on prison policies and programs were little more than unenthusiastic rehashings of positions taken previously by Goree. He did maintain the contacts that had been established with the National Prison Association but did not enjoy the prestige within the organization that had been accorded his predecessor. Like Goree, Whatley condemned the practice of hiring state prisoners to outside parties. It was, he argued, a necessity that could be overcome only with the purchase of farmland by the state to work the prisoners on state account. One has reason, however, to question the degree to which his opposition was genuine. For approximately ten years after his service as superintendent ended, Whatley engaged groups of prisoners to work his farm in Madison County, Texas. From testimony taken during the legislative investigation of 1909–10, conditions on Whatley's farm appeared no better than those that prevailed in other camps.[16]

[14]Frederick H. Wines to James S. Hogg, Apr. 6, 1891, Governor's Letters Received, Hogg Papers.

[15]L. E. Daniell, *Personnel of the Texas State Government with Sketches of Distinguished Texans, Embracing the Executive and Staff, Heads of the Departments, United States Senators, Representatives, Members of the Twenty-first Legislature* (Austin: Smith, Hicks, and Jones, State Printers, 1889), p. 349; *Members of the Legislature, 1846–1939,* pp. 131, 138, 142.

[16]*Proceedings of the Annual Congress of the National Prison Association of the United States Held at Denver, Colorado, September 14–18, 1895* (Pittsburgh: Shaw Brothers,

As the second term of Governor Culberson came to an end with the elections in late fall, 1898, so did Whatley's tenure as head of the prison. Beset with severe financial problems, he pleaded desperately with the new administration, seeking to retain his position as superintendent. Unfortunately for him the incoming governor, Joseph Sayers, refused the request. Whatley had made the mistake of supporting one of Sayers' opponents during the primary campaign, and, although he later worked for Sayers, his early disloyalty cost him his job.[17]

The three men who served as superintendent after Whatley all had the advantage of having had some experience in prison administration before their appointment to the top job. All three expressed opposition to working state prisoners on private farms, much as their predecessors had done, yet none took any significant steps in that direction. They simply accepted the system as it existed and preferred not to tamper with it except, perhaps, to increase its profitability.

J. S. Rice, who immediately succeeded Whatley, had entered penitentiary service originally in 1894, when Governor Culberson had appointed him financial agent. He was a graduate of the Texas Military Institute and had become very successful in banking and in the sawmilling business. Upon the election of Governor Sayers in 1898, Rice was elevated to the position of superintendent and held the job until April 11, 1902, when he resigned to become president of the Union National Bank in Houston.[18]

Rice's successor, Searcy Baker, was an 1882 graduate of the Agricultural and Mechanical College of Texas. Baker became successful in farming and lumbering, and in 1899 secured a position in the prison financial agent's office. He served as superintendent through the administration of Gov. S. W. T. Lanham, but was replaced after Thomas M. Campbell was inaugurated in 1907. After leaving penitentiary service, Baker became the superintendent of police in Houston.[19]

The last superintendent during the state contract period, J. A. Herring, served with the Campbell administration, 1907–11. Herring had

---

Printers, 1896), p. 357; *Proceedings of the Annual Congress of the National Prison Association of the United States, Held at Milwaukee, Wisconsin, September 26–30, 1896* (Pittsburgh: Shaw Brothers, Printers, 1897), p. 388; *Annual Congress, National Prison Association, 1897,* p. iv; *Biennial Report,* 1892, pp. 3–17; 1894, pp. 5–20; 1900, p. 29; 1902, p. 38; 1904, p. 38; 1906, p. 28; 1908, p. 32; 1910, p. 35; *Report of the Penitentiary Investigating Committee,* 1910, pp. 477–501.

[17] L. A. Whatley to E. M. House, Aug. 8, 1898, Box 2R42, House Papers; R. R. Lockett to E. M. House, Nov. 13, 1898, roll. 112, House Papers.

[18] H. T. Warner, Hugh N. Fitzgerald, T. C. Gooch, T. S. Bonner, J. L. Mapes, and Edmunds Travis, eds., *Texans and Their State* (Houston: Texas Biographical Association, n.d.) p. 269; *Biennial Report,* 1896, p. 1; 1900, p. 17; 1902, p. 15.

[19] Warner et al., *Texans,* p. 292; *Biennial Report,* 1902, p. 14; 1904, p. 10; 1906, p. 4.

gone to work for the prison system initially in 1892 as manager of the Harlem state farm, a position he held until 1899 when he returned to his home in Madison County and managed his agricultural interests. Shortly after his return home, he was elected president of the First National Bank in Madisonville.[20]

During the time that Herring lived in Madison County between his periods of service in the prison system, he, along with former superintendent Whatley, leased state prisoners to work his farms. The joint venture, known as the Whatley and Herring farm, lasted until Herring was named superintendent. Herring remained active in politics throughout his tenure with the prison system. Because of his early support for the nomination of Woodrow Wilson in 1912, he was appointed United States Marshal for the southern district of Texas shortly after Wilson was inaugurated as president.[21]

Material success and political activity, the same factors that figured so prominently in determining the individuals chosen to sit on the penitentiary board or serve as superintendent, also came into play, to some degree, in selecting middle-level administrators. Men of some prestige in the state also became assistant superintendents and inspectors although, as a rule, they were neither as prominent nor as financially independent as higher officers. In most cases, men accepted the middle-level positions solely for the salaries they provided rather than from a sense of civic duty. In addition, much more in the way of continuing political service was required of those appointed to fill these positions. An examination of several of the individuals who served as assistant superintendents and inspectors will illustrate the similarities and differences they shared with higher-level prison administrators.

R. H. Underwood, a native of Alabama, came to Texas in 1883 and established a farm in Bell County. In 1893, President Grover Cleveland appointed him postmaster in Holland, Texas. Six years later, prison superintendent J. S. Rice selected Underwood to manage the Dunovant prison farm near Eagle Lake, Texas, where he remained until 1905, when he returned to Holland and took a position as cashier at the First National Bank. Underwood reentered state service in 1907 when Governor Campbell appointed him assistant superintendent at Huntsville. During his time at Huntsville, Underwood attended national meetings of

[20]Dermot H. Hardy and Ingham S. Roberts, eds., *Historical Review of South-East Texas* (Chicago: Lewis Publishing Company, 1910), II, 841–42.

[21]L. E. Daniell, *Texas. The Country and Its Men* (n.p., n.d.), pp. 763–65; *Biennial Report,* 1900, p. 29; 1902, p. 38; 1904, p. 38; 1906, p. 28; 1908, p. 31; *Report of Investigating Committee,* 1910, p. 257.

the American Prison Association and was elected a vice-president of the American Prison Wardens' Association. He remained assistant superintendent until January, 1911, when a new governor, O. B. Colquitt, replaced him.[22]

E. G. Douglas, who served as assistant superintendent at Rusk under Governor Ross, began his political career as sheriff of Grayson County. He was elected state senator from the county in 1886 and served until January, 1889, when Ross named him to the Rusk position. In 1896 superintendent Whatley placed him in charge of the Burleson and Johns share farm where he remained until 1899, when he was made manager of the Harlem state farm. Early in 1907 he became assistant superintendent of the juvenile reformatory in Gatesville, where he died in December, 1907.[23]

James P. Gibson replaced Douglas as assistant superintendent at Rusk. Appointed initially by Governor Hogg, Gibson served also for both terms of Hogg's successor, Charles A. Culberson. He had first entered politics as county surveyor in Cherokee County, where subsequently he served for thirteen years as county judge. Gibson remained at the Rusk prison until the inauguration of Culberson's successor, Joseph Sayers.[24]

A sampling of the men who served as inspectors indicates that they too brought a variety of experience to their tasks. As a rule, inspectors tended to be persons with considerable local or regional prominence who, through their knowledge of local conditions, could function as political operatives for the administration in Austin. Inspectors frequently were called upon to serve as a vehicle for transmitting the wishes and desires of the governor to the party faithful at the county level and below. The amount of politicking engaged in by inspectors suggests that an aptitude for such activities figured prominently in the selection criteria.

One of the earliest inspectors, Daniel M. Short of Shelby County, did not conform so typically to the later image of inspector as a purely local politico. Short was appointed prison inspector by Gov. O. M. Roberts in 1878 and retained the position until 1886. His job with the prison system was the culmination of a long and active career in state politics.

[22]Hardy and Roberts, *Historical Review of South-East Texas,* II, 811–15; *Annual Report of the Officials of the Texas Prison System for the Year Ending December 31, 1911* (Austin: Von Boeckmann-Jones Company, Printers, 1912), p. 44.

[23]Searcy Baker to the editor, Dallas *Times Herald,* Jan. 14, 1907, Box 2-11/364, Thomas M. Campbell Papers, Texas State Library and Archives, Austin; *Biennial Report,* 1894, p. 59; 1900, p. 11; 1902, p. 20; 1904, p. 18; 1906, p. 13; 1908, p. 86.

[24]Sid S. Johnson, *Texans Who Wore the Gray* (n.p., n.d.), I, 199–200; Frank W. Johnson, *A History of Texas and Texans,* III, 1277–78; James P. Gibson to E. M. House, Dec. 11, 1898, Box 2R42, House Papers.

In 1846, Short and Roberts opened a law practice in Shelbyville, Texas, beginning an association that would last all their adult lives. Short served in the war with Mexico and organized a military company from his county in the Civil War. He served as a member of the eighth and eleventh legislatures of Texas, as a delegate to the Secession Convention and, from 1866 to 1892, as chairman of the Democratic Executive Committee of his district and county. Roberts's appointment of Short, in addition to its inherent political wisdom, reflected the governor's concern that he be kept au courant in prison matters. Roberts wanted the prison system to function according to the rules and regulations, in order to eliminate the causes of public dissatisfaction with the manner in which prisoners were treated. By naming a trusted friend to serve as inspector, the governor demonstrated his desire to receive more reliable reports on conditions, particularly in the outside camps.[25] None of the other individuals who served as inspectors would enjoy the close personal relationship with the chief executive that existed between Roberts and Short.

J. G. Barbee of Wharton appears more typical of the majority of inspectors. Barbee, a merchant and farmer, had been instrumental in reestablishing Democratic party control of Wharton County in 1886. He won election to the House of Representatives of the twenty-third legislature in 1892 and was elected to serve as county judge in 1896. He remained a powerful force in local politics and in 1907 was appointed prison inspector by Governor Campbell.[26]

Another inspector, Wharton Bates, a Brazoria attorney, also developed his political skills in a predominantly local setting. Bates, as a member of the Jay Bird Democratic Association of Fort Bend County, participated in that organization's takeover of county politics in the late 1880s. Bates's work on behalf of the Democratic party came to the attention of state Democratic leaders in Austin and, following Culberson's election in 1894, the governor offered him the position of prison inspector.[27]

It is difficult to overstate the importance of the prison system to the political structure of the state during the late nineteenth and early twen-

[25] Johnson, *Texas and Texans,* III, 2010.

[26] Ibid., pp. 1295–96.

[27] Wharton Bates to E. M. House, September 1, 1894, House Papers, roll 109. The Jay Bird Democratic Association of Fort Bend County was a white political organization established in 1889 to seize control of the county political machinery from the majority black population. See Pauline Yelderman, *The Jay Bird Democratic Association of Fort Bend County. A White Man's Union* (Waco: Texian Press, 1979), pp. 119–44.

tieth centuries. In choosing persons to staff the prison, governors placed a premium on previous political service and the potential for continuing effort on behalf of the Democratic party and incumbent elected officials. Securing a position within the prison system came to be viewed as a reward for faithful political service; but it was a gift that could be withdrawn abruptly if one failed to continue working to further the interests of those who had bestowed the appointment.

How prison officials were expected to perform in the service of political administration came to be patterned very early in this period. In late summer, 1880, Superintendent Goree, acting in concert with former Gov. Richard Coke, intervened to defuse a potential political challenge against the incumbent governor, O. M. Roberts, who was under fire from some Democrats because of his extreme fiscal retrenchment policies. The challenge to the governor came from former Confederate general Jerome B. Robertson of Waco.[28]

Shortly after Robertson took the first tentative steps toward announcing his candidacy, Coke sent "seven or eight of our best men" to talk to the general and attempt to dissuade him. Coke also ordered Goree to meet with Robertson and stress the futility of opposing the reelection of Roberts. After talking with Robertson, Goree realized that the general was intent on running, even though he knew he had little chance of winning. As it turned out, however, Robertson was unable to attract the financial backing necessary to conduct a statewide campaign, so his opposition to Roberts amounted ultimately to very little.[29]

By the 1890s, the Austin-to-Huntsville-to-Rusk political axis, with branches down to the state farms, had become sophisticated enough to oversee electioneering activities at the county and precinct levels if necessary. The man chiefly responsible for monitoring and directing the political efforts of prison employees during that time was Edward M. House, advisor and confidant to Governors Hogg, Culberson, Sayers, and Lanham. These men served consecutively as the state's chief executives from 1891 through early 1907. Beginning with Hogg's campaign for reelection in 1892, House played an active role in distributing the patronage that fell within the purview of the governors.

By the last decade of the nineteenth century, the House family had

[28]T. J. Goree to Gov. O. M. Roberts, Aug. 23, 1880, Roberts Papers, Barker Texas History Center. Opposition to Roberts centered around his sale of public lands at very low prices and his reduction in the state budget, especially for education items, to help reduce the level of state indebtedness. See Alwyn Barr, *Reconstruction to Reform: Texas Politics, 1876-1906,* pp. 58-59.

[29]Goree to Roberts, Aug. 23, 1880, and Richard Coke to Goree, Sept. 3, 1880, Roberts Papers.

become wealthy and influential in Texas society. T. W. House, Sr., who came to Texas from England in 1837, established a general mercantile store in Houston and invested the profits of his business in land. At the time of his death in 1880, he owned in excess of 250,000 acres scattered over sixty-three Texas counties. Cotton and sugarcane were the major crops grown on the House properties.

Upon the death of his father, Edward House managed to parlay his share of the family inheritance into a sizable operation of his own. He counted among his possessions several large farms around the state as well as profitable investments in streetcar, railroad, and oil companies. The income from his business interests provided the wherewithal for him to devote so much of his time to state politics. On at least one occasion, House used his position as advisor to the governors for his own personal profit. Beginning in 1904 and continuing until 1910, House acquired prison inmates to lay track for the Trinity and Brazos Valley Railroad, a company he had founded and in which he owned a majority of stock.[30]

In his capacity as trusted advisor to the chief executives—especially Culberson, Sayers, and Lanham—House kept close tabs, through prison personnel among others, on political happenings around the state. In addition, he used his contacts in the penitentiary service to work on behalf of specific candidates he wished to see win elective office. A good example of the manner in which House used prison employees at election time can be seen in the campaign he directed in 1898 to put Joseph Sayers in the governor's office.

As the election season got under way early in 1898, the major candidates for the nomination of the Democratic party included R. M. Wynne, an attorney from Fort Worth, M. M. Crane, attorney-general under the outgoing Governor Culberson, George T. Jester, Culberson's lieutenant-governor, and Sayers, who at the time was representing Texas in the U.S. Congress. House had helped Sayers win reelection in 1896 and the congressman kept in close touch with his Texas benefactor throughout his term in Washington. The friendship between the two men probably explains, at least in part, House's decision to back Sayers for governor over the other contenders.[31]

House initiated the Sayers campaign by calling on members of the

[30] *Biennial Report,* 1904, p. 38; 1908, p. 31; 1910, p. 35; J. L. Allhands, *Boll Weevil: Recollections of the Trinity & Brazos Valley Railway* (Houston: Anson Jones Press, 1946), pp. 1–7; Rupert N. Richardson, *Colonel Edward M. House: The Texas Years, 1858–1912,* pp. 23–209; Johnson, *Texas and Texans,* IV, 1645–46; Barr, *Reconstruction to Reform,* pp. 209–10; Charles A. Culberson to House, August 23, 1907, roll 110, House Papers.

[31] Barr, *Reconstruction to Reform,* pp. 211–12; Richardson, *Colonel House,* pp. 130–32.

Culberson organization, many of whom owed him their positions, and instructing them to work for Sayers. Among those contacted were several officials in the prison system. Wharton Bates, inspector for the southern part of the state, campaigned for Sayers as he made his way around visiting the prison camps in the counties south and west of Houston. He reported his findings, with recommendations, back to House. Following a trip to Galveston in late February, Bates noted with some concern that Crane supporters had been working long and hard in the island city and had managed to line up the Galveston machine behind the attorney-general. Bates reported that he was doing everything he could for Sayers and asked House to suggest anything extra he might do for the ticket. The financial agent, J. S. Rice, working out of Huntsville, kept the Sayers forces in line in southeastern Texas. In addition, he and "the boys" helped the campaign along with financial contributions.[32]

In the process of waging a political campaign, House looked to every detail. In addition to keeping himself abreast of any shifts in the public mood, he and his coworkers corresponded widely with friends and potential supporters around the state and sent speakers into those areas where their candidate needed help. Friends and acquaintances were also called upon for financial assistance. In the Sayers campaign, money was solicited from some of the individuals who hired the labor of the state prisoners. Inasmuch as they benefited financially from the use of prison inmates, it seemed only fitting that they should repay the favor and come forth at election time with money.[33]

All the effort expended by the House team on behalf of Sayers enabled the congressman to win the June primary. House's personal leadership and the direction he lent to the campaign were crucial. Following the victory, Sayers, who had remained in Washington through the entire period, expressed his gratitude by pledging that he would consider no appointments in his administration without House's approval.[34]

The financial role played in the Sayers campaign by the contractors of the prison labor is indicative of the position of this group in Texas society. For the most part, those who hired the labor of state prisoners were wealthy individuals with large landholdings. They used their financial resources to curry favor with, and perpetuate the control of, political factions and individuals who would not disturb the status quo in the prisons. To the degree that contractors used their influence to pro-

[32] Richardson, *Colonel House,* pp. 137–38; Wharton Bates to House, Feb. 28, 1898, J. S. Rice to House, Mar. 21, 1898, and May 20, 1898, House Papers.

[33] J. S. Rice to House, Mar. 21, 1898, C. G. Ellis to House, Feb. 4, 1898, House Papers.

[34] Richardson, *Colonel House,* pp. 154–55.

tect and maintain their access to low-cost prison labor, they constituted a powerful ring interested only in its own self-preservation.

Throughout the period when Texas prison inmates were worked on the state contract system, a handful of leading citizens in the state predominated in the hiring of prisoners. Beginning with the five-year contracts made in the fall of 1882, just before resumption of state control, one finds among successful bidders a group of persons who retained contracts for prison labor as long as they wanted them. Some of the contractors managed to keep their prison forces until all inmates were placed under state control in 1912. The more prominent employers of prison labor through the late nineteenth and early twentieth centuries included E. H. Cunningham, L. A. Ellis, R. S. Willis, P. J. Willis, T. W. House, the Ball, Hutchings Company, Albert Sidney Burleson, W. T. Eldridge, and T. S. Henderson.[35]

E. H. Cunningham and L. A. Ellis were the principals in the firm of Cunningham and Ellis that had leased the entire prison in 1878. For many years following the revocation of their lease in 1883, both men continued to use prison inmates to work their large landholdings in and around Fort Bend County. Cunningham, who lived most of his life in San Antonio, is considered to have been the principal founder and organizer of the extensive sugar industry in Texas in the area southwest of Houston. He used hundreds of state prisoners to work the cane plantations that provided the raw material for his refinery at Sugarland. As one of the larger contractors of prison labor, Cunningham exerted considerable influence in penitentiary affairs. He was related by marriage to the Brahan family, out of which came the first financial agent appointed following state resumption of control of the prisons. He also contributed to statewide political campaigns and was instrumental at one point in securing the superintendent's job for another businessman, Houstonian J. S. Rice. In 1907 Cunningham sold his sugar refinery to a group of Galveston investors who did business as the Imperial Sugar Company. He died in San Antonio on August 27, 1912.[36]

[35]The competitive bidding process by which prison forces were hired was abandoned after 1887 in favor of a system wherein the state set the price it wanted for prisoners. Those contractors already having a prison force were given first choice in keeping it if they agreed to meet the state's price. See *Biennial Report,* 1888, p. 19; "Minutes of the Penitentiary Board, July 10, 1907," Box 2-11/365, Campbell Papers.

[36]"Sugarland and the Men Who Made It," pp. 1–2 (unpublished manuscript in the Fort Bend County Historical Museum, Rosenberg, Texas); A. J. Sowell, *History of Fort Bend County* (Houston: W. H. Coyle and Company, Stationers and Printers, 1904), pp. 348–50; Clarence R. Wharton, *History of Fort Bend County* (San Antonio: The Naylor Company, 1939), p. 194; T. J. Goree to E. M. House, November 10, 1898, J. S. Rice to House, March 21, 1898, Box 2R42, House Papers; *San Antonio Express,* Aug. 28, 1921;

L. A. Ellis, like Cunningham, continued to utilize prison labor on his South Texas plantations, but moved to Austin following revocation of the lease and sold his interests at Sugarland to Cunningham. He still maintained an involvement with the state sugar industry, however, as evidenced by his election as vice-president of the Texas Sugar Growers' Association in 1890. After moving to Austin, Ellis and George W. Littlefield, a wealthy cattleman, established the American National Bank in that city. A few years before his death in December, 1896, Ellis turned over the management of his business interests to his sons, who continued to use state prisoners to work the farms in Fort Bend County.[37]

Other major contractors of prison labor also associated closely with the early sugar industry in Texas included T. W. House, R. S. Willis, P. J. Willis, and W. T. Eldridge. All were men of wealth and influence in the state. The importance of the prisoners to these sugarcane growers is illustrated best by noting the precipitate decline of the sugar industry in the state following the end of the contract system in 1912.[38]

T. W. House had perhaps the most influence on politics in Austin thanks to the position of his brother Edward. T. W. owned and operated several large farms in the cane-growing areas of the state and at one time was a major refiner of sugar. Two of his larger holdings were the Darrington farm in Brazoria County and the Arcola plantation in Fort Bend County.[39]

The Willis brothers, P. J. and R. S., were natives of Maryland who came to Texas in 1836. They opened a small mercantile store in Montgomery, Texas, which by the late 1850s had grown to be "one of the largest houses in the state." After the Civil War, they moved the business to Houston and Galveston, where it operated under the name of P. J. Willis and Brother. P. J. died in 1873, after which his brother as-

---

Biennial Report, 1882, pp. 36–37; 1884, p. 29; 1886, p. 36; 1888, p. 28, Exhibits; 1890, p. 56; 1892, p. 29; 1894, p. 32; 1896, p. 31; 1898, p. 29; 1900, p. 29; 1902, p. 38; 1904, p. 36; 1906, pp. 27–28; 1908, p. 31.

[37]"Sugarland," pp. 1–2; *Austin Statesmen,* Dec. 11, 1896, p. 12; *Biennial Report,* 1882, pp. 36–37; 1884, p. 29; 1886, p. 36; 1888, p. 28, Exhibits; 1890, p. 36; 1892, p. 29; 1894, p. 32; 1896, p. 31; 1898, p. 29; 1900, p. 32; 1902, p. 38; 1904, p. 38; 1906, pp. 22–28.

In 1890, L. A. Ellis's son, C. G. Ellis, made a spirited attempt to lease the Louisiana prison system. Even though he offered a substantial annual sum for the lease, his friends in the Louisiana legislature could not carry the vote for him. See Mark T. Carleton, *Politics and Punishment: The History of the Louisiana State Penal System,* pp. 60–63.

[38]A number of other factors also conributed to the demise of the raw sugar industry in the state: competition from duty-free raw sugar from abroad, disease, and unpredictable weather. See William R. Johnson, *A Short History of the Sugar Industry in Texas* (Houston: Texas Gulf Coast Historical Association, 1961), pp. 58–60.

[39]Ibid., p. 57; Richardson, *Colonel House,* pp. 23–24. The Darrington property ultimately became part of the holdings of P. J. Willis and Brother. See *Biennial Report,* 1896, p. 31.

sumed full control. R. S. Willis later served as president of the Galveston National Bank, the Texas Guarantee and Trust Company, and was one of the founders of the Gulf, Colorado, and Santa Fe Railroad. He also was elected a vice-president of the Texas Sugar Growers' Association. The Willis plantations were located in Brazoria County.[40]

W. T. Eldridge, who owned extensive farms near Sugarland, began his business career as a merchant and builder of the Cane Belt Railway, which ran from Sealy to Matagorda, Texas. In 1903 the railroad was sold to the Santa Fe system. At one time Eldridge owned the City National Bank of San Antonio, where he also had other business interests. Eldridge and the Kempner family of Galveston were the principal parties involved in the formation of the Imperial Sugar Company that bought out the Cunningham properties.[41]

The last large contractor with extensive landholdings in the sugar-growing areas of the state, the Ball, Hutchings Company of Galveston, owned farms in Brazoria County. The firm had been established in 1854 by John H. Hutchings, George Ball, and John Sealy as a dry goods and commission business. Within a year or so, however, the dry goods operation was phased out in favor of private banking. The company made all three men enormously wealthy and enabled them to invest in railroads and other businesses.[42]

The men who hired the labor of state prisoners to develop the sugar industry in Texas exerted a powerful influence on prison system policies for reasons other than their collective wealth. Inasmuch as more prisoners by far worked on sugar farms than at any other type of outside labor, the men who owned those farms could demand that their voices be heard in Austin during any executive or legislative deliberations concerning penitentiary matters. Contractors recognized that their use of prisoners on the cane plantations represented a rather substantial source of revenue to the state, therefore entitling them to some consideration from elected officials. And because the low-cost labor was so vitally important to the continued well-being of the sugar industry, it would only be natural that growers would work together harmoniously to make certain the outside contract system endured.

Although the sugar growers formed the largest and most significant

[40] Johnson, *Short History of the Sugar Industry,* p. 51; Brown, *Indian Wars,* pp. 374–75, 589–90; *Biennial Report,* 1896, p. 31; 1898, p. 29.

[41] Johnson, *Short History of the Sugar Industry,* pp. 66–68; undated obituary of W. T. Eldridge in Fort Bend County Historical Museum, Rosenberg, Texas.

[42] Brown, *Indian Wars,* pp. 152–59; *Biennial Report,* 1880, p. 51; 1882, p. 36; 1884, p. 29; 1886, p. 36; 1888, p. 28, Exhibits; 1890, p. 56; 1892, p. 29; 1894, p. 31; 1896, p. 31; 1898, p. 29.

bloc of prison contractors, other well-known figures also profited from the labor of state prisoners. Two of the more prominent of this group were Thomas S. Henderson and Albert S. Burleson. Both of these men enjoyed long political careers and ultimately occupied positions of considerable influence in state affairs.

Thomas S. Henderson, who leased state prisoners between 1906 and 1912, was an attorney from Cameron, Texas. He was admitted to the bar in 1879 and served successively as county attorney and district attorney in Milam County. He also represented the county in the House of Representatives of the twenty-third legislature, which met in the spring of 1893. Governor Culberson appointed Henderson to the board of regents of the University of Texas in 1895. He remained on the board for sixteen years and for more than ten years was its chairman.[43] The length of Henderson's tenure as a university regent speaks adequately of the quality of his political connections.

Albert Sidney Burleson carried even more political weight than Henderson. Originally from San Marcos, Burleson attended both the A&M College of Texas and the University of Texas. He was admitted to the state bar in 1884 and began his political career as Austin city attorney. Burleson went on to represent the Ninth Texas Congressional District from 1899 to 1913, and from 1913 to 1921 served as postmaster-general of the United States.[44]

Beginning in the mid-1890s, Burleson and his brother-in-law, C. D. Johns, operated a 3,000-acre share farm in Bosque County using a large labor force of approximately 150 state prisoners. The shares on the farm were divided so that the state received 60 percent of the crop. The farm provided a substantial source of income for its owners.[45]

Events in the summer of 1900 demonstrated very clearly the value of the farm to Burleson and Johns when, for a time, it appeared their contract for the prison work force might not be renewed. Burleson contacted E. M. House and stressed that a termination of the labor agreement with the prison would do him "irreparable" financial damage. He asked House to intervene with prison authorities to ensure continuation of the contract. Burleson emphasized that he had been faithful to the administration in Austin and therefore was entitled to favorable con-

[43] *Members of the Legislature, 1846–1939,* p. 154; Johnson, *Texas and Texans,* IV, 1664–65; Hardy and Roberts, *Historical Review of South-East Texas,* II, 740; *Biennial Report,* 1906, p. 28; 1908, p. 31; 1910, p. 35.

[44] Seth S. McKay and Odie B. Faulk, *Texas after Spindletop* (Austin: Steck-Vaughn Company, 1965), p. 38; Walter Webb, ed., *Handbook of Texas* (Austin: Texas State Historical Association, 1952) I, 248–49; Adrian Norris Anderson, "Albert Sidney Burleson: A Southern Politician in the Progressive Era," pp. 1–39, 127–28.

[45] Anderson, "Albert Sidney Burleson," pp. 40, 56; *Biennial Report,* 1902, p. 38.

sideration. He spoke in no uncertain terms of the "great injury" he would suffer if the prison work force were taken from him.[46] House, fearing a breach in the solidarity of his organization if Burleson was not placated, acceded to the congressman's wishes and the contract was renewed. Burleson, deeply grateful to House for the assistance, kept his prison force until all such contracts ended in 1912.[47]

In addition to the private individuals who contracted for the labor of prisoners, several railroads also took advantage of the state's prison policies to avail themselves of a relatively inexpensive, dependable supply of labor. For reasons already discussed, state officials did not like to make contracts with the railroads, but did so despite their misgivings because they were a source of revenue and provided a means to keep prisoners busy. As a result, there were always a few inmates detailed to railroad construction trains and wood-cutting forces.

During the span of time covered by this study, a total of twenty-one different railroad companies made use of Texas prisoners for varying lengths of time. The twenty-year period from 1880 to 1900 saw the most extensive activity. During this period railroads laid sufficient track in the state to establish Texas as the national leader in total railroad mileage.[48]

Despite the considerable amount of railroad construction during the last two decades of the nineteenth century, only a relatively small number of state prisoners engaged in such work. On average, the railroads used only 215 prisoners per year in the period from 1880 to 1900. This figure stood far below the number hired by the large planters in the coastal counties.[49] Perhaps because they employed such a relatively small share of the available prisoners, no indications could be found that the railroads exerted any significant pressure to maintain existent prison contracting policies.

The influence of the major employers of prison labor and their willingness to step forth and guard their privileged position account, in large part, for the durability of the contract system. The large landowners and entrepreneurs joined with those political forces in the state that

[46] A. S. Burleson to E. M. House, July 6, 1900, roll 109, House Papers.

[47] Burleson to House, July 23, 1900, roll 109, House Papers; *Biennial Report,* 1896, p. 32; 1898, p. 21; 1900, p. 29; 1902, p. 38; 1904, p. 38; 1906, pp. 27–28; 1908, p. 32; 1910, p. 35; *Annual Report,* 1911, p. 32.

[48] Joseph Stricklin Spratt, *The Road to Spindletop: Economic Change in Texas, 1875–1901,* pp. 32–33.

[49] *Biennial Report,* 1880, p. 51; 1882, pp. 36–37; 1884, p. 29; 1886, p. 36; 1888, p. 28, Exhibits; 1890, p. 19; 1892, p. 29; 1894, p. 32; 1896, p. 31; 1898, p. 29; 1900, p. 29; 1902, p. 38; 1904, p. 38; 1906, pp. 27–28; 1908, p. 31; 1910, p. 35.

sought to maintain a status quo in which their mutual interest could be protected and extended. The strength inherent in such a coalition made reform of the prison system exceedingly difficult.

The host of individuals who staffed the prison and administered policy joined with the forces resisting change. Most prison employees, especially at the upper management levels, were chosen because of their political record and the promise of continued political service. They brought little professionalism to the task of administering the rules and regulations. Those very few who argued sincerely for substantive reform found themselves hopelessly outnumbered by the comparative multitude who viewed their selection for prison employment as a reward that carried with it the understanding that one should not upset the established order. This combination of entrenched privilege and bureaucratic inertia did not begin to come apart until the serious attacks leveled against it early in the twentieth century by various forces that coalesced to demand significant changes in penitentiary management.

CHAPTER VII

THE END OF LEASING

The Texas that entered the twentieth century had undergone many changes since the end of the Civil War. In addition to a sizable increase in population, the growth of urbanization, and diversification of the economy, the state underwent a political transformation of sorts. The traditional conservatism of the Bourbon Democrats in the 1870s and 1880s gave way in the 1890s to a moderate reform impulse, elements of which carried over into the first decade of the new century and created a political and social milieu that fostered further reforms.

The nature of this reform movement, the forces that composed it, and its effect on prison policies will form the focus of this chapter. An examination will be made of the influence exerted by splinter political parties and factions that forced the dominant Democratic party to accommodate and compromise with groups demanding change. Reform-minded persons and organizations that acted independently of any obvious political affiliations will be scrutinized also to determine the role they may have played in developing a climate in which change became possible and desirable.

In the course of looking at the forces that advocated changes, it will be useful also to examine the public attitudes and assumptions that tended to thwart or delay reforms. Popular perceptions of convicted felons and of their appropriate treatment contributed significantly to an apparent public apathy toward prison conditions. Such indifference logically coincided with the interests of those who favored the status quo in prison affairs.

Public attitudes toward taxation and state spending for public institutions also must be considered a factor in prison reform. Abolition of the contract system involved not only additional outlays for prisoner care but the loss of a substantial amount of income as well. Elected leaders of the state had to move slowly and cautiously to avoid any irrevocable action that would not be supported by the voters. The fact that the public ultimately came to accept an end to the practice of hiring out prisoners to private individuals attests to the magnitude and intensity of the reform movement.

In looking at the forces that sought to bring about changes in the administration of the state prisons, it is necessary to differentiate between those which exerted a relatively minor influence and those which exhibited more substantial and, therefore, effective power. Of the former, it can be said that they spoke first in behalf of prisoners and showed great persistence. What they lacked in terms of power to effect change they made up for in perseverance. The group of less influential advocates for prison reform included various voluntary associations such as a prison reform society, women's clubs, organizations of racial minorities, and labor unions.

The Prison Reform Association of Texas came into existence in the early 1870s, thanks primarily to the efforts of the Reverend B. A. Rogers, rector of St. David's Episcopal Church in Austin from 1866 through 1874. Originally from Philadelphia, Rogers came to Texas sometime shortly after the Civil War to help Texans recover from the wounds of the conflict. He became active in a number of charitable efforts and in 1872 attended the first meeting of the International Prison Congress, held in London. Upon his return from England, Rogers organized the Prison Reform Association and persuaded a number of lawyers and legislators to join.[1]

During the spring of 1873, the Prison Reform Association of Texas petitioned the state legislature for action. The poor financial condition of the state, however, left little money available for serious reforms of state-dependent institutions. Indeed, the state treasury needed the revenue from the Ward-Dewey lease.

Another problem besetting Rogers and his group in their reform efforts was an apparent inability to focus their attention clearly on the state prison system. In a memorial to the legislature in January, 1873, for example, the organization urged state action to improve the county jails, especially the one in Austin. It made no mention of the state prison system. A subsequent letter to the lawmakers included the subject of prison problems, but presented the issue along with appeals for mercy for two condemned murderers in the Travis County jail, a request for a state poorhouse, and a house of correction for juvenile offenders. Had the Prison Reform Association restricted its efforts solely to seeking improvements in the state prison system and tried to come up with some

[1] Federal Writers' Project of Texas, *St. David's through the Years* (Austin: St. David's Guild, 1942), pp. 49–55: *Proceedings of the Annual Congress of the National Prison Association of the United States,* pp. 66–67, 104–105.

alternative sources of income, it might have been more successful in its program.[2]

In late December, 1874, because of poor health, Rogers resigned his position at St. David's and left Austin. He lived on a ranch in Williamson County for several years and moved finally to Houston, where he died in 1904. Although he remained active in the cause of prison reform until his death, the Prison Reform Association he founded disappeared after he left Austin.[3]

Other early criticism of existing prison policies came from leading members of the black community in the state. No doubt because blacks made up such a disproportionate share of the prison population, black leaders scored not only prison conditions but also the inequities in the legal system that left minorities at the mercy of white judges and juries. The net effect of protests from the black community, like those from the Prison Reform Association, was nil.

It should be noted that there was some division of opinion among blacks regarding state prison policies. Some spoke out against the large numbers of black citizens in the prison system and the types of labor to which they were put. Others were satisfied with the way in which prisoners were treated. It seems fair to state that most black Texans disliked state prison policies, but the issue was not one of overriding importance to them. Rather, they listed it as one of many grievances in support of improving their position in Texas society.

As early as July, 1879, in a conference in Houston, black leaders from around the state gathered to air common grievances and discuss the wisdom of leaving the state and joining the exodus to Kansas. In the course of their meeting no reference was made to prison policies as a source of dissatisfaction. Conference members objected specifically to discrimination in railroad travel, the lack of a good public school system in the state, and the generally arrogant attitude manifested by whites toward other racial groups. The absence of any mention of prisons, however, should not be taken to mean that blacks in the state did not object to the relatively large numbers of blacks incarcerated. One black farmer

[2] "Memorial of the Prison Reform Association of Texas. To the Legislature of the State of Texas, January 23, 1873," Texas State Archives and Library, Austin: Austin *Daily Democratic Statesman,* Mar. 15, 1873, p. 2. Roger's efforts to get a new jail for Austin reached fruition in 1876 when "one of the State's most modern jails" was constructed in the city. See Federal Writers' Project, *St. David's,* p. 48.

[3] Frank Brown, "Annals of Travis County and of the City of Austin from Earliest Times to Close of 1875," XIII, 71, Austin Public Library, Austin; *Proceedings of the Annual Congress of the National Prison Association of the United States,* Held at Austin, Texas, December 2–6, 1897 (Pittsburgh: Shaw Brothers, Printers, 1898), pp. 66–67, 104–105.

who joined the exodus to Kansas complained that he did so, at least in part, because so many young persons were being "sent to the penitentiary and hired out on sugar farms," and he feared the situation would get worse. Probably, the omission of the prison from the list of conference concerns simply reflected the fact that other matters were considered more important and in greater need of immediate attention.[4]

The most forceful statement of black opinion regarding the prisons came during a state convention of black citizens held in Austin in July, 1883, shortly after the termination of the leases of the state prisons. The committee on grievances at the convention drew up a list of five complaints it wished to bring to the attention of the elected leaders of the state. The five areas of dissatisfaction and the order in which they were listed were: (1) opposition to the state miscegenation statutes, (2) criticism of funding shortages for black public schools, (3) complaints against the manner in which state prisoners were treated, (4) criticism of the broadly accepted policy of denying to black citizens equal access to the services provided by railways, inns, and taverns, and (5) opposition to the exclusion of blacks from jury service.[5] The priority given to opposition to the state's miscegenation laws stemmed from a disagreement with the fundamental social assumption underlying such laws. Black leaders believed that the penalties for miscegenation manifested a deeply held conviction by whites of the social inferiority of blacks. In the opinion of the convention, all discrimination against blacks by white Texans derived from the social attitudes inherent in the laws against intermarriage between the races.

With specific reference to prisons, the convention did not condemn the contract system or publicly favor its abandonment. It did, however, criticize the manner in which prisoners on the farms were treated as compared with the generally good conditions inside the walls. Protests were directed at the brutal conduct of guards and the excessive amounts of work required of prisoners. Complaint also was lodged at the lack of any reformative efforts in the outside camps. To remedy the situation, the convention called upon state leaders to appoint a black inspector of outside prison camps to make certain all rules and regulations were followed according to the spirit and letter of the law. Elected officials also were urged to appoint at least one black to the board of

[4] *Galveston Daily News,* July 3, 1879, p. 1; July 4, 1879, p. 1; Thomas Michael Parrish, "A New Species of Slavery," unpublished paper delivered at the fall meeting of the East Texas Historical Association, Sept. 27, 1980, Nacogdoches, Texas.

[5] Herbert Aptheker, ed., *A Documentary History of the Negro People in the United States* (New York: Citadel Press, 1951), pp. 686–91.

prison commissioners. Presumably, black inspectors and commissioners would safeguard the interests of black prisoners more diligently than did their white counterparts.[6]

Only one black, Strother Green, who served briefly as a commissioner under E. J. Davis (see chapter II, above), received appointment to prison service during the period of this study. In part, the reason there were no others lay in the assumptions by whites of black inferiority, the very attitude castigated by the members of the 1883 convention. More importantly, however, the political nature of penitentiary appointments excluded blacks from serious consideration. Because blacks in the late nineteenth century were diminishing rapidly as a significant political force, they also were losing any rights of patronage, such as to prison jobs.

A year or so after the 1883 convention in Austin, a black member of the legislature spoke at some variance with the earlier charges made against the prison. R. J. Moore, who represented Washington County in the House of Representatives in the eighteenth, nineteenth, and twentieth legislatures, served in 1885 as a member of a legislative committee examining the prisons. The investigation found nothing seriously amiss in prison management and had much praise for the leadership of Superintendent Goree. Following the investigation, Representative Moore pronounced himself "perfectly satisfied with the treatment of colored prisoners."[7]

It is difficult to reconcile Moore's statement with the criticisms of the 1883 convention, or with the conditions that were known to have existed in the outside camps. It might have been that although life in the camps was intolerable it was no harder on black prisoners than on any others. All farm inmates were subjected to the same deplorable treatment with no distinctions made because of race. The report of the 1885 investigation makes no mention of visiting the outside camps, so perhaps the members of the investigating committee preferred to restrict their remarks solely to what they saw inside the two prisons where living and working conditions were known to have been better.[8]

The early efforts by prison reformers and black leaders to focus pub-

[6]Ibid., pp. 687–90.

[7]Dallas *Weekly Herald,* Feb. 19, 1885, p. 2; *Members of the Legislature of the State of Texas from 1846 to 1939,* pp. 113, 122, 129.

[8]*House Journal, Nineteenth Legislature, 1885,* pp. 190–93. Representative Moore was himself a former inmate in the Texas prison. He had served time for attempted murder in the early 1870s. Upon expiration of his sentence he was given a full pardon by Governor Davis and had all rights of citizenship restored. See *Galveston Daily News,* Feb. 23, 1885, p. 1.

lic attention on the prisons failed to generate any substantive response. They own the distinction of having spoken out first but received little reward for their initiative. The forces resisting change were simply too formidable to yield to groups that stood clearly outside the mainstream of public opinion.

The average Texan in the later decades of the nineteenth century apparently thought very little about persons serving time in the state prisons. Most Texans were too busy with their own problems to give much attention to convicted felons incarcerated in geographically isolated institutions. On those relatively few occasions when the public did speak out about prisoners, it criticized state leaders for allowing proven lawbreakers—persons who had demonstrated their contempt for society—to work outside the prison, thereby depriving law-abiding citizens of needed jobs. The lack of public concern for conditions in the prisons goes far toward explaining how the system could deteriorate to the deplorable levels uncovered by the several legislative investigations. Public apathy toward the prisons and the general ignorance of prison conditions prevailed almost from the inception of the lease period. Shortly after the beginning of the Ward-Dewey lease, an editorial in a leading newspaper of the state lamented the general lack of interest in prison affairs: "Our people are too much in a hurry in the modes of their own life to bestow earnest and well-digested thought upon the . . . effects of . . . penal justice, and the duty of adopting reformation measures in behalf of condemned criminals."[9]

The several former prisoners who wrote of their time spent in Texas prisons also mentioned the prevailing level of ignorance about prison life among the public at large. Indeed, the very fact that former inmates felt compelled to describe their experiences in print arose from their belief that most Texans did not know much about prison life and the conditions under which the inmates lived. J. L. Wilkinson wanted to "burn into the minds of the people" of Texas the terrible ordeal suffered by prisoners. If Texans knew how bad things truly were, changes would come. Henry Tomlin wrote that the disgraceful conditions in Texas prisons would change only when the public became fully informed of the vile nature of prison life. Charles Campbell warned Texans that their state would continue to suffer rebuke and scorn from other parts of the nation "until the sure enough civilized of this state take closer notice of what is going on here [in the prisons] and devise means for a general cleaning out of officialdom."[10]

[9] *Galveston Daily News,* May 4, 1873, p. 1.

[10] J. L. Wilkinson, *The Trans-Cedar Lynching and the Texas Penitentiary,* p. 95; Henry

Unfortunately for those who urged reform, some Texans who did pay attention to prison conditions expressed feelings antagonistic to significant change. Shortly after the establishment of the Prison Reform Association, an outcry went up against all the "talk about prison reform in this country," which would make prisoners "the subject of fashionable sympathy": "Prisons ought not to be made desirable, nor criminals glorified as martyrs to cruel laws. A prison, at best, should be an object of horror, that men may be deterred from the commission of crime by the fear of getting in it."[11]

Opponents of prison reformers conceded that prisoners deserved "a sufficiency of plain food and comfortable clothing," and should not be treated cruelly. Beyond these basic needs, however, they were not willing to go.[12]

The belief that prisons should not be places of comfort also enjoyed currency among some of those citizens most vehement in their objection to the lease and contract systems. John N. Henderson, a judge of the Court of Criminal Appeals in Austin, emerged as a prominent prison reformer in Texas in the late nineteenth century. Exhibiting the most enlightened approaches to penology of the age, Henderson abhorred the practice of hiring state prisoners to private parties and wanted all inmates under exclusive control of the state so that the full array of reformative influences could be provided. He disagreed vigorously, however, with those "sentimentalists who would scatter [a prisoner's] pathway with roses." Addressing a meeting of the National Prison Association in 1897, Henderson argued: "The treatments of the convicted felon should be humane, but firm; his labor should be arduous and his treatment and discipline so severe that he would forever dread the prison walls. His punishment should not only be a deterrent as to himself, but it should be such as to deter others."[13]

Much of the animus for making prisons as uncomfortable as possible arose from the belief that convicted felons, because of their transgression of society's laws, were not entitled to undue concern for their creature comforts. Upon their conviction, prisoners lost the right to expect anything other than what society chose to give them. The prevailing mindset considered prison inmates as outside all but the most minimal levels of compassion. Such feelings provided the rational un-

---

Tomlin, *Henry Tomlin. The Man Who Fought Brutality and Oppression of the Ring in the State of Texas For Eighteen Years and Won,*p. 251; Charles C. Campbell, *Hell Exploded. An Exposition of Barbarous Cruelty and Prison Horrors,* p. 11.

[11] *Austin Daily Statesman,* July 17, 1873.

[12] Ibid.

[13] *Proceedings of the National Prison Association, 1897,* pp. 303–304.

derpinnings for the "convict bogey" apparition that saw prison inmates as loathsome, dangerous creatures who, for the safety of honest citizens, had to be kept locked up and out of sight.[14]

One Texas prisoner, traveling to Huntsville with others in the custody of the state transport contractor, described the attitude of free citizens sharing the same railroad car. They stared at the recently convicted felons and no one made any attempt to start conversation. The prisoners were regarded as "wild beasts" whom the public wanted watched "with sufficient care as to preclude the possibility of escape." An inmate in the prison system was "despised" and denied any "sympathy" from citizens "of the world at large."[15]

The most graphic example of the hostility and contempt exhibited by some members of society toward state prisoners occurred in early summer, 1879, when passengers on a train in northeast Texas witnessed the shooting of a young prisoner who had attempted to escape from a railroad construction crew. After the shooting, the guard dumped the young man, still alive, at a "shanty to rot and die." Some of the onlookers were appalled at such a display of callousness; others, however, simply shrugged their shoulders and said, "he is nothing but a convict."[16]

The public perception of prison inmates as objects of scorn made the task of reformers doubly difficult. As long as a sizable segment of society remained unwilling to concede to prisoners a degree of humanity, it was impossible to make any serious assault upon leasing. The problem became compounded even further when citizens realized that a tax increase would likely ensue if the state attempted to reform the prison system by ending contract labor.

Texans of the late nineteenth and early twentieth centuries enjoyed relatively low levels of taxation. The state had never had a strong tradition of spending for public institutions and the fiscal distress ushered in by the collapse of the Confederacy did little to alter long-standing customs. Texas citizens preferred reductions in public services if necessary to maintain low taxes. Prior to 1860, state income came primarily from the sale of indemnity bonds. Additional operating funds became available to state officials in the form of the $5 million Texas received as part of the Compromise of 1850. Although the state levied taxes on both real and personal property, on occupational licenses, and for use

[14] Harry E. Allen and Clifford E. Simonsen, *Corrections in America,* 2nd ed. (Encino, Calif.: Glencoe Publishing, 1978), p. 63.

[15] A. L. George *The Texas Convict: Thrilling and Terrible Experiences of a Texas Boy,* pp. 105, 115.

[16] Austin *Daily Democratic Statesman,* May 2, 1879.

of the polls, confused and poorly administered assessment and collection procedures resulted in little revenue. In 1860, for example, from a free population of approximately 420,000 persons, the total tax receipts of all taxing jurisdictions in the state came to only $533,265.[17]

The Republican Reconstruction government in Texas, headed by E. J. Davis, attempted to reverse the traditional pattern by increasing taxation and state spending for education, transportation, and law enforcement, but met considerable hostility, primarily from Democrats. Notwithstanding the positive intentions of the Republican programs, or the benefits that likely would have accrued from them, many citizens thought they were too costly and concentrated too much power in the hands of the governor. Critics of Governor Davis and his party wasted little time in voicing their objections to his policies.[18]

In late September, 1871, opponents of the Republican program met in a protest convention in Austin. Calling themselves the Taxpayers' Convention of the State of Texas, the assembled delegates claimed to speak for the citizens of ninety-four Texas counties. Although the convention stated that it represented "no particular political party" and would tolerate "no partisan discussion," it demonstrated a more than obvious political bias against Davis and his brand of Republicanism. Convention members scored the Republicans for increases in taxation levels that had raised ad valorem property levies from $.15 to $2.17½ per $100 valuation. The delegates wanted taxes reduced to one-third of 1 percent for state needs and half that amount for county purposes. In calling for such drastic reductions in state income, Davis's opponents contemplated a much smaller and less expensive state government.[19]

Because of the ease with which taxes could be evaded, the Republican taxing system ultimately failed to accomplish its goals. The state had to sell bonds to obtain operating revenue, thus increasing the debt. More importantly, however, the experience under the Davis administration further fastened in the minds of a majority of citizens the conviction that taxes should be kept as low as possible and state spending regulated accordingly. Low taxes and limited state government became

[17]Edmund T. Miller, *A Financial History of Texas,* pp. 18–26, 95–97, 107–13.

[18]Carl H. Moneyhon, *Republicanism in Reconstruction Texas,* pp. 129–67.

[19]*Proceedings of the Taxpayers' Convention of the State of Texas, Held at the City of Austin, September 22nd, 23rd, and 25th, 1871. Also a Memorial to the Legislature, and an Address to the Taxpayers of Texas* (Galveston: News Steam Book and Job Office, 1871), pp. 5–23. Future prison commissioner Walter Tips, chosen as one of two assistant secretaries of the convention, represented Comal County, and Thomas Goree spoke for Madison County.

articles of faith for the Democratic party when it recaptured control of the legislature in 1872 and the Governor's Mansion in 1874.[20]

After their return to power in the 1870s, Texas Democrats maintained their control of state politics throughout the remainder of the century and the period covered by this study. Uninterrupted Democratic rule, however, did not mean that the party enjoyed complete unity. On the contrary, splinter groups arose during the late nineteenth century to challenge majority policy within the Democratic party and force it to accommodate divergent interests. Demands for change in the shaping of government appeared very shortly after the Democratic party returned to power in the state. Disgruntled agrarian elements among the population, suffering the financial distress that accompanied the economic panic of 1873, spoke out first.

That farmers should have taken the lead in seeking political reform comes as no surprise given their strength in Texas society at the time and the problems they were suffering. In 1870, approximately 70 percent of the state population engaged in some form of agriculture or an occupation related to agriculture. This number remained fairly constant and by the turn of the century had dropped by only five percentage points. Through the later decades of the nineteenth century, farmers endured falling prices, growing indebtedness, increasing dependence on middlemen, and railroad rates that producers considered to be too high. All these problems combined to convince farmers that powerful combinations of monopolistic capital were conspiring to reduce the agricultural classes to a state of peonage.[21]

Through the last quarter of the nineteenth century, farmers increasingly turned to political leaders to seek improvement of the farmer's position in society. The state constitution ratified in 1876, with its provisions for extreme retrenchment in government spending and services, accurately reflected the efforts of the large agrarian element that had authored it. Following the adoption of the constitution, Texas agriculturalists actively entered the political life of the state, hoping to maintain their view of the proper function of government. During the 1880s, first the Greenback party and then the Farmers' Alliance took up the cudgel in behalf of the state's agricultural classes. The Greenbackers, who first began to organize in Texas in 1876, favored expansion of the currency by incorporating into the money supply greenbacks in amounts equal to treasury notes then in circulation. They opposed the demone-

[20]Miller, *Financial History,* pp. 166, 193; Roscoe C. Martin, *The People's Party in Texas. A Study in Third Party Politics,* p. 18.

[21]Martin, *People's Party,* pp. 16–21; Moneyhon, *Republicanism in Texas,* pp. 194–96; Alwyn Barr, *Reconstruction to Reform. Texas Politics, 1876–1906,* pp. 176–92.

tization of silver, land grants to railroads and corporations, and state taxes on occupations. They also maintained: "The honest mechanic and laborer of the country should not be forced into competition with gangs of convicts sentenced to penitentiaries for crimes and we demand that the contract system for this class of labor shall be abolished, and that all convicts shall be confined within the prison walls." The Greenbackers entered candidates in state political races in the late 1870s and early 1880s, but despite some early successes, by 1884 the party was fading from the political scene.[22]

The Farmers' Alliance, which had appeared originally in the 1870s, enjoyed a major resurgence of strength in the mid-1880s. Although the alliance did not run its own candidates for office, it threw its political support to those office seekers who demonstrated sympathy for farmers. Alliance members favored railroad regulation and the adoption of the subtreasury plan, and opposed convict leasing. The alliance's position on lease came about as part of an effort to broaden its base of support by reaching out to groups, like labor, with which it felt a commonality of interest.[23]

Joining the farmers in the opposition to leasing came the Republican and Prohibition parties. At its 1882 state convention, the Republican party, containing a large percentage of blacks, wanted all prisoners confined within the walls of prisons. Party members said nothing concerning any type of work prison inmates should do, or that they be self-sustaining. In addition, Republicans favored the establishment of "houses of refuge or correction for juvenile offenders." Six years later, the Prohibition party, which had been established in 1884, called for abolishing the practice of hiring prisoners to private contractors. The party favored placing all inmates within prison walls. Like the Republicans, the Prohibitionists made no mention of having prisoners work to pay for the prison operating costs.[24]

[22] Barr, *Reconstruction to Reform,* pp. 9–10; Seth Shepard McKay, *Seven Decades of the Texas Constitution of 1876* (Lubbock: Texas Technological College Press, 1942), pp. 47–48, 68–70; Ernest Wallace, *Texas in Turmoil,* pp. 226–27; Ralph A. Smith, "The Grange Movement in Texas, 1873–1900," *Southwestern Historical Quarterly,* 42 (Apr., 1939): 298; Roscoe C. Martin, "The Greenback Party in Texas," *Southwestern Historical Quarterly,* 30 (Jan., 1927): 161–68.

[23] Martin, *People's Party,* pp. 21–24; Barr, *Reconstruction to Reform,* pp. 93–110. The subtreasury idea called for the establishment of branches of the national treasury (subtreasuries) throughout the country. In conjunction with the subtreasuries there would be government warehouses where farmers could store farm goods until prices improved. See Robert C. McMath, Jr., *Populist Vanguard. A History of the Southern Farmer's Alliance* (New York: W. W. Norton and Company, 1975), pp. 90–91.

[24] Barr, *Reconstruction,* pp. 85–93, 180–92; Ernest William Winkler, ed., *Platforms of Political Parties in Texas,* pp. 213, 255.

By 1890 the agricultural classes in Texas prepared to enter what would be a very active decade for them. In that year, Texas agrarians enthusiastically supported James Stephen Hogg, who campaigned for governor on a platform calling for a state commission to regulate railroads. Following Hogg's lopsided victory over his opponents, elements of the farmer constituency broke with the governor over disagreements as to the membership of the regulatory body and the manner in which commission members were to be selected. The disaffected farmers provided the nucleus around which the People's party in Texas would be built.[25]

Texas Populists formed the strongest of the farmer movements in the state. They supported the objectives of their parent organization at the national level, especially the incorporation of silver into the currency base, and tighter controls over railroads. They also favored property tax revision, a graduated income tax, and significant salary reductions for all government officials. Drawing on the experience of the Farmers' Alliance, Texas Populists encouraged others to join their movement. They incorporated into the various party platforms provisions designed to broaden the base of popular support, particularly among workers. For wage laborers, the party sought an eight-hour workday, the creation of a state bureau of labor and board of arbitration, and a prohibition against arresting unemployed workers for vagrancy. They also sought to remove convict labor from competition with free workers.[26]

The Populist appeal found ready converts in Texas. Party membership grew dramatically, and by early 1892, over two thousand Populist clubs had been formed around the state. Two years later, the Populist candidate for governor polled 160,000 votes out of a total of 376,000 cast. In the same balloting, the party elected twenty-two representa-

[25] Barr, *Reconstruction,* pp. 117–21; Martin, *People's Party,* pp. 26–27. On the subject of prison labor, Hogg came up with the novel idea of having state prisoners manufacture the same goods as those produced by the trusts and monopolies operating in the state. Nothing ever came of the suggestion, for the state had decided to emphasize outside farm labor over manufacturing in the prisons. See Robert C. Cotner, *James Stephen Hogg: A Biography* (Austin: University of Texas Press, 1959), p. 225.

[26] Martin, *People's Party,* pp. 47–53. There is reason to question the sincerity of the Populists in calling for an end to competition with prison labor. At the same time that the party appealed for the votes of free workers, it also advocated using state prisoners to build a publicly owned railroad to run from the Gulf of Mexico to the Red River and open the central parts of the state. Party ambivalence on this issue mirrored the activities of party members in other parts of the country who, though condemning the competition from prisoners, nevertheless urged that convicts be used to build roads. See Dan T. Carter, "Prisons, Politics and Business: The Convict Lease System in the Post–Civil War South," p. 98.

tives and two senators, an impressive number but not enough to control legislation.[27]

Following the strong Populist showing in 1894, Texas Democrats stole much of the thunder of the third party. In the state convention in the summer of 1896, the Democrats came out in favor of silver monetization, a graduated income tax, and the direct popular election of United States senators. They registered their opposition to monopoly control and trusts, and to existing tariff policies that offered protection to manufacturers but free trade to agriculturalists. The preemption of much of the Populist program left it with less to entice voters. Many of the farmers returned to the Democratic party that had seemingly changed and begun to adopt a reform posture.[28]

Populist strength waned quickly in the late 1890s and by the turn of the century had ceased to be a formidable factor in state politics. Thus it suffered the customary fate of third parties in American history. Its failure to capture control of state government, however, is not, perhaps, the best measure of its lack of success. As party members looked back over their struggles in the 1890s they could point with justifiable pride to the changes they had wrought in state politics. The Democratic party of the Bourbons, which had practiced an extreme form of limited government and fiscal retrenchment to the point of parsimony, had yielded its control and philosophical orientation to a new generation of political leaders flexible enough to permit a gradual expansion of government to meet the needs of a maturing state.[29]

Although the farmer groups had managed to bring about fundamental alterations in the outlook of the dominant Democratic party, they had wrought little change in the party's position toward placing state prisoners in contract labor camps. As early as 1878, Democratic platform writers had deprecated the necessity of keeping state prisoners outside prison walls and had urged an end to such practice "as soon as practicable." These practical considerations remained of supreme concern to the party throughout the state contract period. In 1894, state Democrats condemned the hiring of prisoners to "corporations and private individuals" and wanted the practice stopped "at the earliest practicable moment consistent with the best interest of the State." By 1902 the party had come to a different decision:

> [To] favor the enactment of laws providing for the employment, as far as practicable, of short time State convicts on the public roads in counties mak-

[27]Martin, *People's Party,* pp. 40–45; Barr, *Reconstruction,* pp. 157–59.
[28]Barr, *Reconstruction,* pp. 161–72.
[29]Martin, *People's Party,* pp. 266–67.

> ing suitable provisions therefor, and the employment of State penitentiary convict labor on work not in competition with free labor, as far as practicable, and that such prisoners be employed in the walls of the penitentiary and on farms operated by the State on its own account.[30]

There is no question but that money matters formed the major concern of Democratic officials with regard to prisons. To end outside contracts would have required heavy expenses to make up for the lost income. This did not seem "consistent with the best interest of the State."

As the People's party spent itself late in the 1890s, state politics went through a hiatus of reform. The two governors who served during the 1898–1906 period, Sayers and Lanham, were both former Confederates and conservative Democrats who concerned themselves primarily with cooling political tempers and reuniting the Democratic party. Both men owed and acknowledged much of their electoral success to the organization built and run by Edward House, who persistently shied away from any political or legislative innovations that would tamper seriously with the existing governmental apparatus. House and his people, although not opposed to all changes, manifested a much more favorable attitude toward business and political stability. They used their considerable powers over patronage to ensure that people of similar philosophy received appointment to state jobs.[31]

Despite the seeming placidity of state politics at the turn of the century, the spirit of reform and the desire for changes to improve society remained alive. During the Sayers-Lanham regnum new groups that sprang from Texas towns and cities and from the industrial establishments in the state joined with the remnants of the agricultural movement of the last quarter of the nineteenth century to throw their weight into a new march of progressivism. In the 1906 gubernatorial elections, the revived reform forces coalesced behind the candidacy of Thomas M. Campbell, who appeared to promise a break with the business-as-usual government of the preceding eight years.[32]

Campbell opened his campaign for the Democratic nomination with a speech in Athens, Texas, on April 21, 1906. The tone of the address

[30] Winkler, *Platforms*, pp. 185, 341, 448. One contemporaneous observer of Texas politics during the late nineteenth century wrote that efforts to end leasing and reform the prisons in the state failed because most Texans refused to accept the increased costs that would have accompanied an end to the highly profitable leasing system. See George W. Cable, *The Silent South Together with the Freedman's Case in Equity and the Convict Lease System*, pp. 156–158.

[31] Barr, *Reconstruction*, pp. 220–22; Lewis L. Gould, *Progressives and Prohibitionists: Texas Democrats in the Wilson Era*, pp. 11–15.

[32] James Aubrey Tinsley, "The Progressive Movement in Texas," p. 66.

hinted at the kind of administration he hoped to lead. More importantly, Campbell couched his appeal for votes in the emotional terms he believed would attract the most voters. He described for his listeners the forces in the state that sought to keep him out of the governor's chair: "Those who would debauch popular government and make it the instrument of avarice and greed, who would make our constitution the toy and the plaything of monopoly, our laws the hiding places of trusts and the shield of grafters, and those who would make Texas only a 'breeding ground for more millionaires and more paupers. . . ."

Campbell warned the crowd that "organized corporate wealth" sought "to fasten its iron hold" upon state government. The trusts were "forging their merciless shackles upon the industry and energies of the people of this commonwealth." Campbell expressed his pleasure that the citizens of Texas, aware of the pernicious actions of great wealth, were "again manifesting a disposition to take an active and firm hand in public affairs [so] that present evil tendencies may be checked." He exhorted his listeners to join the fight with him and not permit themselves to be duped by the "corporations and the trusts" who wanted to use "decoy" issues such as prohibition and local option to divert public attention away from the more legitimate concerns in the campaign.[33]

After making the customary pledge to use tax money in an efficient, businesslike way, Campbell outlined his policies in certain key areas of public affairs. With regard to prisons, he argued that convicted felons should receive "suitable care and humane treatment" from the state. In addition, prisoners "should be required to work, of course, and they should be made self-sustaining." He opposed the use of prison inmates to "enrich individuals and corporations" and called for the abolition of the "system of leasing and otherwise employing convicts in competition with the farmers and wage earners of Texas." As a solution to the prison labor problem, Campbell came out in favor of employing prisoners on the public roads of the state. "Good roads enhance the value of farms, make life in the country more attractive and increase the trade of the towns and cities." Echoing former governor Hogg, he suggested that those prisoners confined within the walls of penal institutions should be put to manufacturing goods to compete with the products offered by the trusts and other monopolistic concerns operating in the state. Convicted felons, in the words of the future governor, "should never be used to drive free labor from the mines, the factories and farms of Texas."[34]

[33]Thomas M. Campbell, *Speech of Thomas M. Campbell Opening His Campaign for Governor of Texas, at Athens, Texas, April 21st 1906 and Press Comments* (Palestine, Tex.: Palestine Printing Company, 1906), pp. 3–31.

[34]Ibid., pp. 13–14.

In other parts of his address Campbell spoke in favor of a constitutional amendment to permit counties to levy an ad valorem property tax to support rural schools, those most in need of additional funding. He also praised voluntary associations of farmers and workers founded to obtain for their members a more equitable reward for the fruits of their labor. He denied that such associations constituted a type of trust that sought monopolistic control: "Their purposes are for the moral and intellectual development and the material prosperity of its members and all mankind. Self preservation and the general uplifting of mankind are inherent in these organizations."

Before concluding his remarks, Campbell declared his support for tax revision to ease the burden on small landowners, a graduated income tax, and stricter regulation of railroads. He opposed railroad mergers and consolidations, the issuance of free railroad passes, professional lobbyists, and the occupation tax except for those persons "enjoying special governmental advantages and franchises."[35]

The shopping list of policy statements Campbell presented to the citizens in 1906 demonstrated that protected wealth and special privilege had come a long way toward supplanting the Republican party as the bête noire of Texas politicians. Indeed, the very fact that he lambasted the monopolies and trusts and made such an open and direct appeal to farmers, workers, and the progressive element among the citizenry suggests the size and power of the anticorporate bloc in the electorate. Texas voters, sensitized by the agrarian reform campaigns of the last decades of the nineteenth century, joined together in 1906 to renew the reform effort.

The state over which Campbell would preside during his administration had changed considerably since the 1870s in areas other than political orientation. The impoverished, heavily indebted commonwealth of the immediate post–Civil War period had worked its way out of its financial morass and enjoyed a growing prosperity as the twentieth century dawned. The conservative fiscal policies of the late nineteenth century had strengthened the state economy, albeit, and regrettably at times, by neglecting the development of public institutions like schools and charitable agencies.

By the turn of the the twentieth century, changes in the Texas economy had made more money available for public spending. Agriculture, engaged in by well over half the adult citizenry in 1900, had expanded as settlement reached the western areas of the state. Between 1890 and 1900, the percentage of state land committed to farming increased from

[35]Ibid., pp. 14–28.

21.6 percent to 74.9 percent, with a corresponding increase in the valuation of farms, lands, and buildings from $170,468,886 to $1,843,203,395. Accompanying the tremendous growth in agriculture came a sizable increase in manufacturing in the state. In 1900, industrial production remained well below that of the farms, but had increased some 800 percent since 1870. Lumbering, the processing of cottonseed, and flour milling formed the largest industries at the turn of the century.[36]

On January 10, 1901, with the discovery of the large oil field at Spindletop, near Beaumont, the economy of the state entered a new and more prosperous era. Opportunities and entrepreneurs converged on southeastern Texas and sank additional wells to tap into the large underground reservoir. Oil production increased dramatically. From a thousand barrels per year in the late 1890s, the output grew to 4.4 million barrels in 1901 and approximately 21 million barrels in 1902.[37]

The growth of the oil industry stimulated the state economy in ways other than just the increase in the number of barrels produced. It boosted urbanization and all its associated industries, brought investment capital into the state, and spurred the development of oil-related products and services. Along with industrial growth came remarkable increases in bank deposits and tax receipts for state government. During the period from 1890 to 1910, the amount of money on deposit in Texas banks increased from $2 million to well over $262 million. State tax receipts during the same period grew from just over $3 million to more than $17 million.[38]

The tremendous economic growth of the late nineteenth and early twentieth centuries made additional funds available for public charitable institutions. State leaders continued to speak of the necessity of curbing expenses and keeping taxes low, yet during the 1881–1915 period the amount spent by the state for social services increased from 36 percent of total expenditures to 82 percent. The fiscal flexibility that came with the increase in tax receipts made it possible for Texas to extend services to all its citizens, even convicted felons and, at least to some degree, made the Campbell reforms possible.[39]

The coalition that supported the new governor consisted of a variety of groups, some familiar to the Texas political scene, others relatively new. With specific reference to prison problems, the labor organizations

[36]Miller, *Financial History,* p. 241; Joseph Stricklin Spratt, *The Road to Spindletop. Economic Change in Texas, 1875–1901,* pp. 281–82.

[37]Ibid., p. 283.

[38]Ibid., pp. 282–84; Miller, *Financial History,* pp. 242–43, 264.

[39]Miller, *Financial History,* pp. 248–49.

of the state and the genteel reformers of the towns and cities represented the two most important new elements. Both these groups had come into existence as political forces during the late 1890s and early 1900s. They formed a vital addition to those seeking change in prison policies.

Although Texas laborers as early as the republic period had united periodically to try to correct local disputes in which they felt wronged, only with the arrival of the railroad in the 1870s did conditions in the state reach a point conducive to the formation of labor unions. The railroads brought with them the labor organizations of railway employees. One of the earliest strikes by these unions, against the Houston and Texas Central in the early summer of 1872, drew attention to some of the problems of the early unions in Texas but failed to achieve any substantive results. The organizations were too small, too weak, and lacked the dynamic, dedicated leadership that could sustain them through times of distress.[40]

By the early 1880s, the Knights of Labor, one of the early national labor organizations, had begun recruiting among Texas workers. Within a few years, membership had reached approximately thirty thousand, a figure that probably included many farm laborers as well as urban workers. Recruitment drives in the state achieved such results that by early 1886 only Boston, Columbus, Ohio, and New York City had larger enrollments in the union.

The Great Southwest Strike, a signal event in the history of Texas labor, took place from early March to early May, 1886. Dissension within the union ranks, coupled with poor leadership, became apparent very early in the standoff and the strikers lost everything they sought. As the strike collapsed, so did the fortunes of the Knights of Labor.[41]

During the late 1880s and early 1890s, workers in Texas either expressed their grievances through the Farmers' Alliance and the People's party or, in the case of the crafts, went into the American Federation of Labor (AFL). In 1898 representatives of the craft unions established the State Federation of Labor and affiliated with the AFL. Because only skilled tradesmen could become members of AFL locals, membership grew rather slowly, especially in comparison with the earlier growth rate of the Knights of Labor. In one of its earliest conventions, the state federation expressed strong denunciation of the "uses of convict labor in factories making goods to be sold in competition with products of

[40] James V. Reese, "The Early History of Labor Organizations in Texas, 1838–1876," *Southwestern Historical Quarterly,* 72 (July, 1968): 1–20.

[41] Spratt, *Road to Spindletop,* pp. 240–42; Ruth Allen, *Chapters in the History of Organized Labor in Texas,* pp. 20–21.

free labor and the leasing of convict labor for work outside prisons." Federation members wanted state prisoners employed on public works projects around the state or making clothes for use within the prison system. The union expressed strong feelings on this issue, which formed a major element of the workers' legislative program.[42]

State federation arguments against competing with prisoners derived primarily from economic motivations and, thus, did little to raise the level of debate on the subject. Like others before them, members of the State Federation of Labor contented themselves with simply objecting to the profitable use of prisoners. They offered no suggestions as to how to deal with the dilemma of keeping prisoners busy and self-sustaining yet not in competition with any segment of the free labor force.

Despite the obvious shortcomings in their argument, however, the influence of organized workers on the prison problem cannot be discounted. Although industrial laborers made up only 1.6 percent of the Texas population in 1900, they were well organized and committed to importuning legislators on behalf of favorite issues. The Texas Federation of Labor, unlike its parent organization, the AFL, decided very early to establish legislative committees and maintain regular contact with elected officials. Labor, therefore, added its support to the cries of others seeking changes in state prison policies.[43]

Another group actively supported the cause of prison reform, although its influence is difficult to measure. The Texas Federation of Women's Clubs, founded in 1897 in Waco, focused its early efforts on campaigns to establish libraries around the state and to end the killing of rare tropical birds for their plumage. The women also spoke out for the establishment of a state industrial school for girls. Shortly after the establishment of the state organization, it underwent something of an identity crisis. Although the women appeared to care deeply about a number of problems in the state, they decided to avoid "even the appearance of meddling in matters political." Evidently, the women thought it would appear unseemly for them to make an active bid to influence public policy directly.[44]

Within a few years, club members chose to cast aside their earlier aversion to politicking. In 1905 they selected Mrs. Cone Johnson of Tyler, Texas, wife of a former state senator, to serve as their president.

[42] Allen, *Chapters,* pp. 123–24; Grady Lee Mullenix, "A History of the Texas State Federation of Labor," pp. 25–30.

[43] Mullenix, "History," pp. 37–38, 46, 66, 142–43; Allen, *Chapters,* pp. 132–36.

[44] Stella L. Christian, ed. and comp., *The History of the Texas Federation of Women's Clubs,* pp. 19–37, 44–45.

Mrs. Johnson was succeeded by Mrs. J. B. Dibrell, spouse of a former state senator from Seguin, Texas. Both of these women, committed to seeking change through the political process, drew on their husband's experience and knowledge of the legislative machinery to obtain what they wanted. Under the leadership of these two women, the state federation adopted a more activist posture and endorsed the movement to reform Texas prisons.[45]

Prison problems also engaged the attention of the Texas division of the Society for the Friendless, the state branch of a national organization of the same name. The society was a voluntary body supported entirely by private contributions. The state executive board consisted of Anson Rainey, chief justice of the Court of Civil Appeals in Dallas; the Reverend Luther Little, pastor of the First Baptist Church in Galveston; Dr. L. M. Keasby, head of the School of Political Science at the University of Texas; J. L. Long, principal of the Dallas Public Schools; Rabbi Samuel Marks, from San Antonio; E. G. Douglas, superintendent of the Gatesville Reformatory; Rev. J. M. Kirwin, rector of St. Mary's Cathedral in Galveston; and Rev. H. A. Boaz, president of the Fort Worth Polytechnic College. In its attitude toward crime and the treatment of criminals, the society placed itself firmly in the philosophical tradition of the early nineteenth-century prison reformers. The best way to reduce crime was to attack its causes, which, according to the society, lay in "the failure of the fundamental institutions (the home, school, church, society, etc.) to keep individuals above the crime line." With this assertion as its basic premise, society members urged Texans to support its programs to keep young persons in school, prevent child abuse, intervene early in the criminal careers of juvenile offenders, provide for evangelical missions in jails and prisons, and assist released prisoners as they made their way back into society.[46]

With particular reference to Texas prisons, the society in the summer of 1907 pronounced itself generally satisfied. The prison buildings, "with the exception of some unavoidable conditions in convict camps," were sanitary, and prisoners received "wholesome food in abundance" and were "well-clothed." Furthermore, thanks to the efforts of senior prison officials, "the prisoners' statutory rights are held inviolate regardless of political, financial or personal considerations." To improve the state's penal institutions, the society recommended that the governor extend the privilege of parole to "worthy Negro convicts," that female prison-

[45]Ibid., pp. 40, 140, 197, 225–53.

[46]*First Annual Report of the Society for the Friendless, Texas Division, 1906–1907* (Dallas: Live Oak Printing Company, Printers, 1907), pp. 6–14.

ers in the outside camps be supervised by a matron, and that "all of those instrumentalities for intellectual and moral improvement" be extended to inmates in the outside camps. It also urged that insane prisoners be removed to hospitals and that "as fast as practicable" the contract system be abolished.[47]

It is difficult to assess the importance of the Society for the Friendless to the prison reform movement in Texas. Society members claimed to have visited almost every location in the state where convicts were kept and yet their descriptions of what they found bore virtually no resemblance to the horrible situation that existed. In a sense, therefore, their activities constituted a disservice to the people of Texas, particularly because the organization was headed by such a distinguished body of men.

The combined effort of all the groups that had called for changes in state prison policies since the beginning of the lease period could not dislodge the idea that prisoners should serve as a source of revenue to the state. The allure of money from private contractors, coupled with the belief that arduous work on the farms helped reform inmates, proved to be virtually impossible to change. Not until a large percentage of Texas citizens became aware of the ghastly conditions in the prison labor camps did reform forces gain the momentum they needed.

The stimulus that brought all reformers together and unified their campaign for changes in prison management came in the fall of 1908. The Reverend Jake Hodges, chaplain of the Huntsville unit, made the acquaintance of George Waverley Briggs, a young reporter for the *San Antonio Express*. Hodges told the young newsman of the many problems within the prison system and of the obstacles he had encountered as a chaplain trying to perform his duties.[48]

Hodges had been a thorn in the side of prison administrators for quite some time prior to his meeting Briggs. Superintendent Herring had complained to Governor Campbell earlier that the chaplain had interfered repeatedly in disciplinary matters and had questioned the circumstances surrounding every instance of corporal punishment of a prisoner. According to Herring, Hodges was easily influenced by the sorrowful stories convicts would relate to him of their treatment and used his position as chaplain to initiate requests that prisoners wanted to relay to the governor and members of the prison board.[49]

Hodges's notoriety extended even to the prison board itself. W. F.

[47] Ibid., p. 15.
[48] Tom Finty, Jr., "The Texas Prison Investigation," *Survey,* 23 (Dec. 18, 1909): 387.
[49] J. A. Herring to Thomas M. Campbell, Sept. 26, 1907, Thomas M. Campbell Papers.

Ramsey, chairman of the board, on one occasion wrote to A. M. Barton, secretary to Governor Campbell, expressing concern about Hodges and suggesting possible ways to deal with the chaplain. Ramsey believed Hodges to be an "indiscreet" individual who had "permitted his sensitive nature to lead him to do a good many things he shouldn't do." Ramsey wanted Barton to persuade the governor to reprimand Hodges and tell him that he "must mend his ways." The chaplain had to be made to understand that "we cannot stand for anything to undermine discipline or cause trouble at Huntsville or anywhere else along the line."[50]

Hodges's displeasure with the prison administration continued a long tradition of dissatisfaction exhibited by other ministers who had earlier worked in various capacities within the penitentiaries. Chaplains found that despite all the official pronouncements of support and commitment to the religious training of inmates, little could be done if it interfered with the earning potential of prisoners. Chaplains could do little more than hold Sunday services in the main prisons and hope their messages had a positive impact. They were discouraged from attempting to involve themselves in matters like discipline or care and treatment of prisoners, which guards and sergeants felt to be their sole responsibility. Moreover, the chaplains received no support in their efforts from the churches they represented. The largest religious denominations in the state demonstrated no concern for the problems of prisoners. Southern Baptists and Methodists of turn-of-the-century Texas reserved their reform energies for campaigns in favor of prohibition, Sabbath observance, and strengthening family life, while opposing gambling, interracial relationships, and "worldly amusements."[51]

At the time Hodges unburdened himself to Briggs, the reporter had been out of school only about two years. The enthusiasm with which he began his investigation into prison affairs strongly resembled efforts of other journalists and writers of the time to ferret out and expose corruption and maladministration in other areas of American life. Briggs visited the penitentiaries and convict camps around the state. Subsequently, he published the findings of his investigation in a series of *Express* articles from December 5, 1908, through January 11, 1909. Among the many criticisms and revelations he presented, Briggs scored most severely the fact that the system was geared almost exclusively to making money, with very little effort expended to reform prisoners. To Briggs,

[50] W. F. Ramsey to A. M. Barton, Sept. 30, 1907, Campbell Papers. Shortly after Briggs began publishing the results of his investigation of the prison, Chaplain Hodges was fired. See *Report of the Penitentiary Investigating Committee, 1910,* p. 156.

[51] Katherine Brown, "A Social History of Texas Baptists since 1865"; John Daniel Barron, "A Critical History of the *Texas Christian Advocate,* 1849–1949."

the administration of the state prisons appeared "wrong and harmful not only to the criminal himself but to the society that is as deserving of protection as the moral defective is of treatment." He argued that the spirit of the age demanded a fundamental change in the way Texas prisons were operated so that they would "more nearly accomplish the will of the people, effect their protection and execute the precepts of humanitarianism . . . [toward inmates]."[52]

At first, state leaders expressed great skepticism about Briggs's contentions. Governor Campbell, in a message to the legislature in January, 1909, asserted that his prison officials had all performed their respective duties in an exemplary manner: "The reports of the Board of Commissioners, the Superintendent and other officials show that the affairs of the system have been for the past two years more efficiently managed, that the convicts are properly housed, clothed and fed, and that they have at all times received considerate and humane treatment."[53]

Campbell went on to admit, however, that the "persistent character" of the "recent agitation" had led him to believe that a thorough investigation of the prison should be undertaken: "The good name of the State demands that this be done. Such investigation should be searching, sweeping, and effective, to the end that any abuses, if found, can be speedily arrested, and that trusted officials may be vindicated if free of fault or wrong."[54]

Responding to the governor's challenge, the leadership of the legislature established a committee to investigate the prison system. Reporters from several leading newspapers of the state traveled with the investigating committee to the various prison camps. Others papers picked up their reports so that word of the investigation enjoyed wide dissemination. According to one source, by the time the committee had finished its labors, the "people and the press" of the state favored "genuine prison reform in Texas." It remained only for public pressure to be brought against the politicians, who, "as usual," were "slow to trust the people."[55]

The information made public by the legislative investigating committee (discussed in chapter V,) revealed a frightening state of affairs in the prisons. Mismanagement, inefficiency, and brutality toward in-

[52] George Waverley Briggs, *The Texas Penitentiary. History of the Texas Convict System and Suggestions for Its Betterment,* p. 5; Finty, "Investigation," p. 387.

[53] *Message of Governor T. M. Campbell to the Thirty-first Legislature of Texas to Which Is Appended the State Democratic Platform Adopted at San Antonio, Texas, August 13, 1908* (Austin: Von Boeckmann-Jones Company, Printers, 1909), p. 21.

[54] Ibid., pp. 21–22.

[55] *Report of Investigating Committee, 1910,* pp. i, v; Finty, "Investigation," pp. 338, 388–89.

mates remained commonplace in 1909, just as they had been since the resumption of state control in 1883. Investigators discovered that many prison employees, especially in the outside camps where abuse of prisoners occurred more frequently, conducted affairs in their respective departments ignorant or unmindful of any regulations that might have governed their conduct.[56]

An independent auditing firm hired to examine the books of the system found that accounting procedures had been so haphazard and careless through the years that a true picture of their financial condition could not be had. The firm discovered, for example, that no permanent daily records had been kept of the industries in the Rusk and Huntsville units. Moreover, very little coordination existed between the outside camps and the financial agent's office so that, in effect, neither knew what the other was doing.[57]

In response to the committee's revelations, newspapers over the state condemned the prison administration and demanded improvement. The *Dallas Morning News* noted that the public had anticipated some few problems in the prison but nothing like what had been uncovered: "Yet, given a political system of irresponsible appointments, where special qualifications count for little and political pull is the all-important consideration . . . what could we expect?"[58]

The Sulphur Springs *Gazette* wrote that even if a certain amount of the testimony were discounted because of exaggeration, there would still be much to condemn. "It really looks as if the State is more intent on making a profit out of its convicts than reforming them."[59] Similar sentiments came from the editors of the McKinney *Democrat-Gazette:* "Leasing out human beings to private corporations and individuals, and allowing them to be treated worse than dogs, is a burning shame and should no longer to tolerated by a civilized people."[60]

Even the Rusk *Press-Journal,* a newspaper one might have expected to take a softer line toward the prison system, heaped criticism on the state officials who permitted abuses in the outside camps "in order that a few men in Texas may grow rich on the blood of these unfortunate men": "These State convict farms are a disgrace to Christian civilization and the man who pokes his head up in Cherokee County as a candidate for the next Legislature and who is not unequivocally

[56]*Report of Investigating Committee, 1910,* pp. 7–15.
[57]Ibid., pp. 133–38.
[58]*Dallas Morning News,* Nov. 10, 1909, p. 8.
[59]Ibid., Nov. 9, 1909, p. 6.
[60]Ibid., Nov. 8, 1909, p. 6.

in favor of abolishing them will be gloriously snowed under at the polls."[61]

The intensity of the public reaction to the newspaper disclosures forced the political establishment into action. Governor Campbell, who had earlier taken a very strong stand against placing prisoners on private farms, found himself having to defend a record that demonstrated just the opposite. By the time the legislative committee began its work late in Campbell's second term, it found that during his tenure of office he had accelerated the shipment of prisoners to outside farms. At Rusk, for example, there were 831 inmates incarcerated when Campbell was inaugurated. By the end of his second term, however, this number had been reduced dramatically to a skeleton force of only 77. The overwhelming majority of the prisoners had been shipped to farms, both private and state-owned, where living and working conditions were equally severe.[62] One inmate wrote that when Campbell came out solidly in favor of penal reform during his first campaign, prisoners had great hopes for an improvement in their lives and encouraged all their "relatives and friends on the outside" to cast their votes for him. Once in office, however, Campbell "put the hardest set of taskmasters over the men known in many years." In addition, the new governor "came near putting all the men out on leases on the farms."[63]

Late in October, 1909, as the legislative investigation of the prison neared its end, many of the state's political leaders gathered in Dallas to attend the state fair and talk shop. After "feeling the public pulse and getting their bearings," for the 1910 elections, the group concluded that the "penitentiary scandal" had aroused more interest and comment among voters than anything else, even prohibition. Popular feeling ran so strong against the system that, according to one reporter, Governor

[61] Ibid., Nov. 2, 1909, p. 6. It should be noted that opposition to placing prisoners in outside camps had been common in Rusk for a good many years. Local citizens believed that the placement of inmates outside the walls, where they would earn more money for the state, was the major reason for the failure of the iron industry at Rusk. See *Galveston Daily News,* Jan. 20, 1885, p. 1.

[62] John L. Wortham to Thomas M. Campbell, Jan. 1, 1907, Campbell Papers; *Biennial Report,* 1906, p. 27; 1910, p. 35. Despite Campbell's poor performance in attacking problems in the prisons, he had supported several progressive measures of interest to reformers. He and his friends in the thirty-first legislature had secured passage of laws limiting the issuance of railroad passes, prohibiting nepotism, and had established a state department of agriculture. They also had enacted bills to tighten even more the state regulation of corporations and had made a start at establishing a uniform ad valorem tax rate. See Gould, *Progressives,* p. 40; Janet Louise Schmelzer, "Thomas Mitchell Campbell: Progressive Governor of Texas," pp. 25–66.

[63] Wilkinson, *Trans-Cedar Lynching,* p. 100.

Campbell had decided to call a special session of the legislature to deal with the prison lease problem.[64]

The Fourth Called Session of the thirty-first legislature met from August 18 until September 10, 1910. Out of this session, and with surprisingly little dissent, came the bill that reorganized the prison system so that all state prisoners were placed under the exclusive control of the state. In the course of formulating the new bill, state legislators paid tribute to the importance of the work done by the newspapers, especially George W. Briggs of the *San Antonio Express,* in bringing to everyone's attention the terrible conditions in the state's prisons. Indeed, the legislators were so impressed with Briggs's work that they requested that he and his press colleagues undertake a similar investigation of the "breeding ground of all crime, the licensed saloon."[65]

The new prison law, which would take effect on January 20, 1911, called for sweeping changes in the structure of prison administration. The legislature stated clearly that the new policy of the state provided for the working of prisoners only "within prison walls, and upon farms owned by the state." The prison board was instructed to "change from the system of leasing and hiring out of prisoners at the earliest practicable time." Under no circumstances would prisoners be hired out or leased to private individuals after January 1, 1914.[66]

The law further attempted to bring a greater measure of managerial expertise into prison affairs. In so doing, legislators sought to demand stricter accountability and competence regarding both the care of inmates and the financial affairs of the system. The positions of superintendent and financial agent were abolished in favor of a three-member board of prison commissioners, each of whom would have full responsibility for one particular aspect of prison operations. One of the commissioners would control financial matters; another would look after the care and treatment of inmates; the third would supervise all officers and employees of the system. All commissioners were to be appointed by the governor, subject to Senate approval, and would be paid $300 per month to work full-time at their prison duties. Each had the authority to dismiss any employees who violated the rules and could themselves be held legally responsible for any failures to enforce the new regulations fully.[67]

[64] *San Antonio Daily Express,* Oct. 31, 1909.

[65] *Journal of the House of Representatives of the Fourth Called Session of the Thirty-first Legislature of Texas* (Austin: Von Boeckmann-Jones Company, Printers, 1910), pp. 1, 207–208, 222.

[66] Tom Finty, Jr., "Troubles of the Texas State Prisons," *The Delinquent,* 3 (Dec., 1913): 4; *Report of Investigating Committee, 1910,* p. vii.

[67] *Report of Investigating Committee, 1910,* pp. viii–ix. The authors of the prison

Early in 1911, the newly elected governor, Oscar B. Colquitt, appointed the new members of the board. They were Ben E. Cabell, former sheriff of Dallas County and mayor of the city of Dallas; Louis W. Tittle, merchant and former county clerk of Cherokee County; and Robert W. Brahan, "who for many years had been connected with the prison system as sales agent and in other capacities." These men, working with the governor, would execute the new law and preside over the demise of the contract system.[68]

On May 11, the new board announced its intention to end outside contract labor before the mandated date of January 1, 1914. Word went out that no contracts would be renewed and that the board would welcome the early surrender of any of the outside forces. By the end of 1911 the number of contracts had been reduced substantially and by late 1912, the contract labor system had been "entirely abolished."[69]

The decision to end the hiring out of prisoners before the scheduled date, though admirable in its intent, placed severe financial strains on the prison system. In the absence of generous appropriations from the legislature to compensate for the lost contract revenue, prison officials found themselves at the mercy of free market forces. They had to "buy supplies at credit prices and sell products at distress prices." Because there was not enough room in the prisons and on the state farms to house and employ all inmates, the board adopted the policy of leasing land for "money rent" from private landowners so that prisoners could be worked under state control. The problems eased somewhat in the summer of 1913 when the legislature voted $500,000 to take care of the system's immediate needs, and granted authorization to issue $1.5 million in prison bonds.[70]

In voting to terminate all forms of leasing, the state assumed full financial responsibility for its convicted lawbreakers. State taxpayers after 1912 began paying all costs incidental to the operation of the prison system. The reasons for such an abrupt change in policy grew out of the process in which the state and its people matured in the decades following the end of the Civil War.

---

reorganization legislation initially had intended to preserve the prison management structure with few changes. As debate on the bill ensued, however, lawmakers succumbed to "an eloquent plea in behalf of the 'commission form of government'" and divided authority accordingly. See Finty, "Troubles of the Texas Prison System," *The Delinquent,* 4 (Jan., 1914): 7.

[68] Finty, "Troubles of Texas Prisons," p. 4. Robert Brahan was the son of former financial agent Haywood Brahan.

[69] Ibid.; *Report of Evidence before Penitentiary Investigating Committee, 1913,* pp. 14–15.

[70] Finty, "Troubles of Texas Prisons," pp. 4–5; *Report of Evidence Before Penitentiary Investigating Committee, 1913,* p. 14.

The indebtedness and relative poverty of the early postwar years, coupled with the public refusal to spend money for any but basic public programs, resulted in a drastic retrenchment in public spending and reductions in all types of taxes. Such thrift in government led to a low priority designation for all institutions, like prisons, that cared for wards of the state. The public contempt for convicted felons further removed penal facilities from the beneficent ministrations of those few farsighted individuals and groups seeking to extend to inmates the care and attention to which the law entitled them.

The last quarter of the nineteenth century brought with it pressures to move away from the traditional conservative view of limited government. Economically hard-pressed segments of society, especially farmers, developed a political activism that forced the dominant Democratic party to forsake the Bourbon ideals of low taxation and reduced services, and accept a more expanded role for state government. The agrarian reform movement, with its allies—the women's clubs, labor unions, and prison reform groups—all from the emerging urban middle class, advocated ending the lease system but offered no substitutes acceptable to elected officials.

Despite all the agitation to improve the treatment of state prisoners, few substantive changes resulted until newspaper disclosures and a major legislative investigation in 1909 revealed for all to see the deplorable conditions in which prisoners lived. Public outcry forced state officials like Governor Campbell to convene a special session of the legislature in the summer of 1910 to bring an end to leasing and establish a prison policy wherein the state would assume all responsibility for the care of its convicted felons. Although the demise of prison contract labor formed an important part of Progressivism in Texas, it came as an afterthought of the movement for change. It was a matter to be corrected only when other more pressing concerns had been dealt with to everyone's satisfaction. That prison problems did not figure prominently in the turn-of-the-century burst of reform simply reinforces the cogent observations made at the time that in everyday affairs most Texans were too occupied with their own personal lives to give much thought to improving conditions in the prisons, especially if such improvements had to be financed with higher tax levies.

CHAPTER VIII

THE TEXAS EXPERIENCE IN PERSPECTIVE

The history of the Texas prison system for the period from 1867 through 1912 may be viewed as the story of the maturation of a large and difficult-to-manage state agency. The phenomenal growth of the prison population over the forty-five-year period presented prison officials with a variety of problems. The manner in which difficulties were resolved demonstrates quite clearly that above all else state leaders consistently sought to exert a greater measure of control over the penal institutions so as to make them more financially profitable.

Beginning with the first leases of prisoners to the railroads in the late 1860s, prison officers and the supervisory legislative committees encountered abuses and maladministration within prison operations that persisted throughout the late nineteenth and early twentieth centuries. The hiring of an inspector and an assistant inspector to look after the state's interests during the Ward-Dewey and the Cunningham-Ellis leases represented an attempt, only partially effective, to secure a more diligent adherence to prison policies. Similarly, the several reorganizations of prison management and the promulgation of more extensive and all-encompassing rules and regulations reflected a commitment to make the prisons a dependable source of revenue for the state. There is little credible evidence to support the contention that long-term lease agreements with private parties represented an attempt to reestablish slavery in a somewhat altered form.[1]

In many of its aspects, the Texas experience with convict lease closely resembled penological developments in other parts of the South. All eleven states of the former Confederacy adopted some form of leasing during the years immediately following the Civil War. It is always difficult, and frequently misleading, to describe in generalities the attitudes and activities supposedly common to any group of persons. Yet to a large degree, the manner in which Southern legislatures governed their prisons in the late nineteenth century demonstrated a considerable una-

[1] Thomas Michael Parrish, "This Species of Slave Labor: The Convict Lease System in Texas, 1871–1914," passim.

nimity of opinion concerning the role of prisons and the objectives of incarceration.

The same factors—growing criminal population, inadequate facilities, and shortages of money—that led Texas to adopt leasing also came into play in the other Southern states. By the early 1870s, the majority of Southern prison inmates labored on railroads, in coal and iron mines, and in turpentine camps. Florida and the Carolinas, not having any permanent penal structures, had to lease their prisoners immediately upon the cessation of hostilities in 1865. Most of the other states adopted leasing in the late 1860s and early 1870s. Alabama and Texas, the two states that had suffered the least wartime damage to their prisons, were the last to turn their penal institutions over to private parties.[2]

Considerable similarity also could be found in the way leasing functioned throughout the South. All the Southern states ultimately realized a net profit from prison labor, even if only in the sense that they were spared the expense of maintaining a prison. Although many of the lease contracts made during the late 1860s and early 1870s did not attain the levels of success the states had envisioned, by the 1880s and 1890s leasing had proven to be very profitable and various state officials welcomed the additional income from prison labor.[3]

The abusive, arbitrary treatment of prisoners, so prevalent in the Texas lease camps, also appeared in other Southern states. From all accounts, prisoners in Florida and the Carolinas, particularly those consigned to turpentine camps, suffered miseries considerably more severe than other Southern prisoners. The absence of any tradition of prison management in those three states probably accounted for the worse than usual conditions.[4]

The best informed and most persistent contemporary critic of prison leasing, the Louisiana writer George W. Cable, has asserted that Alabama and Texas went to greater lengths to safeguard the interests of their leased prisoners than did the other states of the former Confederacy. In part, the comparatively better conditions derived from a system of state inspection that, despite its frequent failures and shortcomings, considerably exceeded any similar efforts in other parts of the South. Cable has also asserted that the two states enjoyed exemplary leadership and guidance from their principal senior administrators during the

[2]Blake McKelvey, "Penal Slavery and Southern Reconstruction," *Journal of Negro History,* 22 (Apr., 1935): 153–62.

[3]Ibid.; Dan T. Carter, "Prison, Politics and Business: The Convict Lease System in Post-Civil War South," pp. 35–55.

[4]McKelvey, "Penal Slavery," pp. 158–66.

period. J. H. Bankhead in Alabama and Thomas J. Goree in Texas, both had taken "the active interest in the best developments [in prison reform] in England and in the North," and had attempted to introduce some of the newer ideas into their respective institutions.[5]

The activities of the few more enlightened and reform-minded administrators could not alter substantially the overall picture of neglect and mismanagement that characterized leasing all through the South. The absence of reliable data on Southern prisons during the period prohibits a detailed look at either the composition of the prison population, or the fate of individual inmates. The scattered evidence available, however, strongly suggests that (1) young black Southerners with little education made up a disproportionately large segment of the prison populations; (2) the individual states made few serious efforts to provide adequate food, clothing, medical care, or reformative training for the prisoners; and (3) the rates of mortality, morbidity, and escape greatly exceeded national norms for the period.[6]

That leasing continued despite opposition from critics came about primarily because of the income it generated for the states. A general public indifference to the fate of prisoners also played a major role. The apparent lack of enthusiasm in nineteenth-century Texas for serious prison reforms also appears to have been evident in the other Southern states. According to one observer, leasing persisted not as a result "of any malicious public intention," but rather because among "the people at large, there is little more than a listless oblivion" toward convicted felons. Once criminal offenders had been caught, found guilty, and sentenced, the public mind was at rest in the belief that "to punish crime, no matter how, is to deter crime; that when broken laws are avenged that is the end; that it is enough to have the culprit in limbo, if only he is made to suffer and not to cost."[7]

The influence wielded by lessees to protect their access to prison workers also came into play to help extend the life of leasing. The efforts of the large sugar growers in Texas to curry favor with the state officials who made prison labor contracts were duplicated by planters, railroads, mining companies, levee construction contractors, and lumbering interests throughout the region. In a few cases, notably Georgia and Alabama, major lessees also occupied the highest positions of elected leadership in the state. Generally, however, prison contractors secured their

[5]George W. Cable, *The Silent South Together with the Freedmen's Case in Equity and the Convict Lease System,* pp. 156–67; McKelvey, "Penal Slavery," pp. 160–62.

[6]McKelvey, "Penal Slavery," pp. 153–79; Carter, "Prisoners, Politics," pp. 61–85.

[7]Cable, *Silent South,* pp. 124–26.

influence with politicians by financial contributions and other support at election time.[8]

The movement to end leasing in the Southern states began to appear in the 1890s with the emergence of the Populist party. The continuing distress of the lower economic classes in the South and their entry into politics foreshadowed fundamental changes in the nature of state governments. The postwar policies of extreme financial retrenchment and limited state government yielded to demands for enlarged governmental activity as the Bourbon Democrats gave way to a new set of political leaders willing to see an expanded role for government. By the first decade of the twentieth century, the Democratic party in all the Southern states had announced intentions of putting an end to the leasing of prisoners as soon as an acceptable substitute could be found.[9]

The end of leasing in the South, during the years immediately preceding World War I, constituted one of the major Progressive reforms in the region. Citizens of the South, motivated by economic and humanitarian concerns and spurred into action by legislative investigations and newspaper disclosures of prison conditions, pressured Southern legislatures to terminate the lease contracts and make other provisions for the employment of state prisoners. In general, the southeastern states put their prisoners to work building and maintaining public roads, whereas the states west of Alabama, following the example of the Harlem and Wynne plantations in Texas, placed their inmates at work on large farms owned and operated exclusively by the states.[10]

The abolition of the lease system in Texas in 1912 represented the culmination of a diverse reform movement that had come together in the early years of the Campbell administration. George W. Briggs, the San Antonio journalist and social critic who spearheaded the 1909 investigation of the prison, acted within the highest traditions of contemporaneous investigative reporting. His articles on prison affairs, plus a subsequent exposé he wrote on housing conditions among the poor in Texas cities, place him squarely within the group of early twentieth-century crusading journalists who played such a prominent part in national Progressivism.[11]

The forces Briggs launched with his articles on prison conditions acted

[8] Carter, "Prisons, Politics," pp. 64–73.

[9] Ibid., pp. 91–107.

[10] Ibid.; Blake McKelvey, "A Half Century of Southern Penal Exploitation," *Social Forces,* 13 (Oct., 1934): 112–20.

[11] George W. Briggs, *Housing Problem in Texas: A Study of Physical Conditions under Which the Other Half Lives,* reprint of articles published in the Galveston-Dallas *News,* Nov. through Dec., 1911, Archives Division, Texas State Library, Austin.

from both economic and humanitarian motives. All agreed that the prison labor earned handsome profits, but at a human cost too high to tolerate. As the Texas citizenry moved to end leasing, it did so in a manner similar to activities in other parts of the region.

The groups leading opposition to prisoner lease in Texas included numerically strong agrarian elements, the politically astute though far less numerous workers, and civic-minded activists from voluntary associations of the emerging urban centers of the state. All these groups faced the task before them from the perspective of a position rooted squarely in the mainstream of Texas society. There is no evidence to suggest that political activity of any extreme variety held any appeal for them. No clearer expression of the fundamentally conservative and tradition-bound nature of the reformers can be found than that which formed the language and provisions of the law passed in 1910 to end leasing.

The new law did not represent a significant departure from the old in most aspects. It did not attempt to restructure every facet of prison life; it did, however, seek to bring about greater control and more stringent supervision of prison activities. Whipping, for example, was not abolished; it was simply restricted to specific cases and under greater supervision. The number of hours prisoners were to work each day was set at ten, but could be exceeded in the event of an emergency. If inmates had to work on Sunday, they were to be paid $1 for their labor. The law did call for better medical care, greater diligence in the preparation of food, more attention paid to prison clothing, and the expansion of the educational and religious opportunities available to inmates. But as in the past, compliance would depend on the quality of inspection and the attitude of individual prison administrators.

The only parts of the new law that represented a substantial departure from previous practice were those that provided for an end to leasing and called for yearly audits of prison financial transactions. Neither of these, it should be noted, posed any serious threat to the earning potential of the prisoners; the state concomitantly committed itself to the purchase of additional state farms on which to work its inmates. Both provisions should be viewed as vital components of Progressive reform in Texas in that they ushered in a period of greater efficiency in the prison system and brought to completion the slowly evolving commitment to bring all convicted felons under the exclusive control of the state.[12]

[12] *Report of the Penitentiary Investigating Committee, 1910,* pp. vii–xxii. The new law also formalized the segregation of inmates by race, a process that had been initiated during the 1890s. Generally, black prisoners were kept separate from whites and Hispanics,

As the legislature and the prison board considered the new directions for the penitentiary, other elements of Progressivism surfaced. In refashioning the prison administration, state leaders chose to delineate the major managerial areas within the system and to place an experienced individual at the head of each division. Responsibility thus would reside with persons competent to handle matters peculiar to the particular area. The adoption of a professional managerial structure to administer the prisons conforms closely to those models of national Progressivism that focused on reform as an expression of greater efficiency and more competent management.[13]

Efficiency-minded Progressives, according to one historian, had witnessed the rapid deterioration of the traditional, personalistic organs of society as the trend toward corporate accumulation and growth accelerated in the late nineteenth century. The reformers sought, among other things, to take the lead in establishing control over state and local agencies that would regulate and direct future growth. Leadership by professionals would ensure that as change occurred among the elements of society, it would be stable, responsible, and directed to serve the best interests of all.[14]

The Texas experience in leasing its prisoners constituted a retrogressive step in the development of the state penal system. Indeed, the decision to adopt leasing placed Texas and the South clearly outside the mainstream of national penological advances. Not until the early decades of the twentieth century did the state begin to take action that eventually would bring its prisons into conformity with national patterns and standards. Even though the negative effects of leasing were considerable, state officials in the late nineteenth century, nonetheless, found it possible to institute some reforms in line with progress in the nation at large.

Superintendent Goree's decision to establish contact with prison officials in other parts of the nation provided a means for infusing into Texas contemporaneous ideas for prison reform. Through membership in the National Prison Association, the principal organization of professional penologists, Goree and his Texas colleagues were exposed to the latest in penal developments. Attendance at the annual meetings of the national professional organization gave state prison officials an opportunity to learn from the experience of others.

---

who were frequently housed in the same camps: ibid., pp. xvii, 14, 151, 604, 647, 648–60, 916, and 930.

[13] Robert H. Wiebe, *The Search for Order, 1877–1920,* pp. 111–12; David P. Thelen, *The New Citizenship: Origins of Progressivism in Wisconsin, 1885–1900,* pp. 55–56.

[14] Ibid.

Through the latter decades of the nineteenth century, the national association worked assiduously to promote a number of reforms, chiefly the adoption of a classification system for prisoners, the use of the indeterminate penal sentence to encourage good behavior, and the construction of special institutions for youthful offenders. Implementation of the indeterminate sentence in Texas in 1883 and the opening of the state juvenile reformatory in 1889 demonstrated that, at least to some degree, Texas found itself able to institute beneficial changes at a time when such reforms were still relatively new and much debated throughout the nation. Texas prison officials could entertain the prospect of reforms and improvements in the prisons as long as such changes posed no threat to the structure of leasing and its revenue-generating potential. Not until the termination of all outside contracts in 1912 did Texas find itself in a position to begin to assume the degree of responsibility for its convicted felons that had become commonplace in some other sections of the country.

AFTERWORD

In December, 1980, some three years after the research for this manuscript was begun, a verdict was rendered in a legal action against the Texas Department of Corrections. In the case of *Ruiz* v. *Estelle,* Federal Judge William Wayne Justice of Tyler ordered sweeping changes in both the way Texas prisons were administered and the manner in which prison inmates were treated. The Justice decision came as a shock to many Texans and, once again, focused an intense public scrutiny on the state prison system.

It is, of course, much too early to assess the long-term effects of the federal judge's orders, but the reemergence of a reform effort directed toward the prison system is simply the latest in a continuum that began in the late nineteenth century and saw the abolition of leasing during the Progressive period as its first major victory. In the mid-1920s and the late 1940s, the attention of Texas citizens and politicians again came to rest on prison affairs. Out of the public debates of the times came legislation that sought to correct the more egregious problems. The administration of O. B. Ellis, who began serving as director in the late 1940s, and that of his successor, Dr. George Beto, represented the culmination of the reform efforts in the first half of the twentieth century. The Ellis-Beto years saw vast improvement in the management of the penal facilities and brought to the state a degree of professionalism and public service that placed the Texas prison firmly among the first rank of such institutions nationwide.

The federal court edict of the early 1980s should serve as a reminder that, despite enormous advances and improvements, public vigilance must be constant in order to guarantee that our prisons are administered according to accepted principles of modern penology. Although the Justice decision continues a very long reform tradition, it differs significantly from earlier efforts in one major aspect. All the successful campaigns for change in prison affairs prior to the Ellis-Beto era came about as a result of the coordinated activities of the more public-spirited citizens of the state who were able to generate a consensus among their fellow Texans and the state legislature that change was both desirable and necessary. With a solid foundation of public support, the reforms enacted were able to endure through the years and form a basis for further improvements. No such coalescence of public pressure for innovation accompanied the federal judge's orders.

In handing down his verdict, Judge Justice acted from a position independent of public opinion in the state, thus causing considerable concern among large segments of the population, and casting doubts as to whether the public would support and fund the changes over the long haul. In addition, intolerably high costs and unacceptable levels of inmate violence within the prisons have followed the judge's decision. If these problems cannot be corrected to the public's satisfaction, the Justice ukase is destined to be short-lived.

One thing is certain: state leaders will have to continue to devote much of their time to try to determine the most efficient way in which to manage the state's penal institutions. Prison requests for funding increases will have to be balanced against demands from other state agencies, such as those concerned with education and social welfare programs, each of which could present equally urgent, and perhaps more valid, claims on the state treasury. The debate that began more than a century ago is far from over.

SELECTED BIBLIOGRAPHY

Any researcher who undertakes a study of the Texas prison system during the late nineteenth century recognizes quickly the crucial importance of this agency to the entire apparatus of state government. Not only did the prison house the antisocial element of society, it also formed a major source of revenue and helped maintain the strength and durability of the dominant Democratic party. For all these reasons, the researcher must attempt to look at everything, published and unpublished, that touches on the economic, political, and social life of the state at the time in order to place the prison system in its proper perspective. In the course of preparing this narrative, much material was examined, and even though it was not incorporated into the body of the manuscript, it was nonetheless important in that it provided a background in which to interpret the more relevant sources.

To list in the bibliography all the materials already cited in the notes would be redundant and would result in a document unwieldy in length. For these reasons, the list of sources that follows contains only those materials deemed to be of particular importance. Anyone desiring to delve deeper into the subject of Texas prisons for the same period will profit from the sources listed and, using notes and citations they contain, will be led to additional materials, most of which were used in this study.

PRIMARY SOURCES

Manuscript Materials

Barker Texas History Center, University of Texas at Austin: Ruth A. Allen Papers; Albert S. Burleson Papers; Thomas M. Campbell Papers; Richard Coke Scrapbook; Charles D. Culberson Papers; James S. Hogg Papers; E. M. House Papers; "Index to Biographical Studies of Texans"; John Ireland Papers; Oran M. Roberts Papers; Lawrence S. Ross Papers.

Texas State Library, Archives Division, Austin: Thomas M. Campbell

Papers; Richard Coke Papers; Oscar B. Colquitt Papers; Edmund J. Davis Papers; Richard B. Hubbard Papers; "Index to the Papers of the Fifth through the Fourteenth Legislatures"; John Ireland Papers.

Office of the Secretary of State, Executive Record Books, 1836–79: Penitentiary Papers; Oran M. Roberts Papers.

Thomason Room, Newton Gresham Library, Sam Houston State University, Huntsville, Texas: Thomas Jewett Goree Papers.

Documents and Reports

The standard reports for the prison system were prepared biennially in the even-numbered years, usually at the end of the month of October. With very minor variations, all bear the same title, beginning with "Report of the Directors, Superintendent, etc.," and can be found in the major libraries and archives of the state. The reports for the years 1866–1912 were used in preparing this study. Similarly, the records of the state legislature, always entitled, "Senate Journal" or "House Journal," are distinguished by the session number and dates. In writing this book I made use of the reports for the years 1866–1910, along with the accounts of all investigations ordered by legislators for the same period. The rules and regulations for the governing of prisons during the years of this study were prepared by the commissioners and approved by the legislature. All the sources generated by the various organs of state government can be found in the Archives Division of the Texas State Library in Austin. And finally, the annual meetings of the National Prison Association published their reports as "Proceedings of the National Prison Association," followed by the name of the city where the sessions were held and the year. These can be found in the larger libraries of the state.

Address of T. J. Goree, Superintendent of Penitentiaries, on the Penitentiary Leases, Delivered before the Penitentiary Committees of the Senate and House of Representatives, Eighteenth legislature in Joint Session, February 14, 1883. Austin: E. W. Swindells, State Printer, 1883.

Governors' Messages, Coke to Ross, 1874–1891. Edited by and for the Archive and History Department of the Texas State Library. Austin: A. C. Baldwin and Sons, 1916.

Members of the Legislature of the State of Texas from 1846 to 1939. N.p., n.d.

The Penitentiary Leases. Speeches Delivered in the House Favoring Their Ratification by Hon. J. Q. Chenoweth, Hon. H. J. Labatt, Hon. R. R. Hazlewood, Hon. A. K. Swan, Hon. W. F. Upton, and Hon. A. J.

Chambers, March, 1883. Austin: Press of Defenbaugh and Company, 1883.

Report of the Lessees of the Texas State Penitentiary, April, 1876. Houston: Telegraph Steam Book and Job Print, 1876.

Speech of Thomas M. Campbell Opening his Campaign for Governor of Texas, at Athens, Texas, April 21, 1906. Palestine, Texas: Palestine Printing Company, 1906.

Books

Briggs, George Waverley. *The Texas Penitentiary: History of the Texas Convict System and Suggestions for Its Betterment.* San Antonio *Express,* n.d.

Campbell, Charles C. *Hell Exploded: An Exposition of Barbarous Cruelty and Prison Horrors.* N.p., 1900.

Finty, Tom, Jr., et al. *Our Penal System and Its Purposes.* Galveston-Dallas *News,* 1909.

Gammel, H. P. N., comp. *The Laws of Texas, 1822–1897.* 10 vols. Austin: Gammel Book Company, 1898.

George, A. L. *The Texas Convict: Thrilling and Terrible Experience of a Texas Boy.* Austin: Ben C. Jones and Company, Printers, 1893.

Paschal, George W. *A Digest of the Laws of Texas: Containing Laws in Force, and the Repealed Laws on which Rights Rest.* Washington, D.C.: W. H. and O. H. Morrison, 1873.

Proceedings of the Taxpayers' Convention of the State of Texas, Held at the City of Austin, September 22nd, 23rd, and 25th, 1871. Also a Memorial to the Legislature and an Address to the Taxpayers of Texas. Galveston: News Steam Book and Job Office, 1871.

Shotwell, John. *A Victim of Revenge or Fourteen Years in Hell.* San Antonio: E. T. Jackson Company, 1909.

Tomlin, Henry. *Henry Tomlin: The Man Who Fought the Brutality and Oppression of the Ring in the State of Texas for Eighteen Years, and Won.* N.p., 1906.

Wilkinson, J. L. *The Trans-Cedar Lynching and the Texas Penitentiary.* Dallas: Johnston Printing and Advertising Company, n.d.

Winkler, Ernest William, ed. *Platforms of Political Parties in Texas.* Bulletin of the University of Texas No. 53, 1916.

Newspapers

Austin Statesman. 1871, 1873, 1874, 1878, 1879, 1883, 1884, 1906, 1912.

Clarksville *Northern Standard.* 1850, 1853, 1856, 1857, 1858.

Dallas *Herald.* 1870, 1871, 1872, 1873, 1874, 1875, 1876, 1877, 1878, 1881, 1882, 1883, 1884, 1885.

Dallas Morning News. 1898, 1902, 1909.

Galveston Daily News. 1867, 1871, 1873, 1875, 1876, 1877, 1882, 1883, 1885, 1886, 1898.

Houston *Daily Post.* 1883, 1904.

Houston *Daily Telegraph.* 1871.

San Antonio Express. 1871, 1881, 1909, 1912.

Texas Siftings. 1883.

Wood County *Flag.* 1879.

Secondary Sources

Books

Allen, Ruth. *Chapters in the History of Organized Labor in Texas.* University of Texas Publication No. 4143 (Austin: Bureau of Research in the Social Sciences, 1941).

Ayers, Edward L. *Vengeance and Justice: Crime and Punishment in the Nineteenth Century American South.* New York: Oxford University Press, 1984.

Barr, Alwyn. *Black Texans: A History of Negroes in Texas, 1528–1971.* Austin: Jenkins Publishing Company, 1973.

———. *Reconstruction to Reform: Texas Politics, 1876–1906.* Austin: University of Texas Press, 1971.

Brewer, J. Mason. *Negro Legislators of Texas and Their Descendants.* Austin: Jenkins Publishing Company, 1970.

Buenker, John D. *Urban Liberalism and Progressive Reform.* New York: W. W. Norton and Company, 1978. [Charles Scribner's Sons, 1973.]

Cable, George W. *The Silent South Together with the Freedman's Case in Equity and the Convict Lease System.* New York: Charles Scribner's Sons, 1885.

Carleton, Mark T. *Politics and Punishment: The History of the Louisiana State Penal System.* Baton Rouge: Louisiana State University Press, 1971.

Casdorph, Paul. *A History of the Republican Party in Texas, 1865–1965.* Austin: Pemberton Press, 1965.

Christian, Stella L., ed. and comp. *The History of the Texas Federation of Women's Clubs.* Houston: Dealy-Aden-Elgin Company, Stationers and Printers, 1919.

Connor, Seymour V. *Texas: A History.* Arlington Heights, Ill.: AHM Publishing, 1971.

Cotner, Robert C., ed. *Addresses and State Papers of James Stephen Hogg.* Austin: University of Texas Press, 1951.

Foucault, Michel. *Discipline and Punish: The Birth of the Prison.* Translated from the French by Alan Sheridan. New York: Pantheon Books, 1978. [Paris: Editions Gallimard, 1975.]

Gould, Lewis L. *Progressives and Prohibitionists. Texas Democrats in the Wilson Era.* Austin: University of Texas Press, 1973.

Grantham, Dewey W. *Southern Progressivism: The Reconciliation of Progress and Tradition.* Knoxville: University of Tennessee Press, 1983.

Hunt, Robert Lee. *A History of Farmer Movements in the Southwest, 1873–1925.* College Station: Texas A&M University, 1935.

Johnson, Frank W. *A History of Texas and Texans.* 5 vols. Edited by E. C. Barker, with assistance of E. W. Winkler. Chicago and New York: American Historical Society, 1914.

McKay, Seth Shepard, and Odie B. Faulk. *Texas after Spindletop.* Austin: Steck-Vaughn Company, 1965.

McKelvey, Blake. *American Prisons: A Study in American Social History Prior to 1915.* Chicago: University of Chicago Press, 1936.

McLaurin, Melton Alonzo. *The Knights of Labor in the South.* Westport, Conn.: Greenwood Press, 1978.

McMath, Robert C., Jr. *Populist Vanguard: A History of the Southern Farmers' Alliance.* New York: W. W. Norton and Company, 1977. [University of North Carolina Press, 1975.]

Martin, Roscoe. *The People's Party in Texas. A Study in Third-Party Politics.* Austin: University of Texas Press, 1970. [University of Texas Bulletin No. 3308, 1933.]

Miller, Edmund T. *A Financial History of Texas.* Bulletin of the University of Texas No. 37, 1916.

Moneyhon, Carl H. *Republicanism in Reconstruction Texas.* Austin: University of Texas Press, 1980.

Potts, Charles Shirley. *Crime and the Treatment of the Criminal.* Bulletin of the University of Texas No. 146, May, 1910.

Rabinowitz, Howard N., ed. *Southern Black Leaders of the Reconstruction Era.* Urbana: University of Illinois Press, 1982.

Ramsdell, Charles William. *Reconstruction in Texas.* Austin: University of Texas Press, 1970. [1910.]

Rice, Lawrence D. *The Negro in Texas, 1874–1900.* Baton Rouge: Louisiana State University Press, 1971.

Richardson, Rupert N. *Colonel Edward M. House: The Texas Years, 1858–1912.* Abilene, Texas: Abilene Printing and Stationery Company, 1964.

Sitterson, J. Carlyle. *Sugar Country: The Cane Sugar Industry in the South, 1753–1950.* Lexington: University of Kentucky Press, 1953.

Spratt, John Stricklin. *The Road to Spindletop: Economic Change in Texas, 1875-1901.* Austin: University of Texas Press, 1970. [Southern Methodist University Press, 1955.]

Steen, Ralph W. *Twentieth Century Texas.* Austin: Steck Company, 1942.

Thelen, David P. *The New Citizenship: Origins of Progressivism in Wisconsin, 1885–1900.* Columbia: University of Missouri Press, 1972.

Walker, Samuel. *Popular Justice: A History of American Criminal Justice.* New York: Oxford University Press, 1980.

Wallace, Ernest. *Texas in Turmoil.* Austin: Steck-Vaughn Company, 1965.

Wiebe, Robert H. *The Search for Order, 1877-1920.* New York: Hill and Wang, 1967.

Wines, Frederick Howard. *Punishment and Reformation: An Historical Sketch of the Rise of the Penitentiary System.* New York: Benjamin Blom, Inc., 1971. [1895.]

Articles

Allen, Ruth A. "The Capitol Boycott: A Study in Peaceful Labor Tactics." *Southwestern Historical Quarterly,* 42 (Apr., 1939): 316–26.

Duncan, J. S. "Richard Bennett Hubbard and State Resumption of the Penitentiary, 1876–1878." *Texana,* 3 (1974): 47–55.

Finty, Tom, Jr. "The Texas Prison Investigation." *Survey,* 22 (Dec. 18, 1909): 387–91.

———. "Troubles of the Texas Prison System." *The Delinquent,* 4 (Jan., 1914): 5–10.

———. "Troubles of the Texas State Prisons." *The Delinquent,* 3 (Dec., 1913): 1–5.

Hiller, E. T. "Development of the Systems of Control of Convict Labor in the United States." *Journal of Criminal Law, Criminology, and Police Science,* 5 (1914–15): 247–64.

———. "Labor Unionism and Convict Labor." *Journal of Criminal Law, Criminology, and Police Science,* 5 (1914–15): 851–79.

McKelvey, Blake. "A Half Century of Southern Penal Exploitation." *Social Forces,* 13 (Oct., 1934): 112–23.

———. "Penal Slavery and Southern Reconstruction." *Journal of Negro History,* 20 (Apr., 1935): 153–79.

Martin, Roscoe C. "The Grange as a Political Factor in Texas." *Southwestern Social Science Quarterly,* 6 (Mar., 1926): 363–83.

———. "The Greenback Party in Texas." *Southwestern Historical Quarterly,* 30 (Jan., 1927): 161–77.

Meyrick, A. S. "Convict Labor and the Labor Reformers." *Princeton Review,* 59 (Mar., 1883): 196–212.

Potts, Charles S. "The Convict Labor of Texas." *Annals of the American Academy of Political and Social Science* (May, 1903): 426–37.

Reese, James V. "The Early History of Labor Organizations in Texas, 1838–1876." *Southwestern Historical Quarterly,* 72 (July, 1968): 1–20.

Richardson, Rupert N. "Edward M. House and the Governors." *Southwestern Historical Quarterly,* 61 (July, 1957): 51–65.

Smith, Ralph A. "The Grange Movement in Texas, 1873–1900." *Southwestern Historical Quarterly,* 42 (Apr., 1939): 297–315.

"The Texas Penitentiary and Governor Campbell." *Farm and Ranch,* 28 (Dec. 11, 1909): 8.

Zimmerman, Jane. "The Penal Reform Movement in the South During the Progressive Era, 1890–1917." *Journal of Southern History,* 17 (Nov., 1951): 462–92.

Theses and Dissertations

Anderson, Adrian Norris. "Albert Sidney Burleson: A Southern Politician in the Progressive Era." Ph.D. dissertation, Texas Tech University, 1967.

Bailey, Lelia. "The Life and Public Career of O. M. Roberts, 1815–1883." Ph.D. dissertation, University of Texas, 1932.

Barron, John Daniel. "A Critical History of *The Texas Christian Advocate,* 1849–1949." M.A. thesis, University of Missouri, 1952.

Blatner, William E. "Some Aspects of the Convict Lease System in the Southern States." M.A. thesis, University of Oklahoma, 1952.

Brown, Katherine. "A Social History of Texas Baptists since 1865." M.A. thesis, Baylor University, 1949.

Brown, Patrick. "A Study of the Laws Passed during the Administration of O. M. Roberts, Governor of Texas, 1879–1883." M.A. thesis, Sam Houston State Teachers College, 1949.

Budd, Harrell. "The Negro in Politics in Texas, 1867–1898." M.A. thesis, University of Texas, 1925.

Carter, Dan T. "Prisons, Politics and Business: The Convict Lease System in Post-Civil War South." M.A. thesis, University of Wisconsin, 1946.

Crow, Herman Lee. "A Political History of the Texas Penal System, 1829–1951." Ph.D. dissertation, University of Texas, 1964.

Farrow, Marion Humphreys. "The Rise of the Democrats to Power in Texas, 1872–1876." M.A. thesis, University of Texas, 1940.

Gildemeister, Glen Albert. "Prison Labor and Convict Competition with Free Workers in Industrializing America, 1840–1890." Ph.D. dissertation, Northern Illinois University, 1977.

Huckaby, George Portal. "Oscar Branch Colquitt: A Political Biography." Ph.D. dissertation, University of Texas, 1946.

Kinsey, Winston Lee. "Negro Labor in Texas, 1865–1876." M.A. thesis, Baylor University, 1965.

McKay, Seth Shepard. "Texas under the Regime of E. J. Davis." M.A. thesis, University of Texas, 1919.

Maroney, James C. "Organized Labor in Texas, 1900–1929." Ph.D. dissertation, University of Houston, 1975.

Martin, Ruby Lee. "The Administration of Governor S. W. T. Lanham, 1903–1907." M.A. thesis, University of Texas, 1937.

Mullenix, Grady Lee. "A History of the Texas State Federation of Labor." Ph.D. dissertation, University of Texas, 1955.

Nielsen, George Raymond. "Richard Bennett Hubbard, 'The Demosthenes of Texas.'" M.A. thesis, University of Houston, 1957.

Norton, Frank Edgar. "The Major Administrative Policies of Oran M. Roberts, with an Introduction to His Life." M.A. thesis, University of Texas, 1925.

Nowlin, James Robertson. "A Political History of the Texas Prison System, 1849–1957." M.A. thesis, Trinity University, 1962.

Parrish, Thomas Michael. "This Species of Slave Labor: The Convict Lease System in Texas, 1871–1914." M.A. thesis, Baylor University, 1976.

Reese, James Verdo. "The Worker in Texas, 1821–1876." Ph.D. dissertation, University of Texas, 1964.

Reynolds, James Robert. "The Administration of the Texas Prison System." M.A. thesis, University of Texas, 1925.

Sandlin, Betty Jeffers. "The Texas Reconstruction Constitutional Convention of 1868–1869." Ph.D. dissertation, Texas Tech University, 1970.

Schmelzer, Janet Louise. "Thomas Mitchell Campbell: Progressive Governor of Texas." M.A. thesis, Texas Christian University, 1975.

Smith, Maggie Ruhamah. "The Administration of Governor John Ireland, 1883–1887." M.A. thesis, University of Texas, 1934.

Tatum, Bowen C. "The Penitentiary Movement in Texas, 1847–1849." M.A. thesis, Institute of Contemporary Corrections and Behavioral Sciences, Sam Houston State University, 1970.

Tenney, James Leighton. "The Public Services of Joseph Draper Sayers." M.A. thesis, University of Texas, 1933.

Tinsley, James Aubrey. "The Progressive Movement in Texas." Ph.D. dissertation, University of Wisconsin, 1953.

Wagner, Robert Lancaster. "The Gubernatorial Career of Charles Allen Culberson." M.A. thesis, University of Texas, 1954.

Webb, Juanita Oliver. The Administration of Governor L. S. Ross, 1887–1891." M.A. thesis, University of Texas, 1935.

Zimmerman, Hilda Jane. "Penal Systems and Penal Reforms in the South since the Civil War." Ph.D. dissertation, University of North Carolina, 1947.

INDEX

"An Act to Provide for the Employment of Convict Labor in Works of Public Utility," 19
agrarian reform movement, 172–73, 176, 190, 195
agriculture, 19, 94, 95n. *See also* farmers; contract system; share farms
Airline Railroad, 21
American Federation of Labor (AFL), 180
American Prison Association, 152
American Prison Wardens' Association, 152
Arcola plantation, 158
Auburn penitentiary system, 7–9, 15
Austin-to-Huntville-to-Rusk political axis, 154

Baker, Searcy (prison financial agent), 150
Ball, George, 159
ball and chain, 50, 82
Ball, Hutchings Company, 157, 159
Bankhead, J. H. (Alabama prison superintendent), 193
Barbee, J. G. (prison inspector), 137–39, 153
Barrett, R. A. (furnace expert), 88
Barton, A. M. (secretary to T. M. Campbell), 184
Bates, Wharton (prison inspector), 153, 156, 163
Beauregard, P. G. T., 148
Beccaria, Cesare (prison reformer), 6
Bell, P. H. (governor of Texas), 16
Bennett, A. J. (prison superintendent), 26–27
Beto, George (prison director), 198
Birbenbine, John (iron production expert), 88
blacks, 18; as prison inmates, 63, 94n, 114–15, 126, 135, 167, 167n, 182, 191, 193, 195n; and prison lease system, 24, 165–67
Blakeley, Bassett, 100
Board of Public Labor, 19–22
Boaz, Rev. H. A., 182
Bounds, F. P. (prison guard), 61
Bowman, ______ (Texas legislator), 137
Brahan, Haywood (prison financial agent), 81, 97, 157
Brahan, Robert W. (prison director), 189
Brazos Branch Railroad, 21
Briggs, George Waverley (investigative reporter), 183–85, 188, 194
Buchanan, A. M. (Texas senator), 58–59, 62
burglary, 20, 120–21
Burleson, Albert Sidney (outside contractor), 157, 160–61
Burleson and Johns share farm, 138, 152, 160
Burnett, James, 25
Burnett, J. H., 47–48
Burnett and Kilpatrick prison lease, 47–48
Bush, J. W. (prison director), 35

Cabell, Ben E. (prison director), 189
Cable, George W., 192
California: and prison lease system, 10
Calvert coal mining camp, 135–37
Campbell, Charles (former prisoner), 140, 168
Campbell, J. K. P. (prison inspector), 35, 40–41, 51
Campbell, Thomas M.: prison appointments of, 137, 146, 150–51, 153; and prison investigation of 1909–10, 128, 133, 136, 183, 185–87, 188; and reform movement, 176–79, 194
Cane Belt Railway, 159
Carey, J. W. (prison director), 64
Carr, John (prisoner), 130–31
Chenoweth, J. Q. (Texas legislator), 76
Cherry and Morrow, 72
Cherry Hill penitentiary system, 6–7
Clemens, William (prison director), 146–47

Clemens state farm, 99, 132, 134
Cleveland, Grover, 151
Coke, Richard: and Thomas A. Goree, 147, 154; and retrenchment policies, 78; and Ward-Dewey prison lease, 35-37, 39-40, 43-44
Coleman, Capt. R. H. (assistant prison superintendent), 132
Colquitt, O. B., 146, 189
Comer-Fairris prison lease, 83-84, 86-87
Compromise of 1850, 170
Consumers Lignite Company, 95
contract system, 10
"convict bogey," 170
convict labor: and coal mining, 95; and construction contracts, 13, 20, 89-91; and farm contracts, 4, 68-72, 77, 91-98, 96n, 112, 126-29, 150, 167, 189; and Huntsville industries, 7-8, 16-17, 23, 26-28, 31, 35-36, 66-69, 83-85, 91, 97; and profits to state, 7-8, 12-15, 22-24, 27-28, 83, 91, 112; and public opposition, 4, 45, 57, 62-66, 75-77, 187, 193-94, 197-98; and railroad contracts, 21-22, 57-58, 64-69, 82, 92, 95, 161, 191; and rehabilitation, 5-16, 28, 55, 121, 124; and Rusk industries, 70, 84-88; and state farms, 78, 80, 96-101, 112, 126-69, 150, 167, 189; and turpentine companies, 95, 95n; as unfair competition, 9-12, 57-59, 62, 67, 76, 85, 90, 168, 179-81, 190, 195. *See also* skills; treatment of prisoners
Cooper, L. W. (judge), 34
Cotton Press Company, 29
Crane, M. M. (Texas attorney-general), 155-56
criminal behavior: attitudes toward, 3, 5-6, 8, 14, 22. *See also* public attitudes
Culberson, Charles A., 98, 147, 149-53, 156, 160
Cunningham, E. H. (prison contractor), 46, 48, 157-59
Cunningham-Ellis prison lease, 46-49, 81, 86, 157, 191; and Goree evaluation, 50-52; possible renewal of, 68-74; profits to state from, 52-53, 65-66, 75, 83; reports of abuse in, 57-64; termination of, 69, 75-77, 79-81

Dallas Morning News, 186
dark cell, 50, 82, 129
Darrington farm, 158
Davis, Edmund J., and origin of lease system, 22, 24-28; and Republican programs, 44-45, 167, 171; and Ward-Dewey prison lease, 33-35
deaths of prisoners, 124
Democratic politics: and fiscal retrenchment, 78, 172, 176; and "pig laws," 115; and prison appointments, 15, 44, 145-56, 167; and prison contractors, 156-62; and prison lease system in the South, 194; and reform movement, 172, 174-75; and Texas Bourbons, 78, 163, 175; and the Ward-Dewey lease, 35, 44-45
deprivation of privileges, 82, 129
Dewey, E. C. (prison contractor), 29, 34, 41
Dibrell, Mrs. J. B., 182
dogs, 130
Donahue, Willie (prison guard), 60
Douglas, E. G. (prison assistant superintendent), 152, 182
Dudley, Col. N. A. M. (prison superintendent), 25-26
Dunovant prison farm, 151

Eastham, Mrs. Delha (outside contractor), 135
Eastham share farm, 135
economy, post-Civil War Texas, 18-19, 45-46, 172, 178-79
education of prisoners, 10, 69, 117, 121-22, 195
Eldridge, W. T. (prison contractor), 157-59
Ellis, C. G., 158n
Ellis, L. A. (prison contractor), 46, 48, 99, 157-58
Ellis, O. B. (prison director), 198
Ellis contract farm, 134
escapes, 21, 41, 51, 82, 90, 124, 193; response to, 60-61, 65, 130, 170
Evans, Ira H., 27-28

farmers: as political force, 172-74, 190
Farmers' Alliance, 172-73, 180
farm labor contracts, 4, 68-72, 77, 91-98, 96n, 112, 126-29, 150, 167
financial agent, 27, 81, 81n
Finley, R. W. (prison financial agent), 98
food, 9, 134, 193
forgery, 120-21
Fourth Called Session, 188

Gaines, I. T. (prison director), 47, 61
Galveston Daily News, 32, 58, 77
Galveston, Houston, and San Antonio Railroad, 92
Gibbs, Sandford, 31
Gibson, James P. (prison assistant superintendent), 152
Giles, Mr. (attorney), 59
Goree, Thomas J. (prison superintendent): and Burnett and Kilpatrick lease, 47, 47n; hopes of, for prison industries, 84, 87–88; and investigation of Cunningham-Ellis, 58–67; as noted prison official, 147–49, 193; and outside labor camps, 51, 61, 64, 66–67, 90–93, 122; and support of Cunningham-Ellis leases, 50–52, 73; and Texas Democratic politics, 148, 154; and Ward-Dewey lease, 35
Granite Cutters' National Union, 90
Great Northern Railroad, 34
Great Southwest Strike, 180
Green, Strother (prison director), 31, 167
Greenback party, 172–73
guards (and sergeants): authority of, 20–21, 63, 133; brutalities of, 33–34, 37–39, 62, 64–66, 79, 127; and female prisoners, 136; killings by, 21, 130, 170; and outside compensation, 30, 71–72, 86, 127–28

Hamby, Gen. W. R., (prison contractor), 71–72
"hanging them in the window," 131
Harlem state farm, 97–100, 130, 152, 194
Harrison, William Henry, 90
Hawkins, Sam (prison inspector), 137–38
Henderson, John N. (prison reformer), 169
Henderson, T. S. (outside contractor), 157, 160
Herring, J. A. (prison superintendent), 100, 132, 150–51, 183
Hodges, Rev. Jake, 131–32, 183–84
Hogg, James Stephen, 93, 98; prison appointments of, 145–46, 148, 152, 154; and reform movement, 174
Hood, Gen. John Bell, 48
"horse" (stocks), 69
House, Edward M., 98, 154–56, 158, 176
House, T. W., Sr., 155, 158
Houston and Great Northern Railroad, 32
Houston and Texas Central Railroad, 32, 92, 180
Howard, John (prison reformer), 6
Hubbard, Richard B., prison appointments of, 145, 148; and prison leases, 43–44, 46–48, 57; and retrenchment policies, 78
Huntsville Penitentiary: beginnings of, 14–16, 22; and Cunningham-Ellis lease, 49–50, 64–65, 65n; industries in, 16–17, 66, 76, 83, 85, 112, 186; and prisoner profiles, 68, 70, 91; and Ward-Dewey lease, 30–39; and Wynne Farm, 96–97. *See also* legislative investigations
Hutchings, John H., 159

immigration, 119
Imperial farm, 99, 134–35
Imperial Sugar Company, 99-100, 159
inspector of prisons, 31, 33–34, 42, 69, 138-39, 142, 151–52
International and Great Northern Railroad, 64, 92
International Prison Congress, 164
Ireland, John, 73–75, 79–81, 89, 146
irons, 82
isolation of prisoners, 5–6

jails, county, 4, 13, 32
Jay Bird Democratic Association, 153
Jester, George T., 155
Johns and Burleson share farm, 138, 152, 160
Johnson, Ed (former prisoner), 59
Johnson, H. W., 129–30
Johnson, Mrs. Cone, 181–82
Justice, William Wayne (judge), 198–99
juvenile reformatory, 36, 72, 72n, 137–38, 152, 164, 182, 197

Kansas report, 37, 42
Keasby, Dr. L. M., 182
Kempner family, 159
Kennon, W. A. (prison guard), 61
Kirwin, Rev. J. M., 182
Kittrell, Norman G., 148
Knights of Labor, 180

labor, organized, 9–12, 173, 179–81, 190, 195
Lane, J. W. (prison director), 28
Lanham, S. W. T., 150, 176
lease law of 1871, 28–29

lease system of prison management, 3–4; opposition to, 9–12, 62–63, 75–77, 173, 190, 195; in post-Civil War South, 191–94, 196; and power of private contractors, 35, 74–75, 156–60, 157n, 193–94; and state finances, 7–10, 13–14, 18, 22–24, 27–28, 53, 65, 143, 189, 193; and Texas legislation, 19–22, 28–30, 43–46, 53–56, 80–83, 188–90, 194–95. *See also* convict labor; treatment of prisoners
Lee, Eugene (prisoner), 131
legislative investigations: of 1875–76, 37–43; of 1879, 58–63; of 1871, 28–29; of 1909–10, 124, 128–42, 185–88, 190, 194; in Reconstruction convention, 22–24
Lenz, John (prisoner), 134–35
Little, Rev. Luther, 182
Littlefield, George W., 158
Long, J. L., 182
Long, James, 60–61
Longstreet, Gen. James, 148
Lowood plantation, 99
Lunatic Asylum, 52

McDaniel, T. F., 62
McKinney Democrat-Gazette, 186
Markham, Dr. Thomas W., 52
Marks, Rabbi Samuel, 182
Massachusetts: and prison lease system, 10
medical care, 9–10, 20, 40, 52, 61, 81, 195
Mewshaw, J. R. (prison director), 146
Mineola incident, 57–64
"money rent," 189
Moore, R. J., 167, 167n
Moore, R. L. (Texas legislator), 28
Morrow, Hamby, and Company, 75, 78–79

National Prison Association, 148–49, 169, 196
neck collars, 124
New Orleans Times, 37
newspapers: and prison policies, 32, 37, 74–75, 128, 133, 185–86, 190, 194
New York: prison management in, 7
"nigger cloth," 27

Oliphant, Dr. H. S. (prison physician), 26, 32
overcrowding: at end of leasing, 189; under first lease, 32; measures to relieve, 4, 22, 28, 36, 81; post-Civil War, 19; and state finances, 45; statistics on, 29, 65, 90–91, 98, 112–13

Patton, Dr. A. L., 61
Patton, Nathan, 24, 29
Pease, Elisha M., 16, 22–25, 29
Penitentiary Act of 1848, 14–16
Pennsylvania: prison management in, 6
Philadelphia Society for Alleviating the Miseries of Public Prisons, 6
piece-price system, 9–10
"pig laws," 115
"poker Legislature," 74
Populist party, 174–76, 180, 194
President's Commission on Law Enforcement and Administration of Justice, 3
prison conditions: 10–11; after Civil War, 20, 25–27; during Cunningham-Ellis lease, 52, 60–61; under state lease management, 141–43, 190, 195, 199; during Ward-Dewey lease, 30, 32, 36–38, 40
prison industries: at Huntsville, 7–8, 16–17, 23, 26–28, 31, 35–36, 66–69, 83–85, 91, 97; at Rusk, 70, 84–88
Prison Reform Association of Texas, 164, 169
Progressivism, 5, 176, 190, 194–96, 198
Prohibition party, 173
public account system, 8, 11
public attitudes: antipathy toward prisoner labor, 9–12, 57, 59, 62, 67, 85, 90, 168, 180–81; antipathy toward prison reform, 163, 169–70, 184; contempt for prisoners, 190; outrage at prisoner treatment, 45, 64, 76, 87, 195

Quakers, 6

racial classification of prisoners, 60, 114, 126, 136, 195
railroads: and convict labor, 21–22, 57–58, 64–69, 82, 92, 161, 191; regulation of, 173, 180
Rainey, Anson (judge), 182
Ramsey, W. F. (prison director), 183–84
Ramsey farm, 99–100
Randle, Ed T. (prison inspector), 32–34
Randle, J. H. (prison sergeant), 60–63
Rawlings, Dr. W. A. (prison physician), 26, 36

Read, B. F., 60
Reconstruction Convention, 23-24, 28-29
Reeves, O. C., 60
reform movement: opposition to, 162, 169; and political splinter groups, 163-64, 166-67, 175-76, 176n, 182; and prisoner rehabilitation, 5-6, 8-11, 16, 121, 124; and prison reforms, 5-6, 39, 77, 183, 190, 193-94, 197-98
Republican politics, 29, 44-45, 171, 173
resumption bill, 43-46
Reynolds, Gen. J. J., 25
Rice, J. S., (prison financial agent), 98, 145, 150, 156-57
Richardson, J. W., Jr. (prison guard), 61
Riddick, C. W., 100
Riddick farm, 99-100
Roberts, Oran M.: and Cunningham-Ellis lease, 57-77; and prison appointments, 145, 152-53; and retrenchment policies, 78, 154
Robertson, Jerome B., 154
Rogers, Rev. B. A., 164-65, 165n
Ross, L. S., 152
Royal, Peter (prison director), 31
Ruby, George T., 24
Ruiz v. *Estelle,* 198
rule of silence, 7-8
Runnels, Hardin, 16
Rusk Penitentiary: as a facility, 36, 65, 83, 91; industries in, 70, 72, 76, 85-89, 186; prisoner arrival at, 124-26
Rusk *Press-Journal,* 186

San Antonio Express, 183-84, 188
Sartartia plantation, 99
Sayers, Joseph, 147, 150, 153, 155-56, 176
Sealy, John, 159
Searcy, I. G., (prison director), 80
Secession Convention, 153
shackles, 82
share farms, 4, 96, 96n
Shepard, James E. (prison director), 47
Sherman Courier, 76
Short, Daniel M. (prison inspector), 58-59, 62, 64, 152-53
Shotwell, John (former prisoner), 140-41
skills: and classification of prisoners, 20, 66, 84-86, 91, 119
Smith, S. R. (prison director), 64
Society for the Friendless, 182-83
sodomy, 132
"solitary" cells, 15
South: prison lease system in the, 5, 10, 192-94
spike (ankle cuff), 82
Spindletop, 179
state farms, 78, 80, 96-101, 112, 130-31, 136, 154, 166, 195
State Library and Historical Commission, 146
Stevenson, Louis W., 27
stocks, 50, 60, 69
subtreasury idea, 173, 173n
sugar industry, 99, 158-59
Sugarland, 158-59
Sulphur Springs Gazette, 186
Swan, A. K. (Texas legislator), 76
S. W. Fuel and Manufacturing Company, 95

taxation: public attitudes, 8, 18, 33, 163, 170-71, 189-90
Taxpayers' Convention of the State of Texas, 171
Terrell, A. W. (Texas senator), 44-45
Texas and Pacific Railroad, 57, 59, 63
Texas Central Railroad, 92
Texas Department of Corrections, 198
Texas Federation of Labor, 180-81
Texas Federation of Women's Clubs, 181
Texas Guarantee and Trust Company, 159
Texas Mutual Life, 29
Texas Siftings, 74-75
Texas Sugar Growers' Association, 158-59
Texas Turpentine Company, 95
textile industry, 7, 16-17, 27, 31, 97
theft: of farm animals, 115-16, 120
Throckmorton, James, 19, 22-23
Tips, Walter (prison director), 80-81, 146
Tittle, Louis W., 189
Tomlin, Henry (former prisoner), 168
transportation of prisoners, 21, 33-34, 44
treatment of prisoners: during Cunningham-Ellis lease, 57-64; during state lease management, 121-24, 129-42, 185-94, 198; during Ward-Dewey lease, 34-42, 44
Trinity and Brazos Valley Railroad, 155
Tubb, Sam (prisoner), 134
turpentine contracts, 95, 95n

Underwood, R. H., 151-52
Union League in Texas, 24

Walker, B. W. (prison director), 35
Walter Tips Company, 146
Ward, A. J. (prison contractor), 29, 30n, 34, 37, 41
Ward, Dewey, and Company, 28, 31, 33, 148
Ward-Dewey prison lease, 164, 168, 191; contractual problems with, 33–35; demise of, 43–46, 49, 52; improvements during, 31–32, 36; investigation of, 39–42; provisions of, 29–30
Whatley, Lucius A. (prison superintendent), 98, 131, 149, 152
Whatley-Herring farm, 130–31, 151
whippings: illicit, 128–32, 139; recommended and supervised, 50, 69, 82; rules on, 82n, 195; for rules violations, 7; of women, 136
White, Henry K., 40, 47, 145
Wiggin-Simpson Company, 83–84, 84n, 87
Wilkinson, J. L. (former prisoner), 140, 168
Williams, D. C., 62
Williamson, Mac (prison sergeant), 131
Willis, P. J., 157–59
Willis, R. S., 157–59
Willis plantations, 159
Wilson, Woodrow, 151
Wines, Frederick H., 148
Wood County Flag, 58, 62
Wooldridge, A. P. (prison director), 146
women prisoners, 135–36, 182–83
women's clubs, 182, 190
Wynne, J. M. (prison director), 64
Wynne, R. M., 155
Wynne farm, 96–97, 194

Zapp, Robert, 28

Penology for Profit was set into type on a Compugraphic digital phototypesetter in ten point Times Roman with two points of spacing between the lines. The book was designed by Jim Billingsley, composed into type by Metricomp, Inc., printed offset by Thomson-Shore, Inc., and bound by John H. Dekker & Sons. The paper on which the book is printed bears acid-free characteristics for an effective life of at least three hundred years.

Texas A&M University Press : College Station